IMAGES
of America

AMAGANSETT

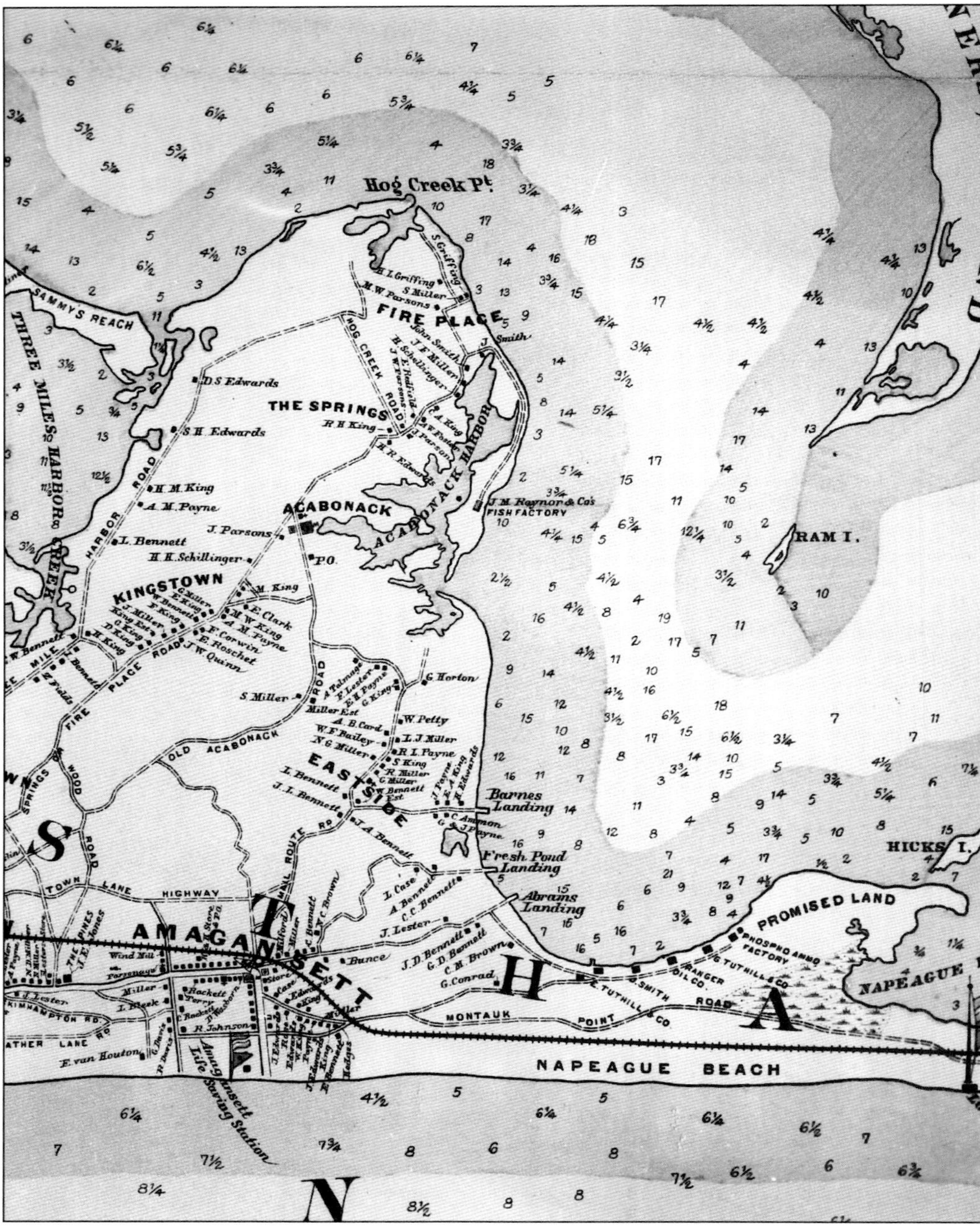

A map of Amagansett, East Side, Napeague, and Springs, showing the tip of Gardiners Island at the upper right.

COVER: Captain Samuel S. Edwards and his bride-to-be, Eva King, in August 1905.

IMAGES
of America

AMAGANSETT

Carleton Kelsey and Lucinda Mayo

ARCADIA
PUBLISHING

ISBN 978-0-7385-9034-9

Published by Arcadia Publishing
Charleston, South Carolina

Printed in the United States of America

For all general information contact Arcadia Publishing at:
Telephone 843-853-2070
Fax 843-853-0044
E-mail sales@arcadiapublishing.com
For customer service and orders:
Toll-Free 1-888-313-2665

Visit us on the Internet at www.arcadiapublishing.com

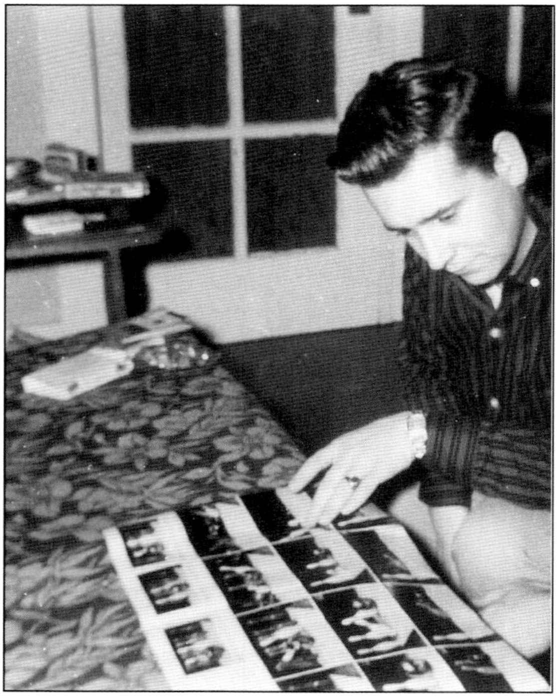

Dedicated to the memory of
Robert Midgett (1937-1978).

Contents

Introduction 7

1. Old and New 9

2. Summer and Winter 23

3. Here and There 37

4. Warp and Weft 47

5. Land and Water 57

6. Roots and Scions 71

7. Thought and Action 81

8. Order and Chaos 95

9. Supply and Demand 107

10. New and Old 117

Photo Credits 128

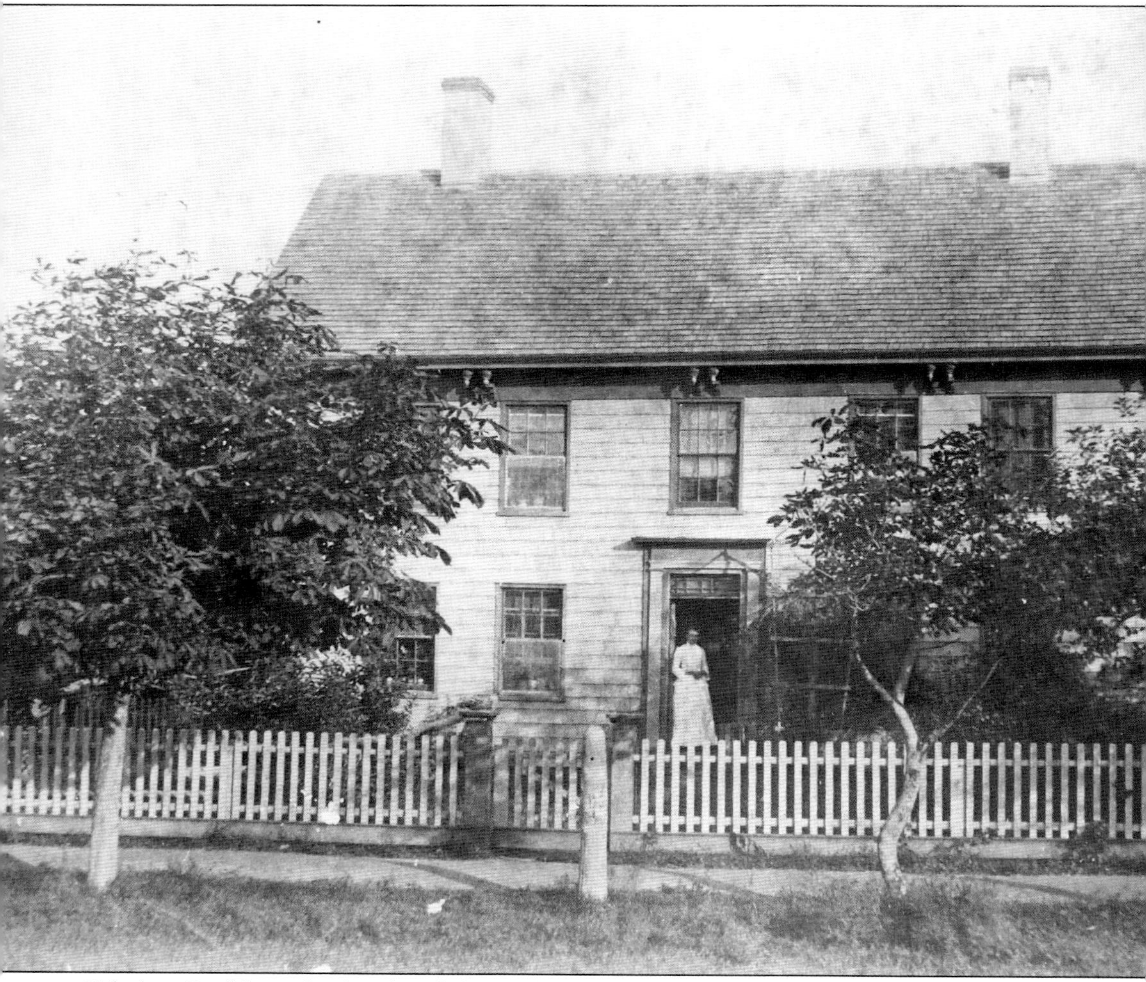

Zebulon Conklin, who lived with his wife, Sarah Mulford, in this house on Main Street, was one of twelve Amagansett men to serve in the Revolutionary War. The others were David and Nathaniel Baker, Jonathan and Matthew Barnes, Daniel and Samuel Conklin, Thomas Edwards, Benjamin Eyres, Nathaniel Hand, and two Samuel Mulfords (a father and his son, who later married Zebulon's daughter Mary). Three of Zebulon's cousins, who lived in Orange County, New Jersey, enlisted on April 25, 1775, and another, a seafarer, was taken by the British in Liverpool at the beginning of the Revolution, interned, and never heard from again.

Standing in the doorway of the Zebulon Conklin house in 1902 is Arletta (Rackett) Conklin, "Aunt Letty." A favorite story is her explanation of how she caught a cold one year, "from turning the pages of the Sears-Roebuck catalogue."

Introduction

In composing the text for these images of Amagansett, I have thought often of a quote from Thomas Wolfe's *Look Homeward, Angel*:

> Each of us is all the sums [s]he has not counted: subtract us to nakedness and night again, and you will see begin in Crete four thousand years ago the love that ended yesterday in Texas.

As we meet the individuals and families who make up the over 300-year social history of Amagansett, and explore their local haunts, no one can be found who is not linked in rich, sometimes aggravating, often delightful, ways to the rest of the community. There is no place in the relatively small hamlet that does not evoke the lives, work, and love that transpired there, and it is nothing odd to hear "voices," speaking far-reaching dialects. Amagansett is a community that has always encompassed a boggling geography, where our sense of the temporal collapses neatly when we least expect it.

I have tried to arrange images which date from 1853 to the present, and which detail life from 1680 to the turn of the next century and beyond, that they might suggest paths for future research. I hope to share the undeserved gift I've received, of captivating work and (nearly) time enough to do it. Being able to work with a fine historian and companionable *raconteur*, a wondrous collection, and a community settled by long-lost—now quizzically recaptured—ancestors, has been a magical experience.

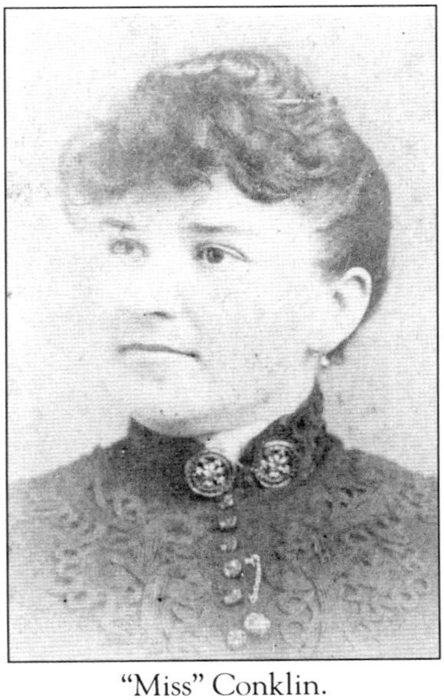

"Miss" Conklin.

The reader will note that we've had several "axes to grind," and we hope we've been able to hone them subtly. The village (it is officially a hamlet, but village is more often used to describe it) was never provincial. Its inhabitants have always been distinctively mobile and valiantly curious. Well before the development of a resort economy, residents measured prosperity in real estate holdings and trade that would compare enviably with any other area's, but also in terms of intellectual wealth and regard for the durability of human connections.

We have selected many of these images to focus on Amagansett "firsts," on the Schellinger-Babcock houses, and as a very small template for a family-by-family social history of the village. Having worked with many school groups over the years, at the library and the museums, we have tried to include text that answers some frequently asked questions, and raises others which might stimulate young people to conduct their own original research.

Conscious of the difficulty in presenting combinations of soft and hard facts, we have had many a lively exchange, and have tried to lean toward primary sources without losing the verve of oral accounts. I have learned much from the ladylike prose of Jeannette Edwards Rattray and the gentlemanly research style of Carleton Kelsey. They are both self-effacing historians who have borne their roles in the midst of local history with dignity. Distilling material by countless writers, I have finally accepted that I am as much a "child of my time" as any, but hope that my interest in Amagansett's "past lives" is sufficient to encourage others in their own explorations. Perhaps the most important thing I have learned while working on this book is that it is gentler to say, "You don't *mean* it!", than to say "Are you *sure*???". I pass the hard-won knowledge along to anyone who might be able to use it.

I want to thank my two favorite Celts—Michael Hogan, whose love and patience have seen me through a decade of more or less sensible projects, and Carleton Kelsey, whose impatience and patience have been equally helpful, because he is ever gracious, and is "my most unforgettable character." I am very grateful to Sarah Maineri, a wise and unflappable editor, and the staff at Arcadia Publishing. And, these images would not have found their way to publication without generous help and encouragement from the following: the Amagansett Historical Association, the Board of the Amagansett Library, the Amagansett School, Russell Bennett, Isabelle Carmichael, Dennis Carr, Allison Cornish, Josephine Crasky, Betsy Cunningham, Diana Dayton, Vito DeMai, the staff at Estia, Sandra Ferguson, Robert Fortin, the Frankel Foundation, Lisa Friscia, Lillian Granger, Laurie Edwards Granitto, Barbara Gray, Beth Barnes Gray, Louise Green, Harbor Heights, Java Nation, Bill Jenkins, Dorothy King, Harold King, Deborah Ann Light, the Long Island Studies Institute at Hofstra University, Mark Mahnken, all the Mayos—James, John, Karen, Kate, Mary Louise (Barnes), Millard, and Stephen, the Morris Studio, Mr. and Mrs. Herb Mulford, Maureen Murphy, Natalie Naylor, Cynthia Osterweil, Tony Prohaska, Alice Ragusa, the John Reed Studio, Anne Roberts, Spinnaker's, Town & Country Photo, Terry Trifari, Richard Wands, Susan Wawryk, and Nancy Wendell.

Lucinda Mayo
Sag Harbor, New York
December 1996

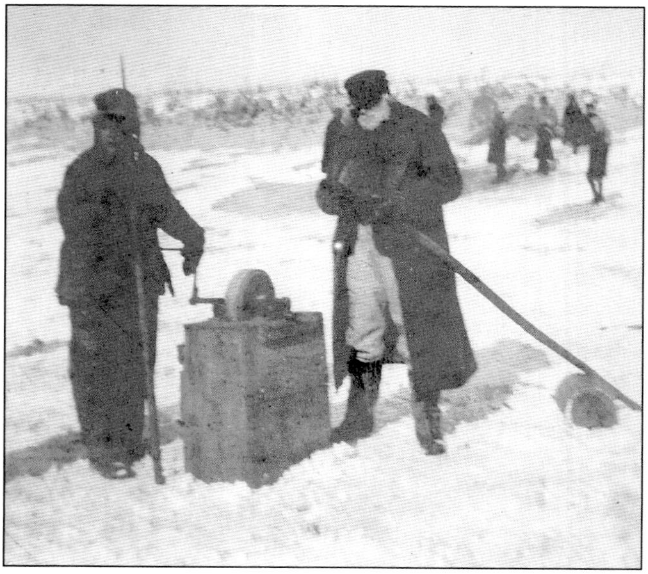

"Capt. Josh" Edwards is standing at a grindstone used to sharpen whaling implements.

One

Old and New

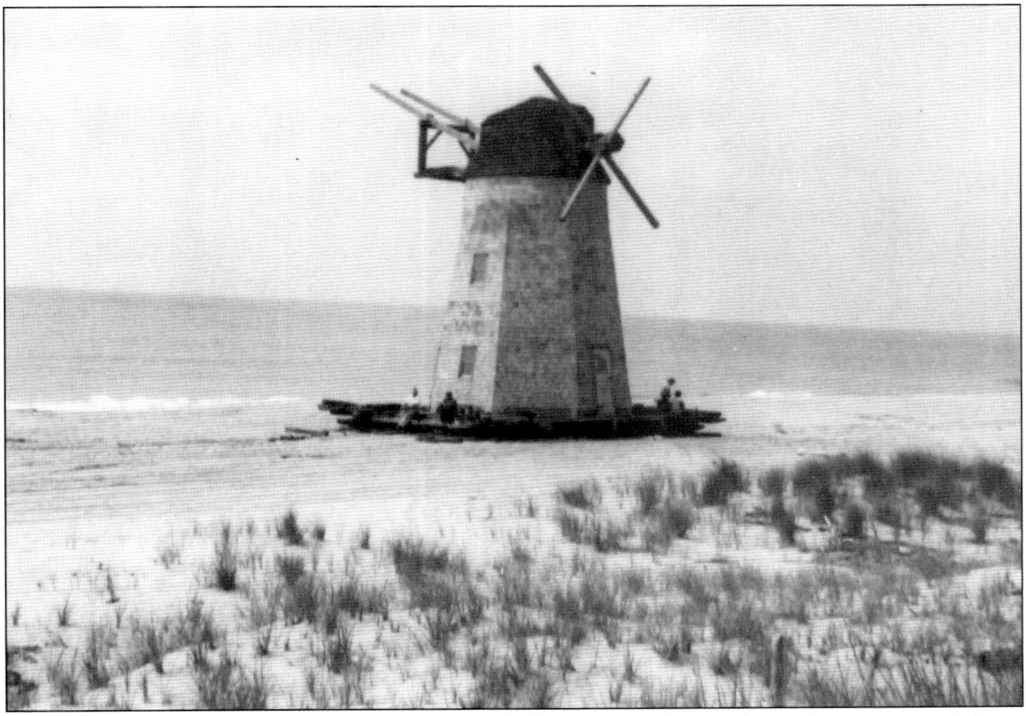

The Hayground mill, built by Samuel Schellinger, is shown here being moved from Bridgehampton to Further Lane. Because they were so heavy, the stones, called the "bed" stone and the "running" stone, would be brought by water, even when the wooden structure came on land.

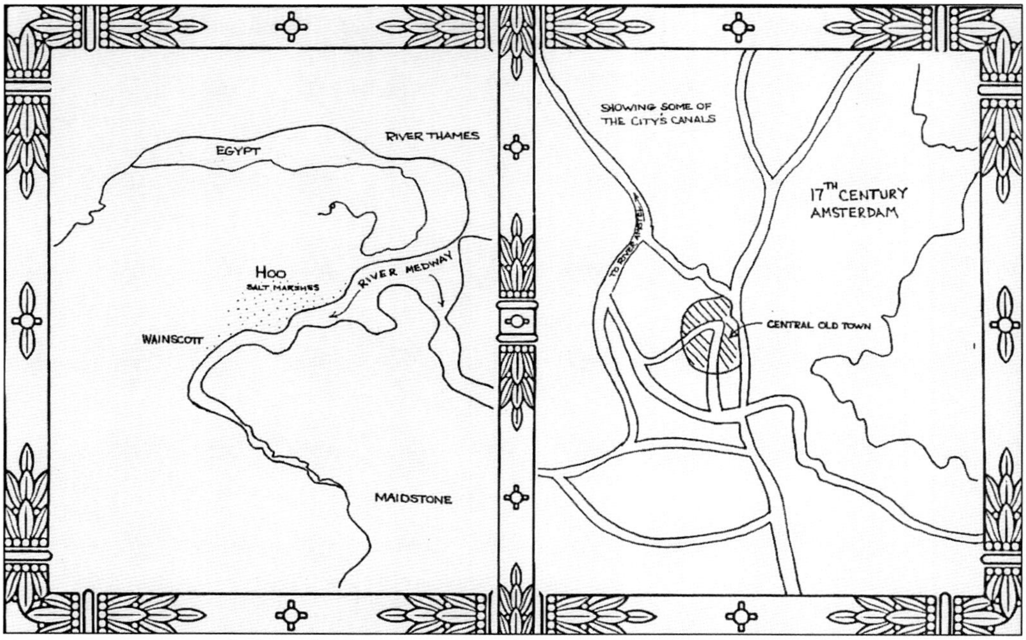

Amagansett was settled in the late seventeenth century by four families: the Bakers, Barnes, Conklins, and Schellingers. The first three of these came from Kent, in England, via Connecticut or Massachusetts. The Schellingers came from another coastal area, Amsterdam (map, right). They settled in Staten Island, and left "Nieuw Amsterdam" when it was taken by the British in 1664. The movement of these families eastward, from East Hampton and Southampton, was affected by primogeniture law and land availability, of course, but also by adventurousness and an aim for greater prosperity. When Jacobus Schellinger and his family, including step-son James Loper, arrived, it was to retrieve merchant fortunes (lost to Dutch taxation and a disastrous fire) in "the whale designe."

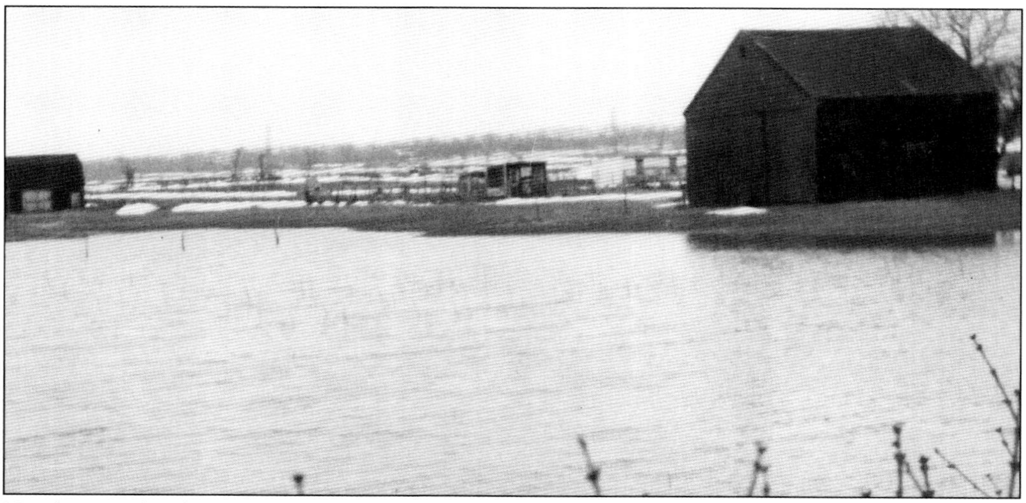

Until recently, the land beside Miss Amelia's Cottage flooded regularly—which likely added to the challenges of the Schellingers' extensive farming . A scene like this may have been the inspiration for an idea that crops up repeatedly in old Historical Association minutes, of establishing an ice skating rink on the property.

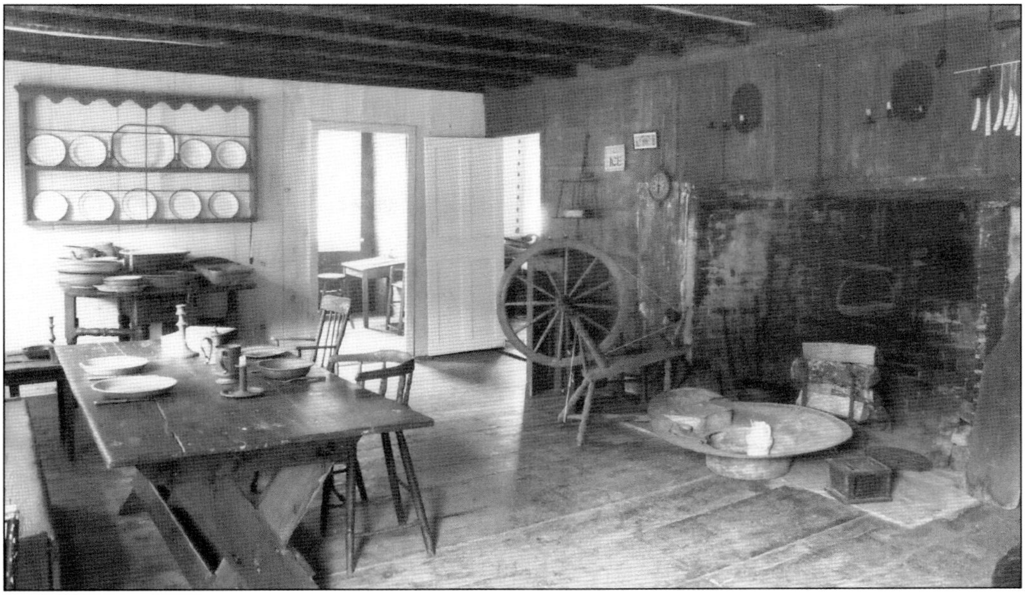

Exactly three centuries after the Schellingers left Staten Island, the Amagansett Historical Association was formed to save their 1725 "cottage" from being razed and supplanted by a supermarket. The only Amagansett house on the National Register of Historic Places, it was built west of what is now Windmill Lane, possibly for Jacobus' granddaughter Catherine when she married John Conkling, and was "skidded" to its present site in 1794. Four more generations of the family lived in the house; the last was Mary Amelia Schellinger, who died in 1930.

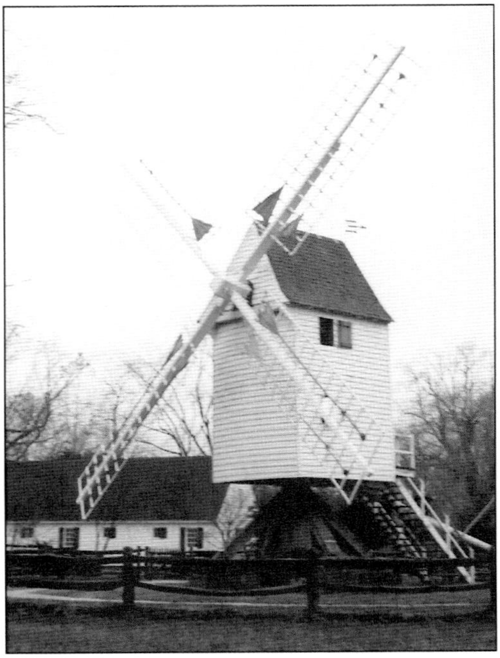

The original windmill in Amagansett was a "post mill" like this one, and stood in the middle of what is now Montauk Highway—the village's "common land." A post mill moves differently from the hood or petticoat mills that became more common: the entire mill structure turns around a center post. In both varieties of mill, special stones are used for wheat and corn (smaller stones for corn.) The first mill was run by Isaac Barnes; after his death it was operated by his son Jonathan and grandson Nathaniel. Several East End windmills have been restored in recent years, so there are many opportunities for residents to study their workings. The only windmills remaining in Amagansett today are the mock mill on the Mill-Garth property, and the one on Quail Hill.

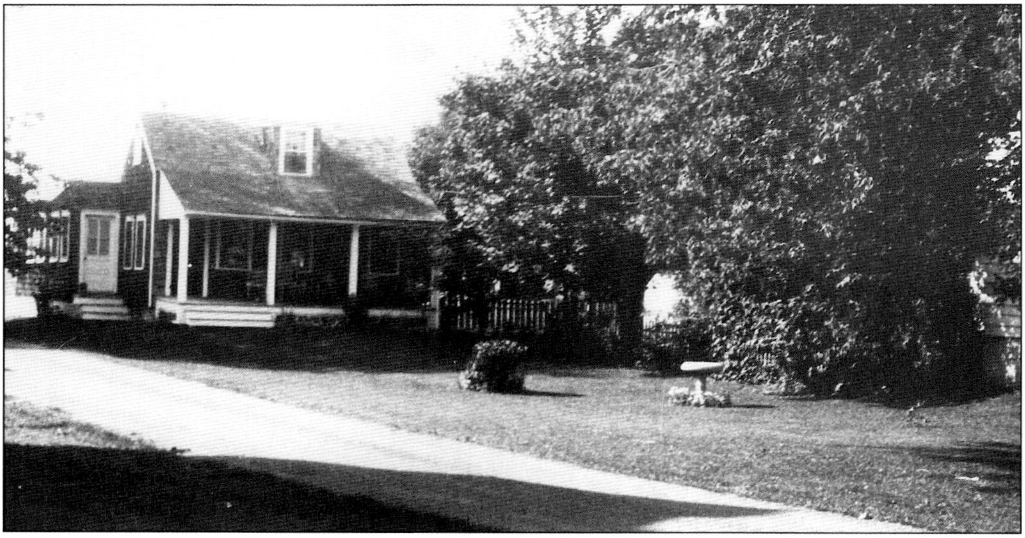

When we read that Nathaniel Baker and his wife, Catherine Schellinger, had eight children, seven of whom survived, it is easy to understand that this was considered a "starter" house—they lived in it just until their "real" family home was built. The oak beams in this first house are said to have come over from Holland as ship's ballast.

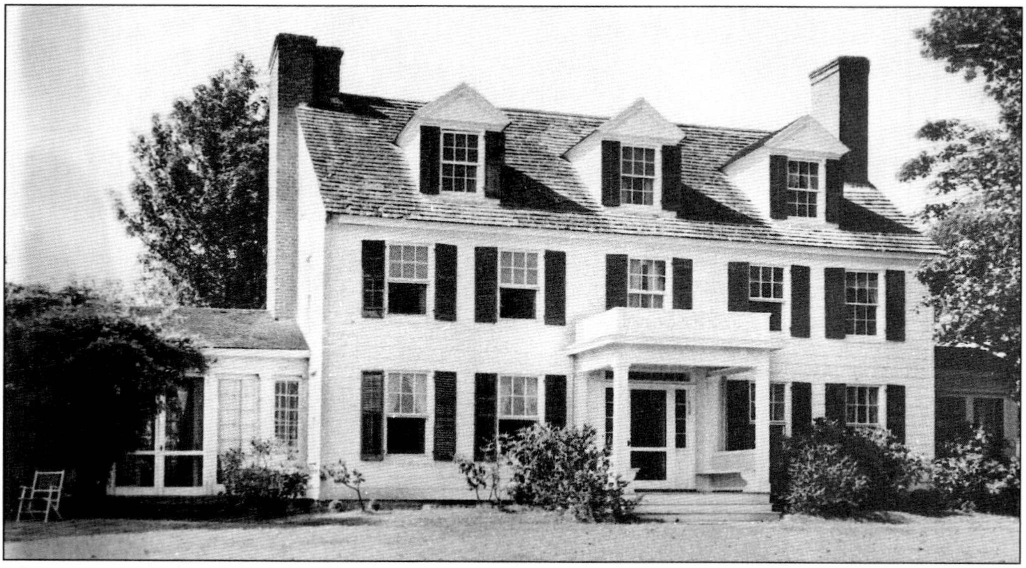

The second Nathaniel Baker home was built in the early 1680s, and "raised," or expanded, in 1797 by Samuel Schellinger. One of many Amagansett homes which have been ambitiously relocated over the years, it was moved from Main Street to Stony Hill in 1913 and for some time sat on a 325-acre dairy farm there. It has recently been purchased by actors Alec Baldwin and Kim Basinger. Several of Nathaniel's children moved to New Jersey at the turn of the eighteenth century, and remained there for generations. Nathaniel's grandson Daniel inherited the Amagansett house in 1740. A contemporary account tells how he drowned in the surf as he, Jacob Schellinger, and a slave approached the shore in their whaleboat. His wife, Mary, had dreamed the night before that "the tide rose so high that it came up to the house, burst open the door and brought in a coffin," and she had asked that he not go whaling that day.

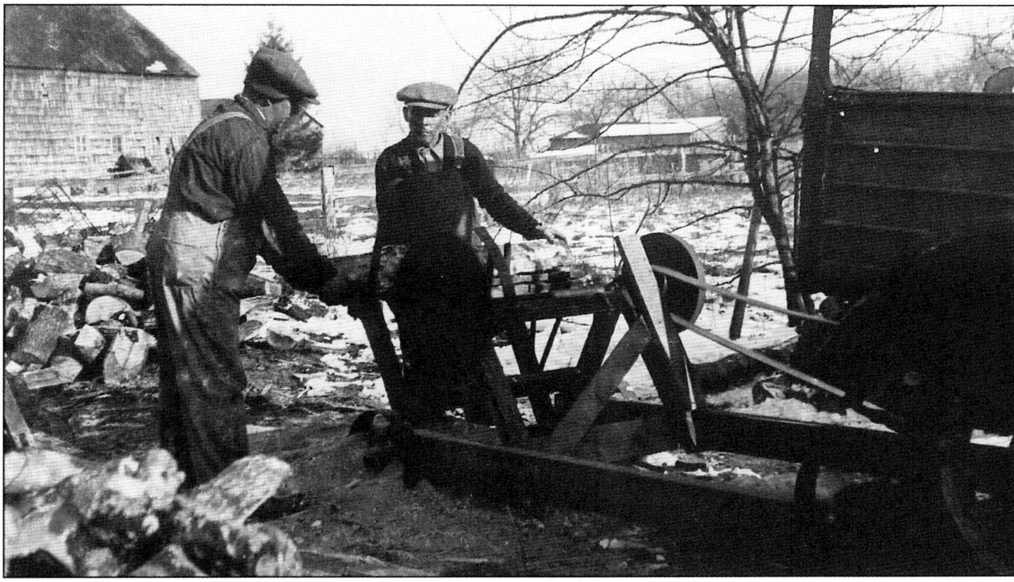

From the earliest days, the cutting and shipping of cordwood was a particularly lucrative enterprise. The many "landings" still appearing on street signs—including Abrahams', Barnes', Northwest, and Settlers'—were originally places where wood was loaded for sale across the Sound. With receipts from the sale of this indispensable cargo, ship owners were able to buy land and livestock (cattle and horses were sometimes shipped back to Amagansett in special slings to keep them "seaworthy"). They were also able to build more sophisticated vessels: Captain Davis Conklin's sloop, the *Traveler,* was appraised for $3,000 in 1812, and he had it built with money raised in the coastal trade.

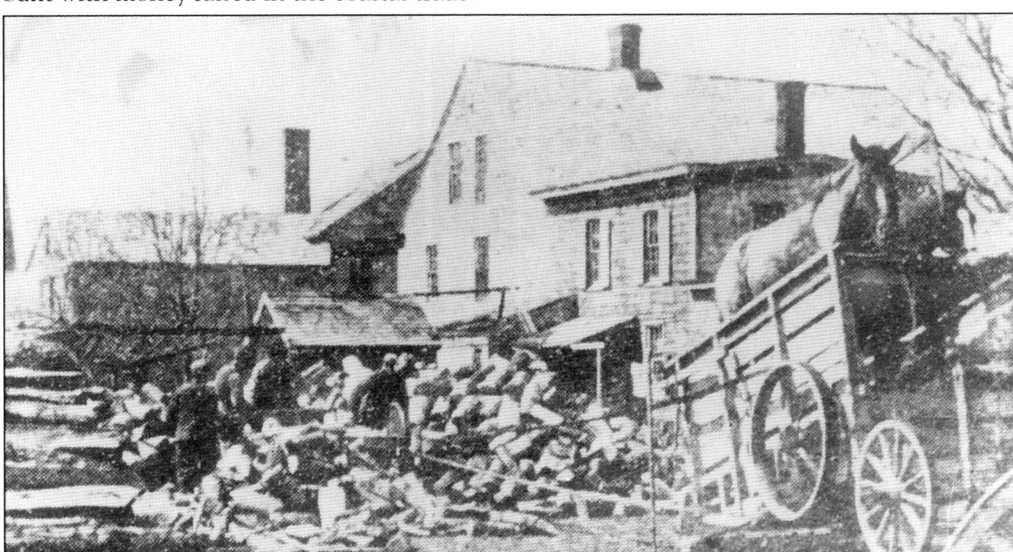

The woods around Amagansett—families owned woodlots as well as their farmlands and house sites—were felled perhaps four times, primarily for firewood and brickyards.Trees in the area were not suitable for ship masts, and, though the land provided for local building, timber was also imported. Such high-energy industries as Isaac Barnes' flourishing brick kiln near Fresh Pond, and "try works" for rendering whale oil, added to the local demand for wood.

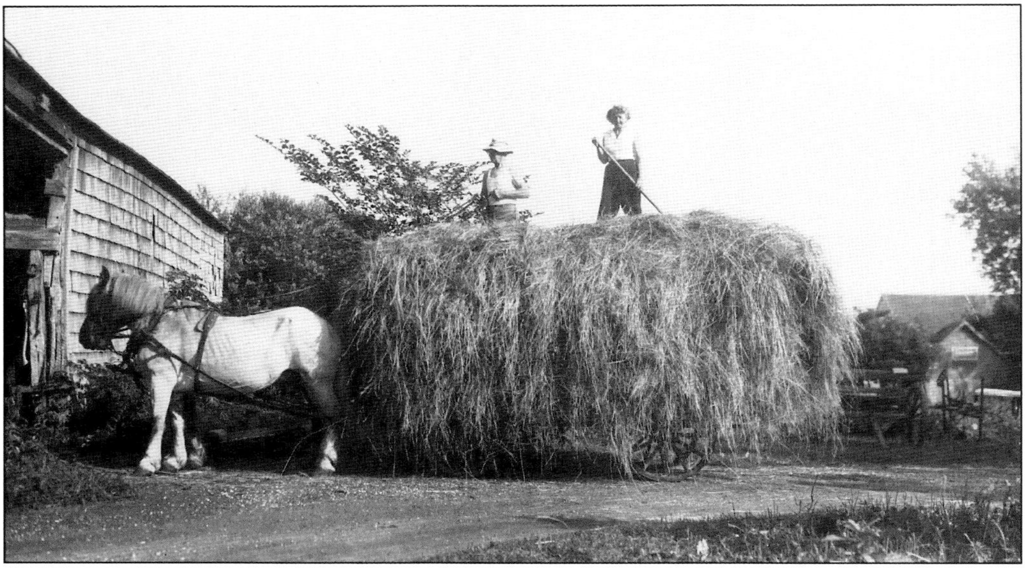

Although trustees' records describe the town's management of Montauk grazing lands—with considerable help from the indigenous Montauks—even before 1700, sustaining work horses and other animals on the village farms required the production and storage of tons of hay. "Salt hay" was also gathered to bank the foundations of village homes, for winter insulation, and for bedding in the stables.

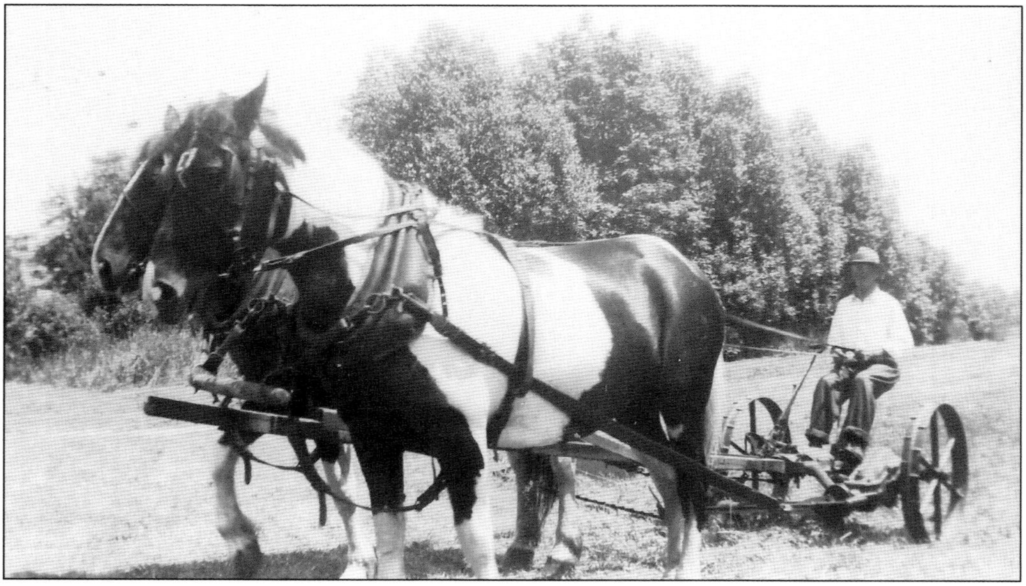

With a team and a single plow, an eighteenth-century farmer could plow 2.5 acres in a day: as Nathaniel Baker's first Amagansett farm of 60 acres was representative, we can see how the horses earned their hay. Along with cultivating beans, corn, potatoes, pumpkins, and squash, the settlers grew apples and pears, and harvested wild beachplums, cranberries, and grapes.

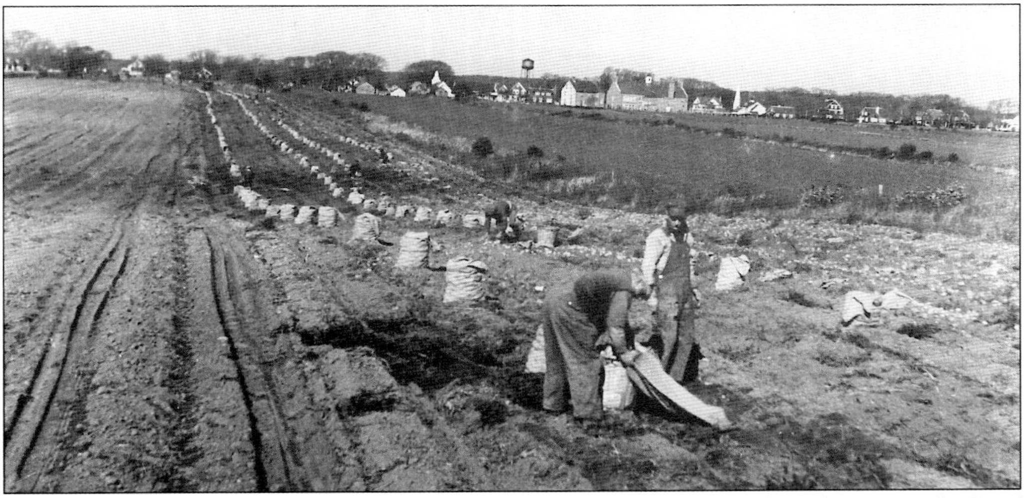

Early Amagansett families also benefited from the cultivation—and cooking—methods of the indigenous Montauks. Along with sharing methods for growing potatoes, the Montauks introduced the Dutch and English settlers to such nourishing uses for corn as the preparation of "samp"—porridge of whole hominy that became Sunday dinner for generations. Sailors, it is said, could tell they were approaching the village because they heard the pounding of samp with mortars and pestles. With the decreased availability of the special hominy in recent years, and with local taste-memories wistful, the growing African-American and Mexican populations reintroduced it to local stores—samp, or whole hominy, is also called *pozole*. Large fields of potato and corn were planted here until the 1950s; they have disappeared except for the flourishing farm at Quail Hill, preserved by the Peconic Land Trust.

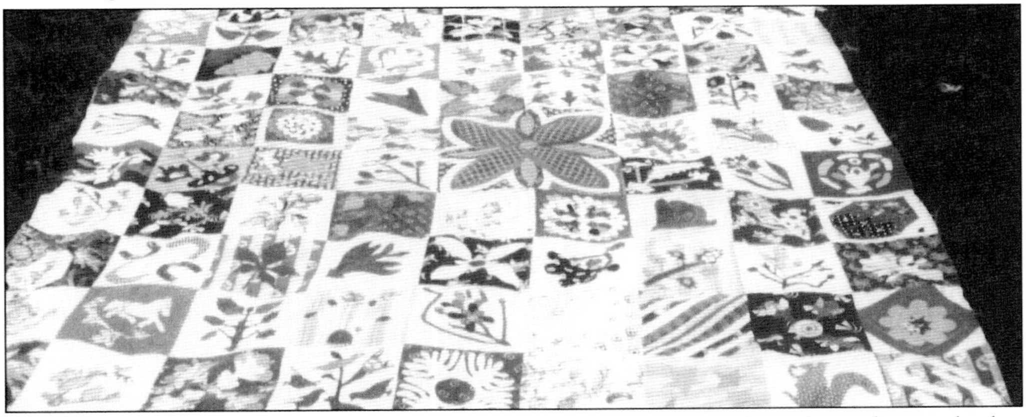

While "men's work" and "women's" were symbiotic, not separate, and textile production both a family enterprise and an industry for Amagansett craftsmen, women were responsible for much bedding and clothing manufacture. One woman said that her grandmother "made her do a stint every day; so many rows of knitting, so much on one of her quilt blocks, before she could go out to play," and if a mistake was made, it had to be done over. "I used to think that the quilts would never need washing, they had been soaked in tears enough to last them a lifetime." Unlike other regions, little competition in "fanciwork" ever developed, though—the "recipe" for an Amagansett quilt might be, "We make 'em quick enough to keep from freezing, and pretty enough to keep our hearts from breaking." This quilt by Mary Ann Bennett is, distinctively, appliquéd—in one corner the maker even stitched little wolves, to memorialize those her husband killed for "bounty."

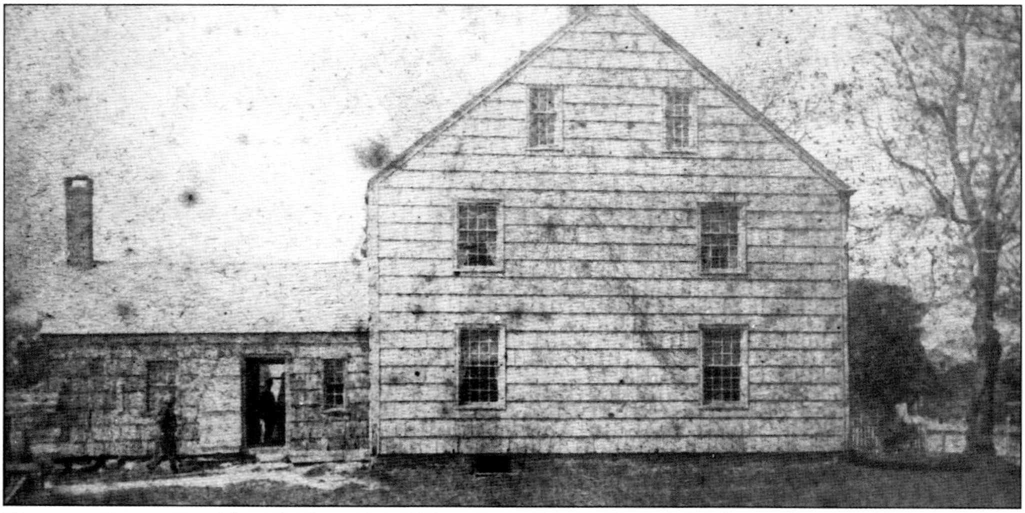

Captain Davis Conklin died in the "Christmas Storm," 1811. Where the weather had been unseasonably mild (one local teamster left a wagonload of oysters outside, and horses in the pasture that night), the northeaster began early in the morning and raged for twenty-four hours. Conklin's *Traveler* was one of more than sixty vessels that foundered on the north shore in that one storm. Samuel Schellinger went to Eaton's Neck to repair and retrieve the sloop. Christmas was not a legal holiday in New York State until 1875, and both seamen and townsfolk often "celebrated" it by working.

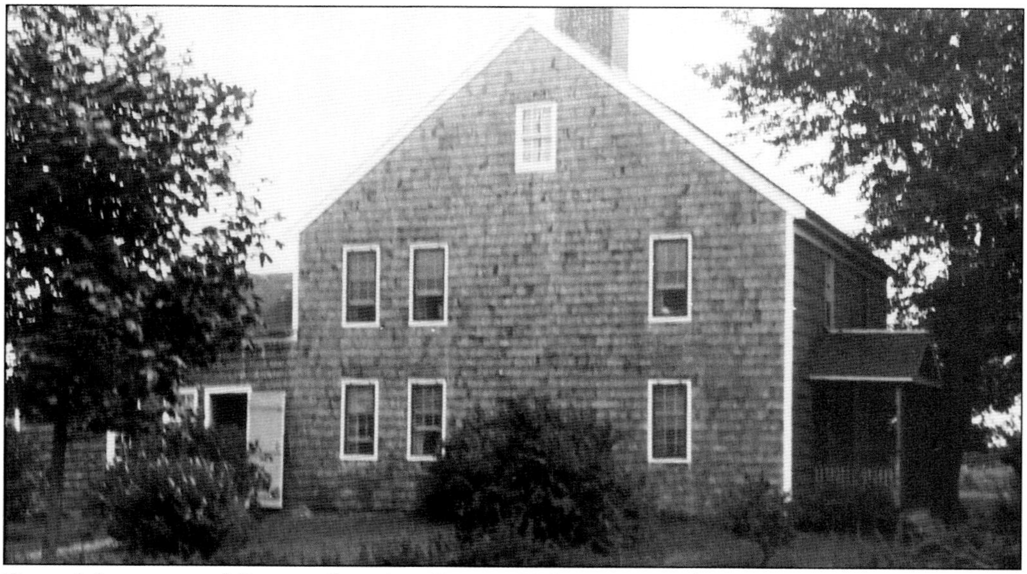

One of three sons of Captain Jonathan Barnes, Talmage was a farmer—he owned 40 acres on Abrahams Landing Road, and later, fields between Main Street and Bluff Road. Like many men and women in days of higher mortality rates, he married twice—to Mary Talmage Hedges and Mary Baker Hand. It is likely that Mary (Hand) Barnes missed having neighbors, so he sold this house on the Abrahams Landing Road and bought a "saltbox" on Main Street. This house was later purchased by Captain Sylvester Miller, a whaler. Carleton Kelsey was born in the front parlor of the Talmage Barnes house. His mother was attended by Dr. Frederick Finch until he became exhausted and called "Dr. Dave" Edwards in to deliver the baby.

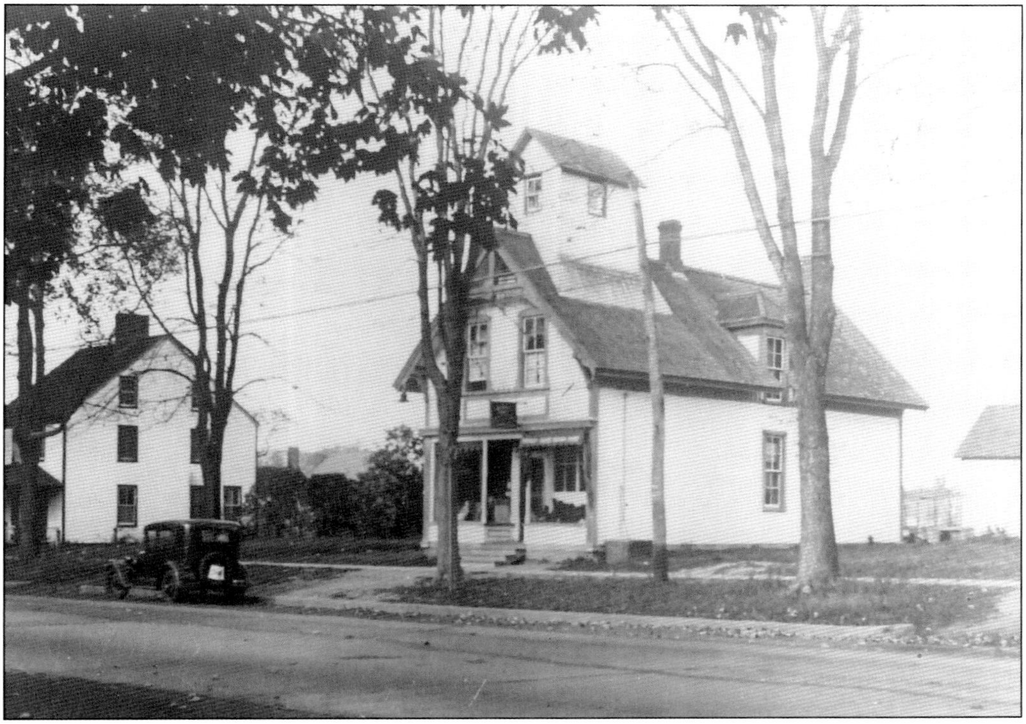

Erastus Barnes, great-grandson of the first Barnes to settle at Amagansett, was a deep-sea whaling captain out of Sag Harbor. His whaling logs, 1830–1852, are in the Pennypacker Collection at the East Hampton Library. His house (left) has been converted into a long-successful restaurant and nightclub, named for "Stephen Talkhouse," one of the most legendary of the Montauk Indians. To its right is the Bluff Road Life Saving Station, which was moved to Main Street and is now LaCarrubba's store.

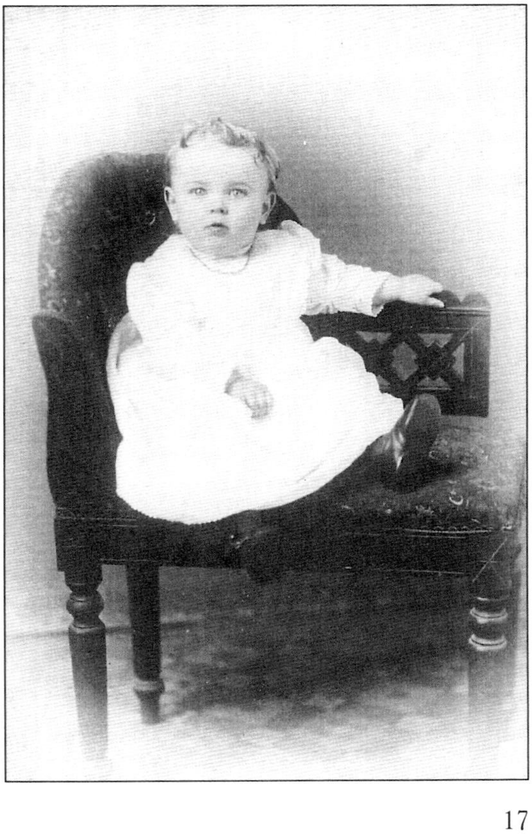

By the time Teunis Barnes was born in 1867, many of the Amagansett Barnes' had sold their land here and moved to East Hampton. Erastus' son Thomas had married one of the East Hampton "gentry," Adelaide Huntting, but she chose to return to her mother-in-law's home for the births of her sons, Teunis and Norman.

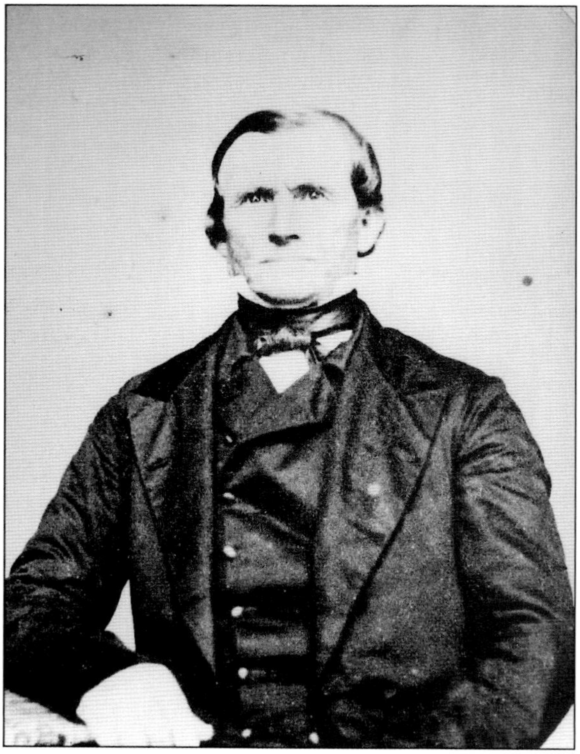

Charles Barnes (1807-1879) was Erastus Barnes' brother (Talmage's nephew).

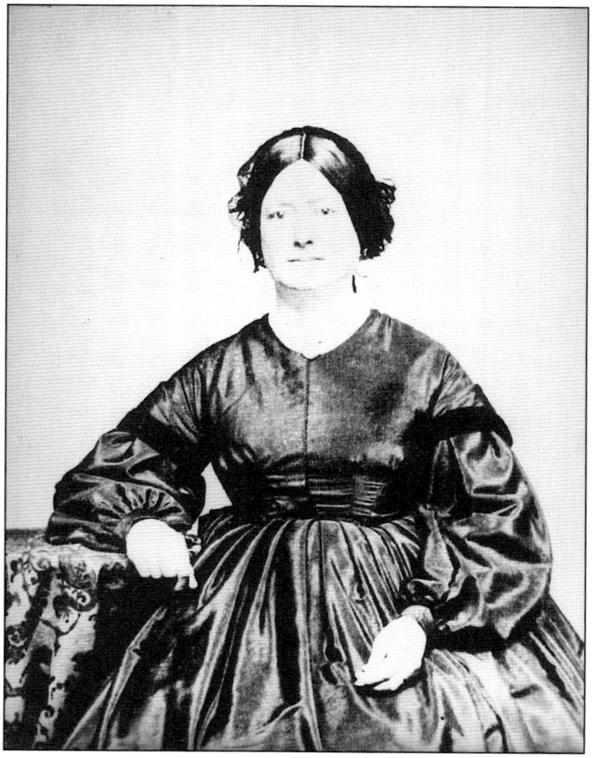

Charles' wife was Mary (Edwards) Barnes.

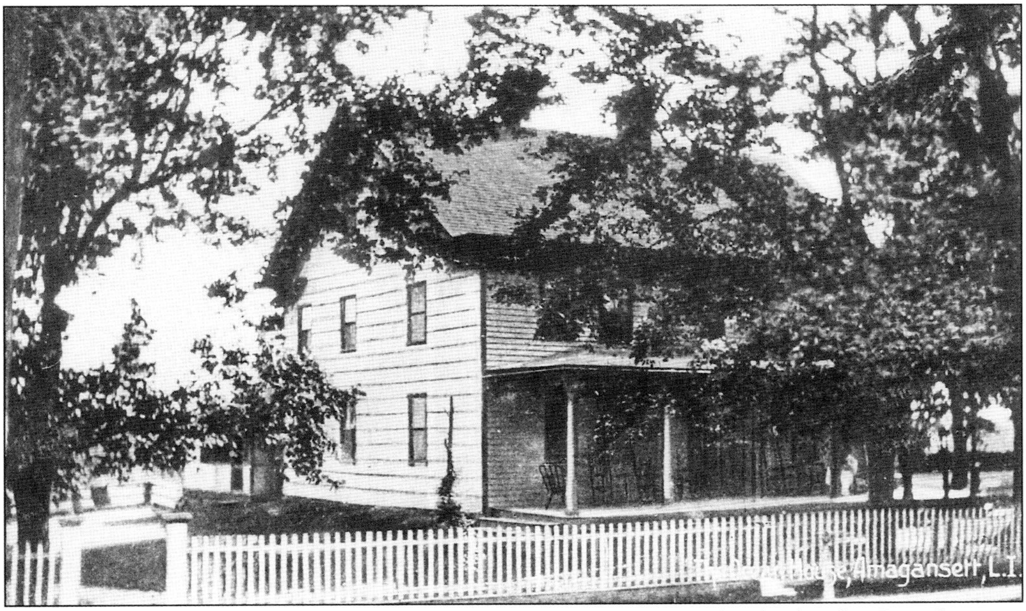

Lieutenant Matthew Barnes was a Revolutionary officer: we know that his brother Jonathan was with the 12th Company of Minute Men in 1776, and later became a captain. The third brother, Nathaniel, moved to Connecticut, and died on a voyage to Charleston, South Carolina. Their father, Isaac, was an energetic tradesman, captain of the militia, and was prominent in town affairs; from 1776 to 1815 he kept an edifying journal.

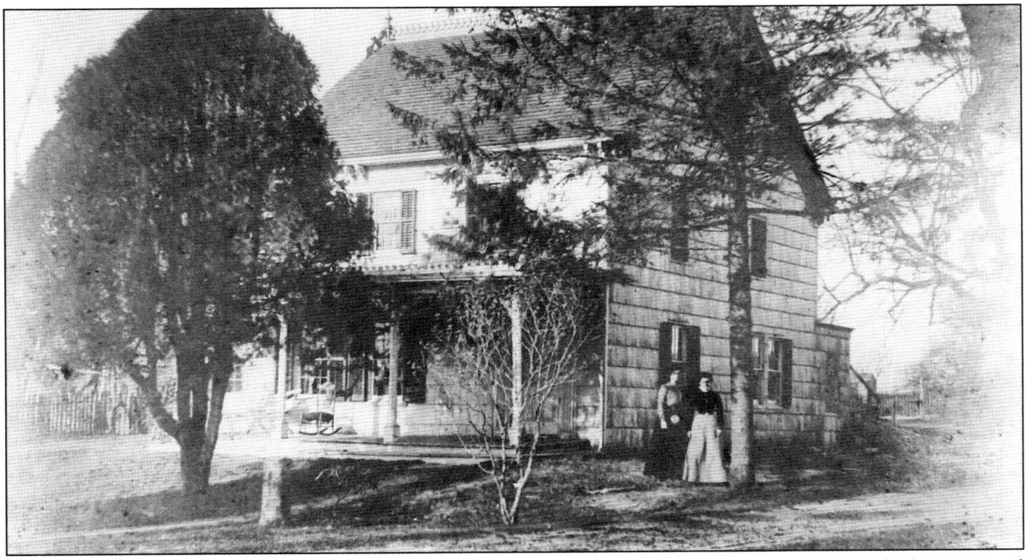

The Baker, Barnes, and Conklin houses pictured were all either built or "raised" by Samuel Schellinger (1765–1848), and he specifically mentions enlarging this, the Jonathan Baker house, in his journal. Two other Schellinger houses were Thomas Edwards', which stood on the north side of Main Street, and Ezekiel Payne's, which was built on the south side. Schellinger was a millwright and house mover as well as a highly skilled builder. His daughter Elisheba married Captain Howell H. Babcock of Sag Harbor, and his grandson and namesake, Samuel Schellinger Babcock, also constructed a number of Amagansett houses.

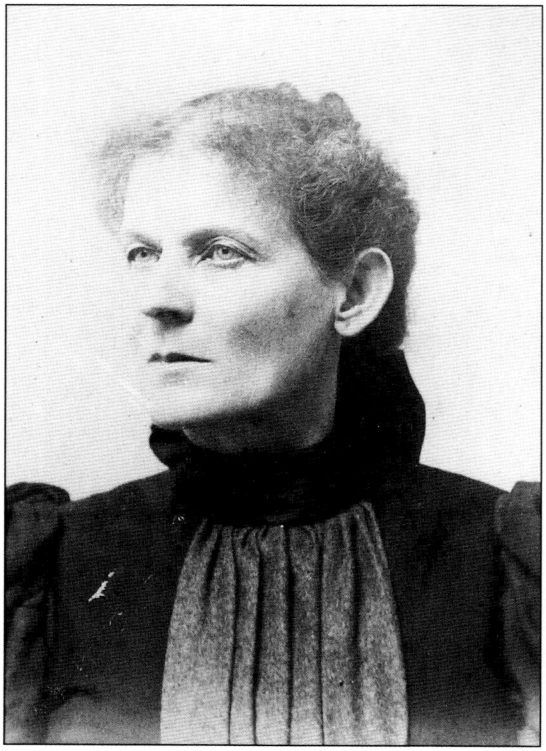 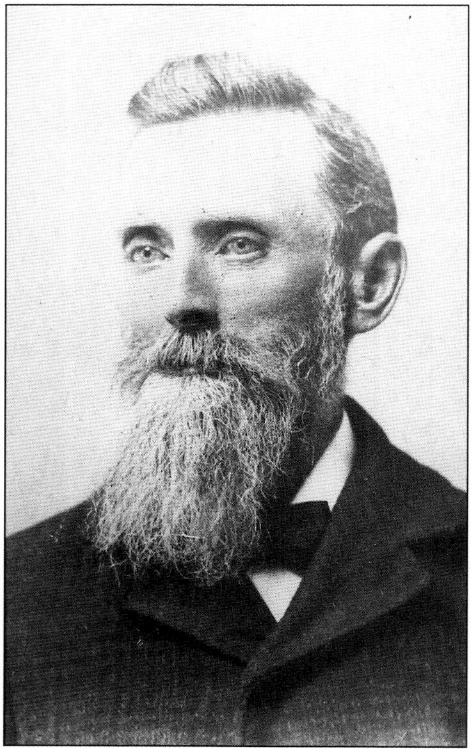

When Althea Barnes Edwards was born in 1846 there were just about fifty houses in the village, and when she married William Terry Baker on Christmas Eve 1869, she carried a large percentage of its "household names." Given that her mother was Thankful *Miller* Edwards, and her daughter Caroline married Jeremiah *Parsons Conklin*, she provides a good example of Amagansett's ongoing interrelatedness. This tapestry of relations made for a far-from-provincial village atmosphere, however: many "younger sons" of local families had moved after the Revolution to "upstate" New York, and other families had gone to New England, New Jersey, and points west, so it was almost as likely that one would marry an out-of-towner with a familiar name as a neighbor. Between merchant and whaling voyages, and adventures like the "Gold Rush" which drew a number of Amagansett men "around the Horn," the village was a lively part of the world.

Samuel Schellinger Babcock supervises his crew, including Lawrence Cartwright, on the construction of the Madison F. King House,1875.

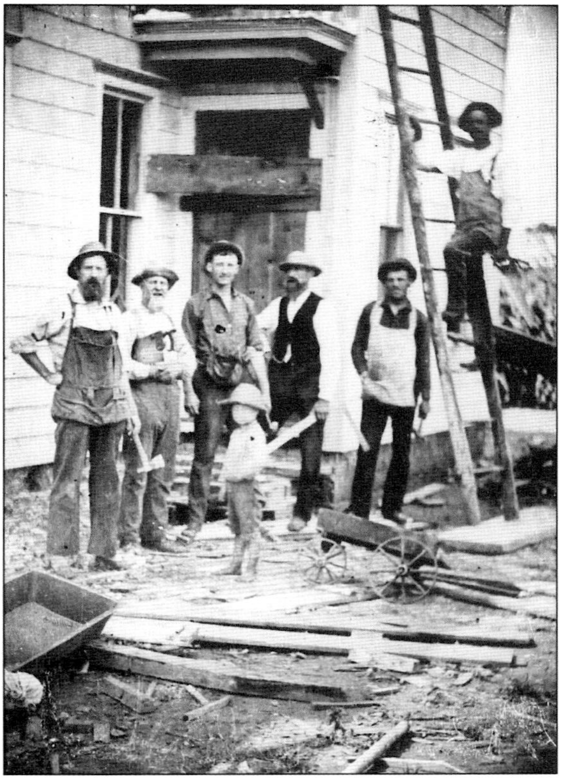

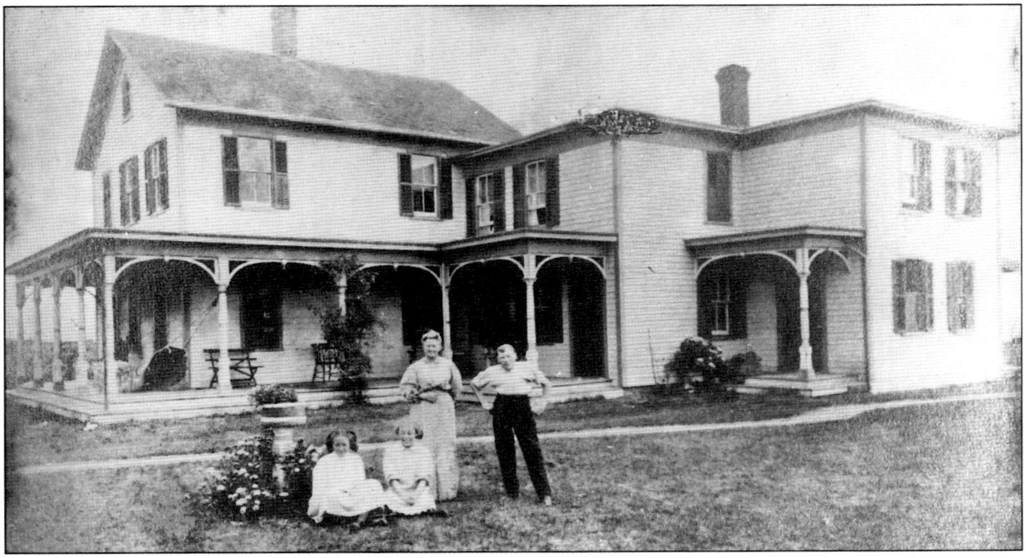

Madison King's father, Clark, made one of his whaling voyages on the *Cadmus* with Captain Hedges Babcock. Madison contracted Samuel Babcock to build this handsome house on what is now Old Montauk Highway. In the early 1900s, "Dora" Bennett King ran a boardinghouse here, for railroad men.

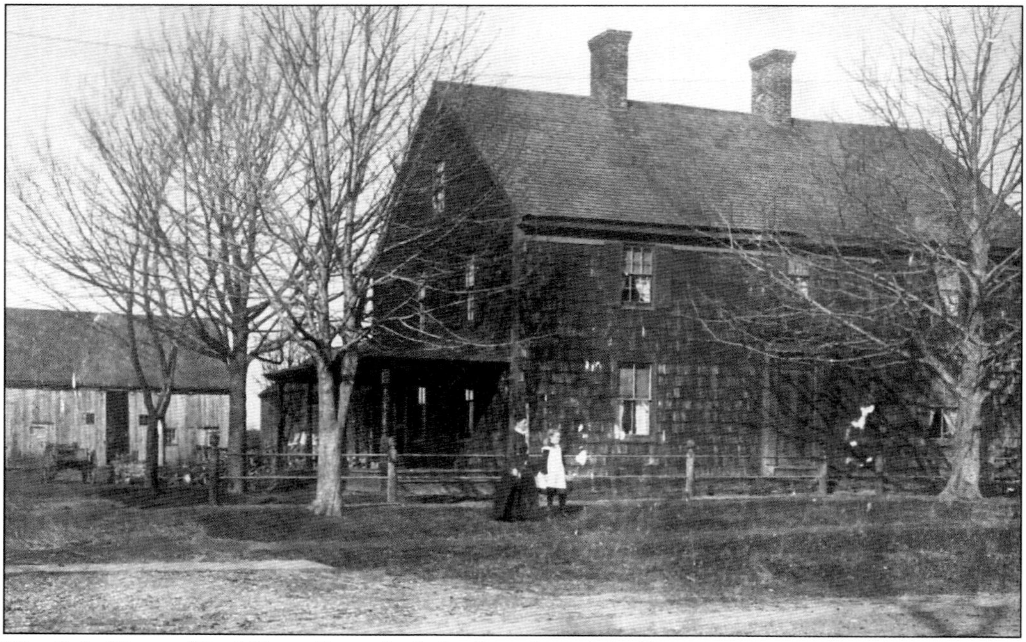

The Schellinger "Red House" was built by Jonathan Schellinger in 1760. Ellen (Schellinger) Parsons, who appears in the last chapter, was born here in 1837. Pictured are Ellen (Oakley), wife of George Stratton Schellinger, and her daughter Eliza. The guest book that the George S. Schellinger's kept for their boarding house here shows visitors from as far away as California.

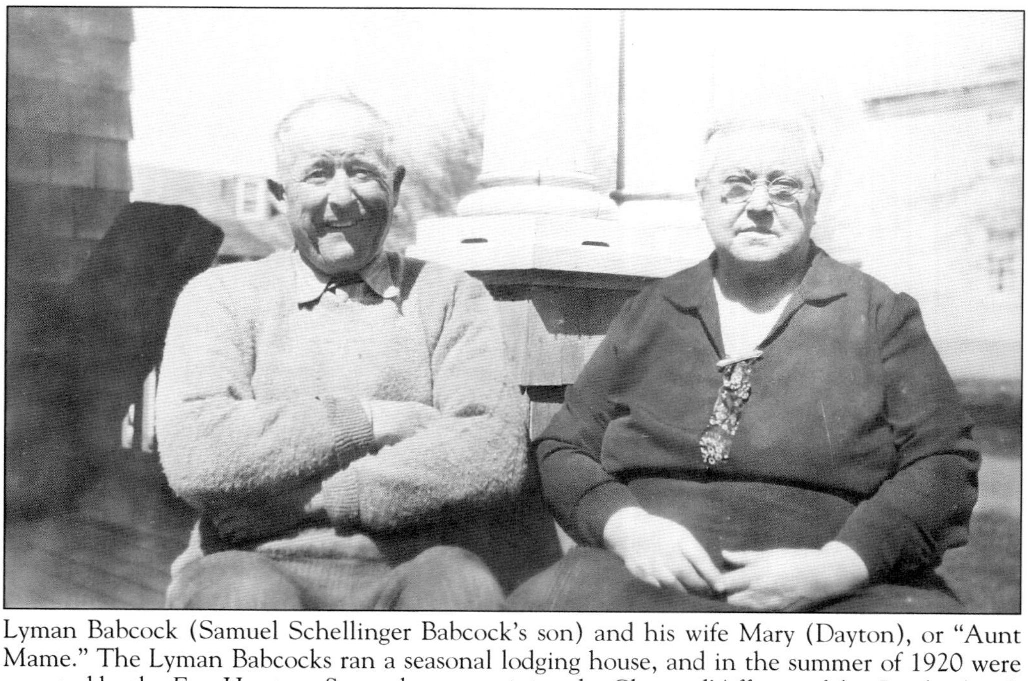

Lyman Babcock (Samuel Schellinger Babcock's son) and his wife Mary (Dayton), or "Aunt Mame." The Lyman Babcocks ran a seasonal lodging house, and in the summer of 1920 were reported by the *East Hampton Star* to be entertaining the Charge d'Affaires of the Czechoslovak Republic, and several of his friends.

Two

Summer and Winter

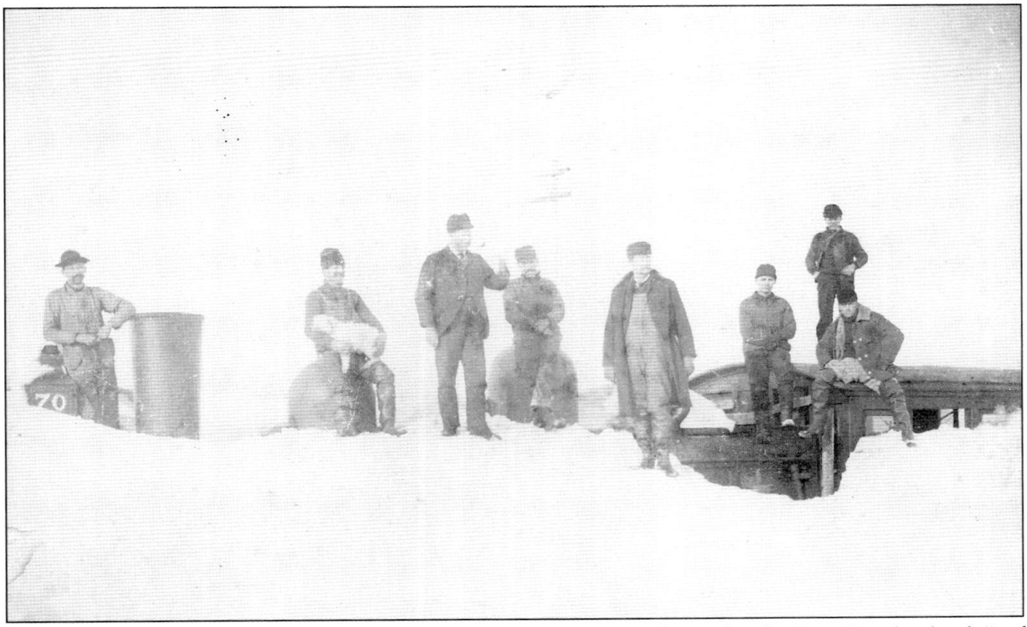

In 1895, Miss Emma Bridgens decided to visit her sister Ruhamah, the "mail-order bride" of David Hunting Miller, a life saver at the Ditch Plains Station. Emma took the train from Beech Creek, Pennsylvania, to Jersey City, New Jersey; she then boarded a ferry for Manhattan, caught a horse car that took her to the East River, and took another ferry to Long Island City, where she bought a ticket for Montauk. After all this she was told that the train would not yet be going any farther than Amagansett, so she contacted her brother-in-law, who agreed to meet her there. At the ticket window later, though, it had been discovered that LIRR President LeBoutelier would be making a VIP inspection of the entire new system that day, and the train would run to Montauk after all. Emma proudly became the first paying passenger from Long Island City to "the end of the line." Those first runs to Amagansett and Montauk were in August: by that winter, lighthearted summer excursions were a dim memory, and crews had to contend with snowdrifts on the strip between the two villages, which is where this photograph was taken.

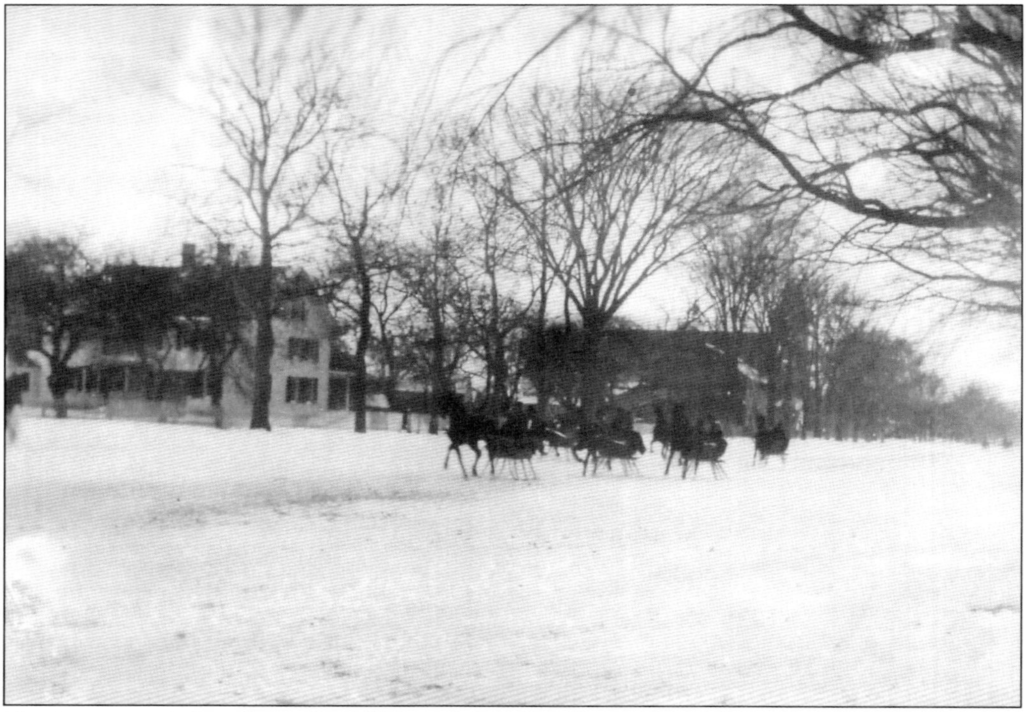

Sleigh races on Main Street, East Hampton, were a popular form of entertainment at the turn of the century.

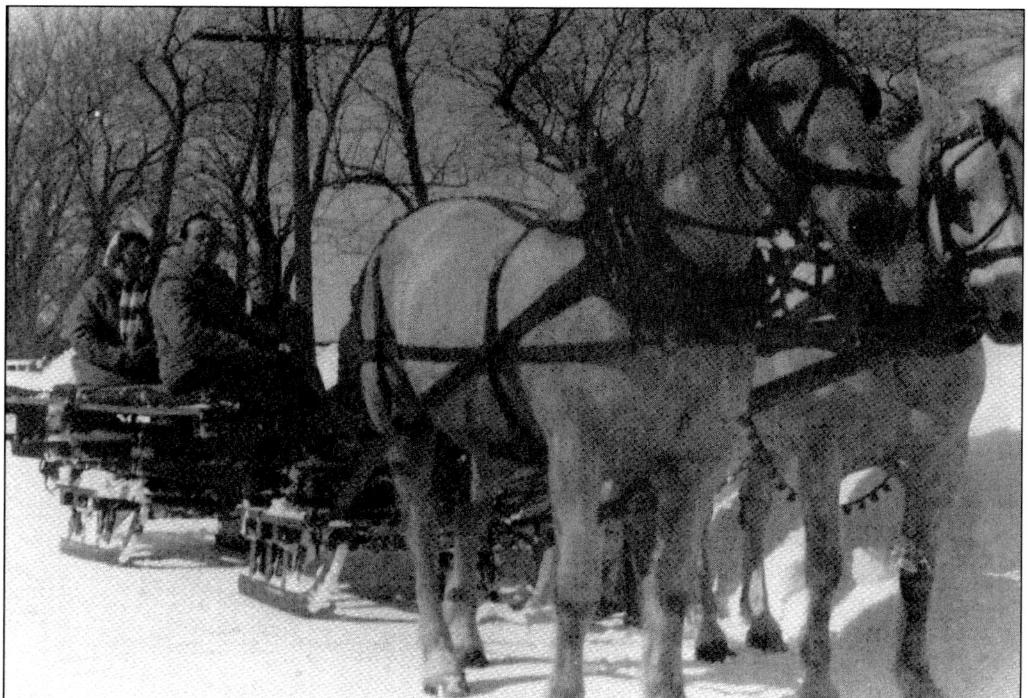

Carleton Kelsey is shown here sleighing with Roy Lester and daughters in the 1940s.

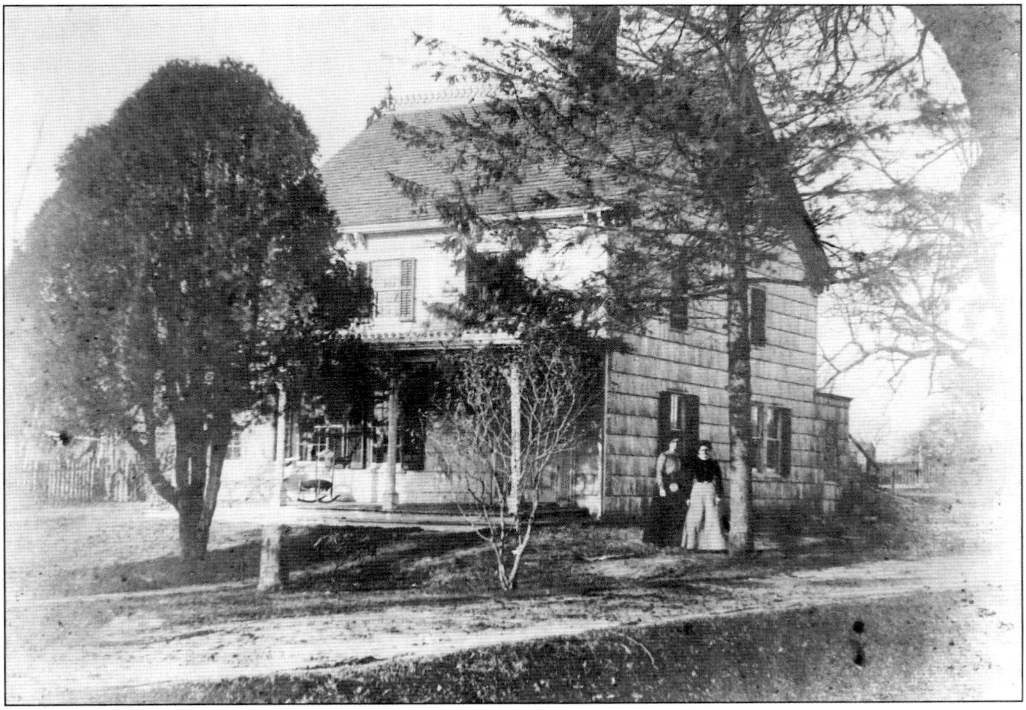

The George L. Baker house is shown here with Baker's granddaughters, Caroline and Ethel, posing out front.

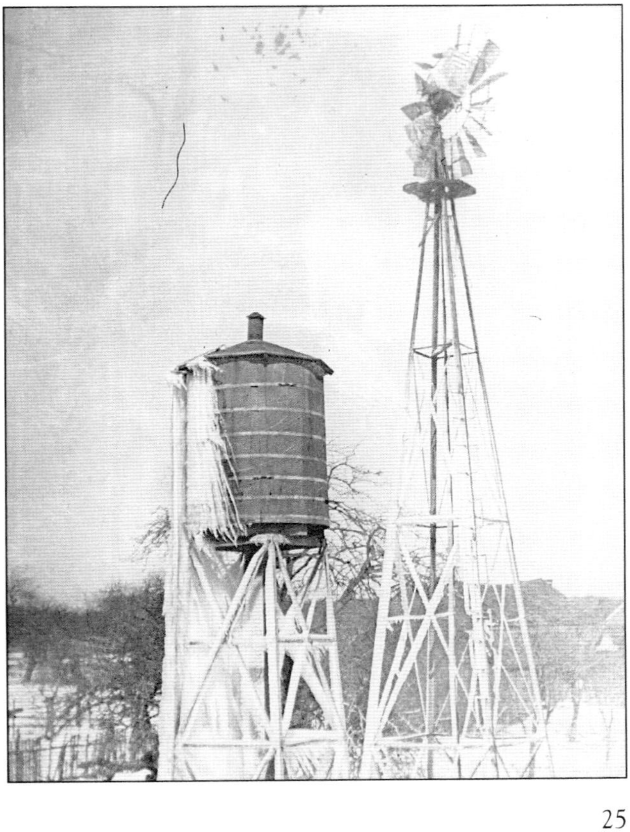

This tower, at Joseph Cozzens' house, provided some of the first domestic running water in the village. For most of Amagansett's history, winter chores included hauling water from the pump at the cistern to the house and the barn. There was an art to "settling" a well. Main Street developed because distance to the water table was most efficient there, in days when wells were hand-dug and lined with brick.

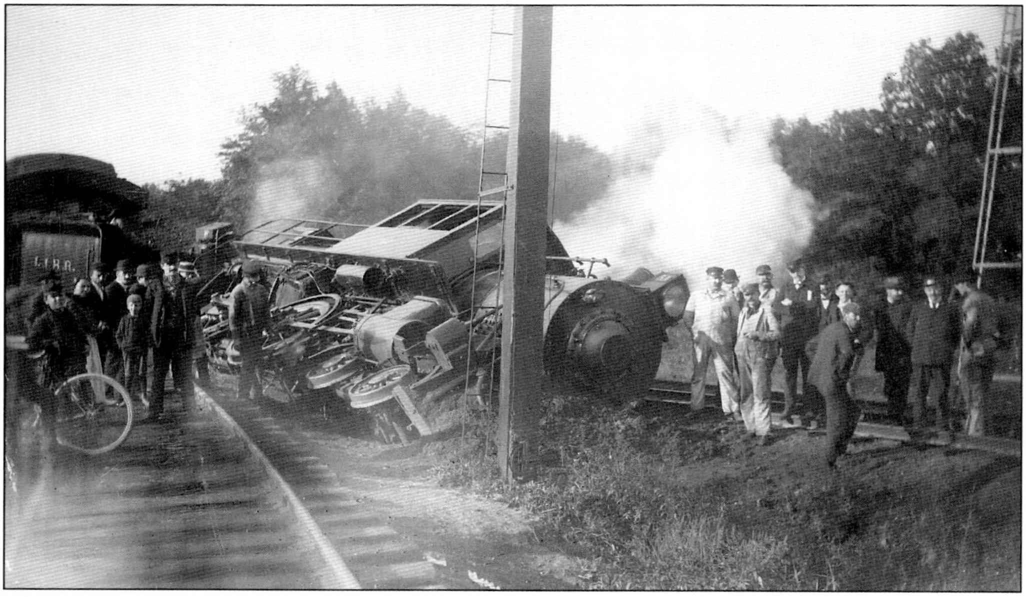

This disaster occurred "up island" as the train headed for Amagansett. The *East Hampton Star* mentions a variety of mishaps within the township, including a derailment that occurred near Hither Woods, between Amagansett and Montauk.

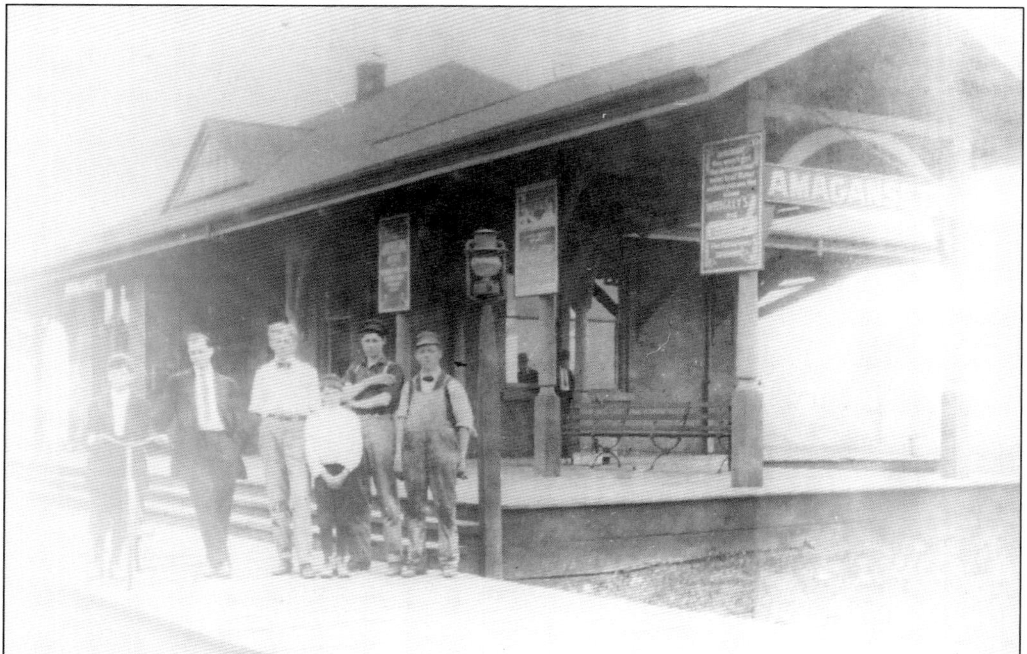

Howard Eichhorn (the Western Union messenger), Ira Baker (stationmaster), Louis Schmidt (telegrapher), Frank Tibbetts, Craven Vaughn, and George Eichhorn are shown here in 1909. There was full Western Union service at the station until Ira Baker's retirement in the 1950s. Baker was a renowned telegrapher himself, and his distinctive touch with the modern "bug" version of the telegraph key was recognizable to dispatchers up and down the island.

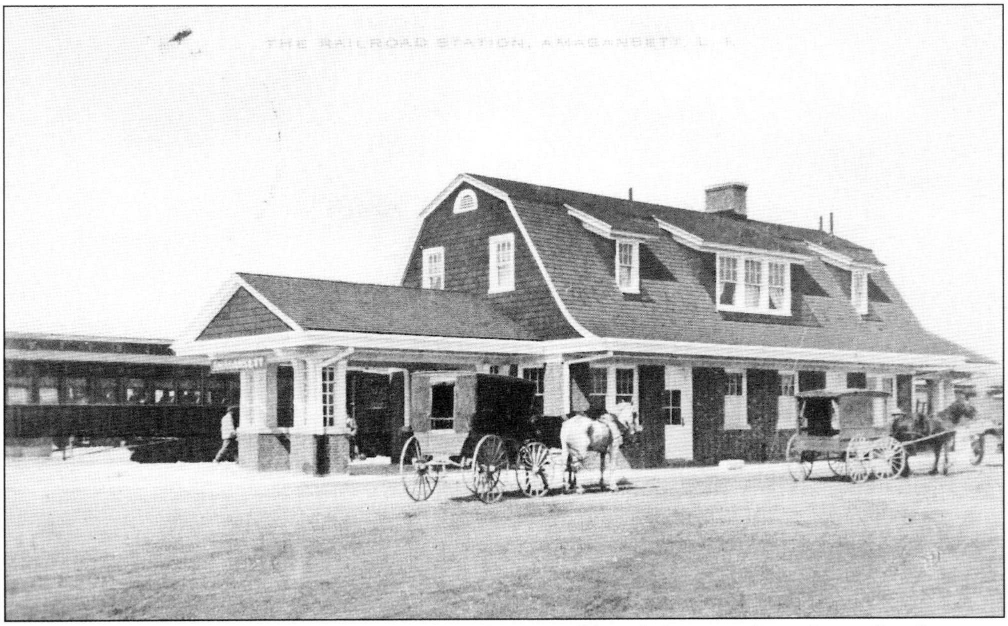

As this postcard shows, the "iron horse" supplemented but did not replace the earlier horse and carriage. At the far right, you may also see an early automobile or "horseless carriage."

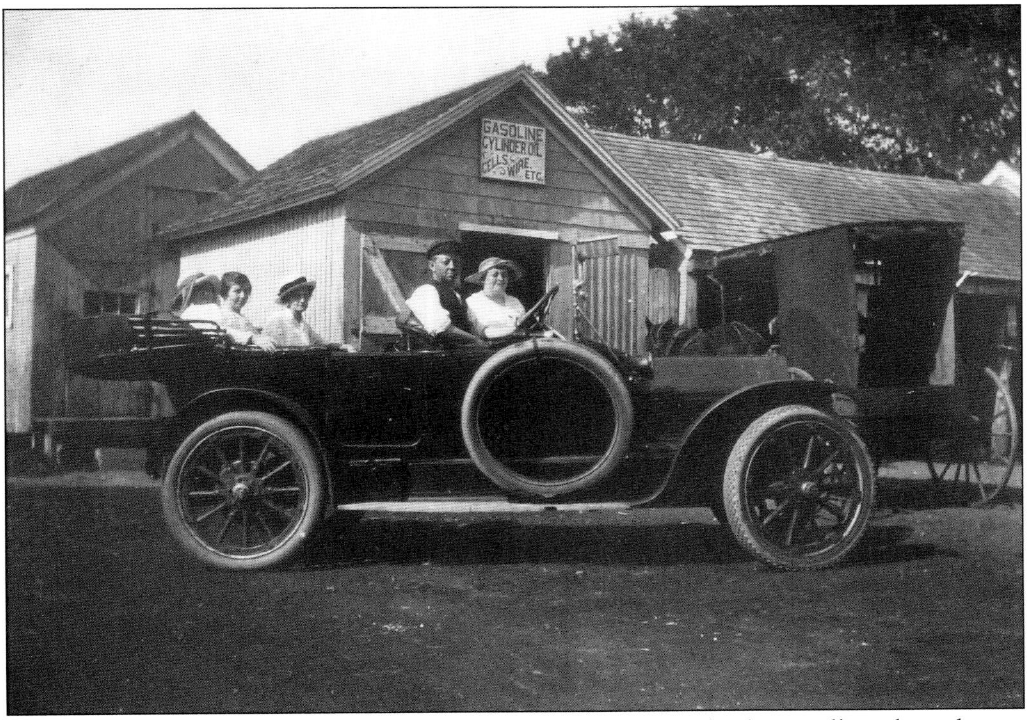

The Eichhorn family pose in their Buick—in 1913 the steering wheel was still on the right.

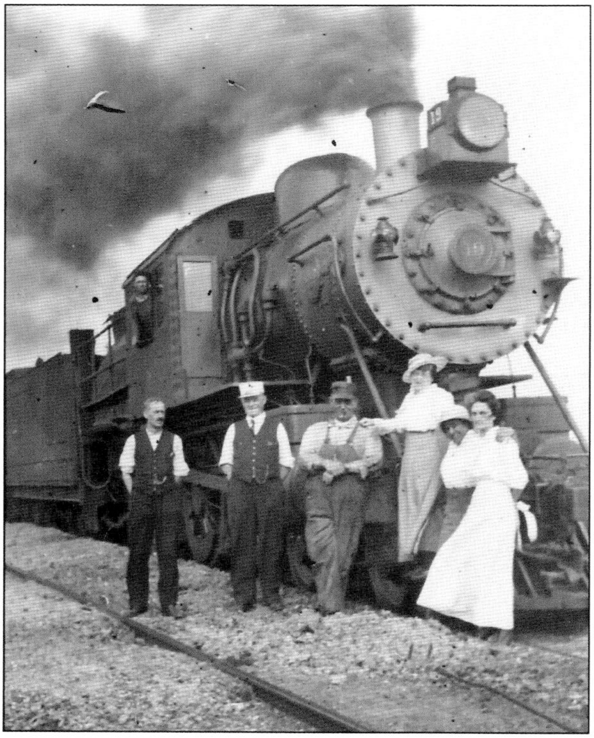

Florence Eichhorn (in hat) poses with members of her family and a railroad crew. Florence served as librarian from 1950 to 1964—in the building which had once been her family home. Before that, from 1910 to 1921, she had been the first New York Telephone Company operator in Amagansett. The telephone exchange was also, initially, in the library building.

Amato (Mike) Dellapolla worked as a "hostler" on the "Scoot." Clem Eichhorn is shown standing on the ground.

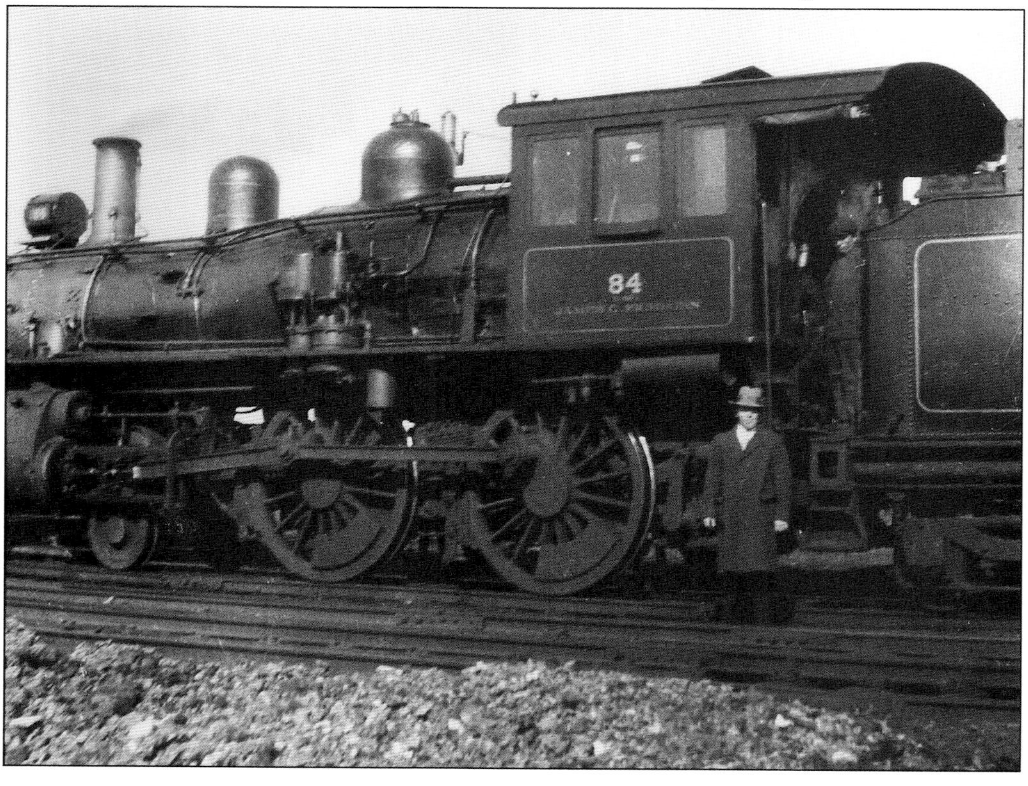

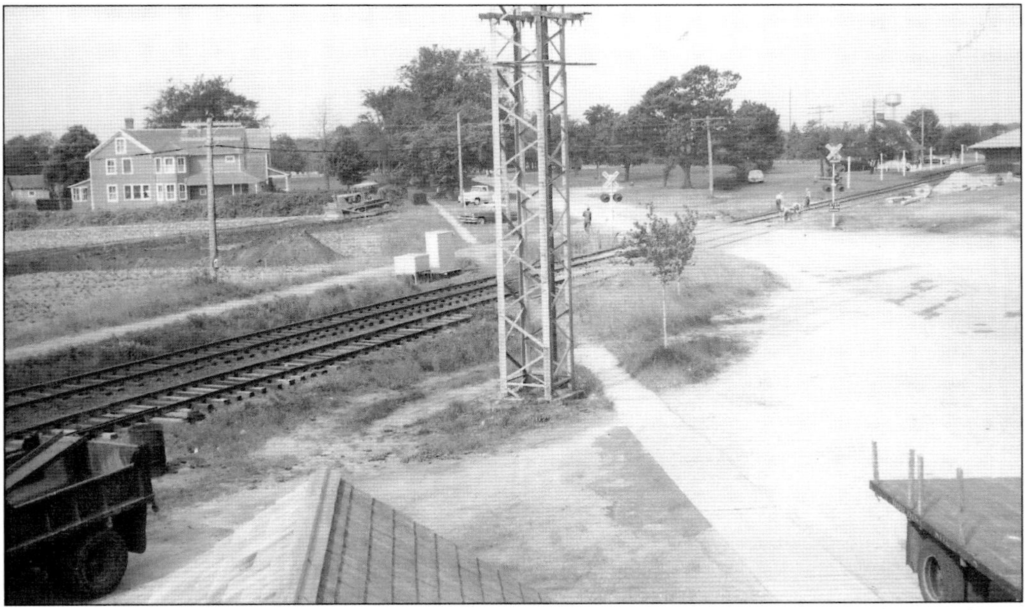

As motor traffic increased, "Old" Montauk Highway, with a turn that required great driver concentration, became especially treacherous. This photograph shows the crossing at the east end of the village before the highway was re-routed in 1957.

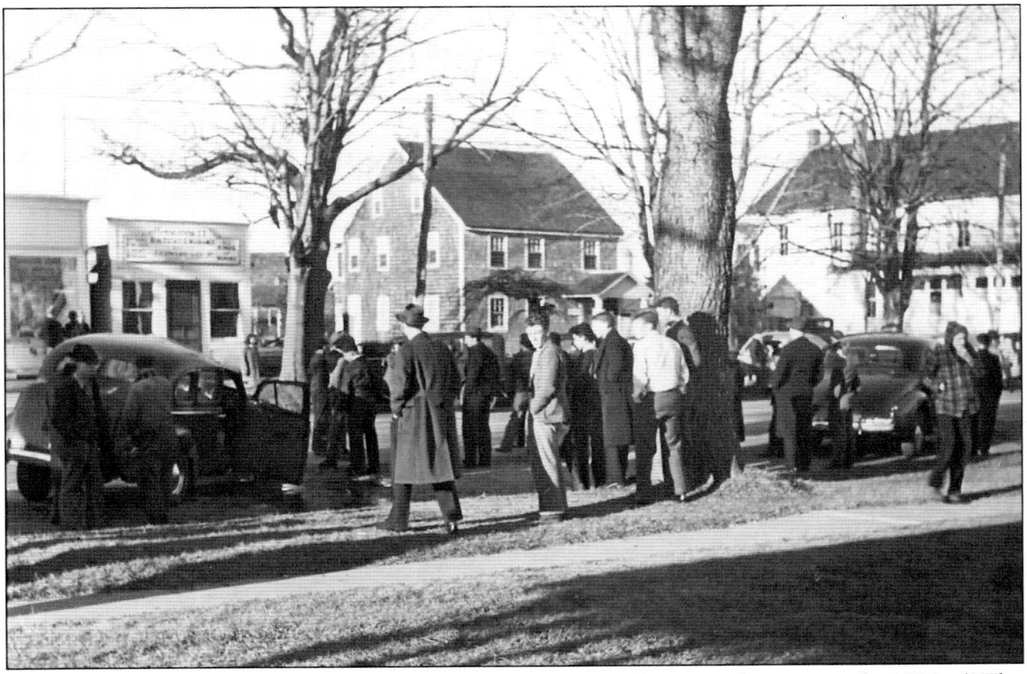

Although the *East Hampton Star* began reporting car accidents in the very early 1920s ("The people of the State of New York should rise up in arms to do something to stop the slaughter of pedestrians by rank, inexperienced drivers," one magistrate was reported as saying), this is the first photograph on file of a fender bender in Amagansett. It took place right in front of the insurance office (now Coach Leather).

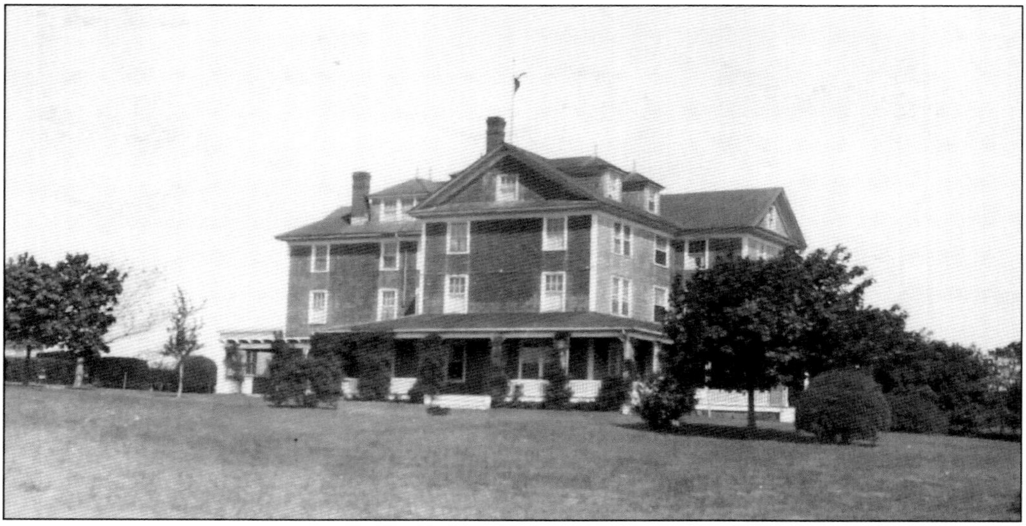

The first summer resort hotel in Amagansett was built in 1898 on the corner of Indian Well Hollow Highway and Further Lane (an area settled before 1700 by the Barnes family). Wealthy summer visitors had begun building homes in this neighborhood in 1884 (the first, built by Hunter College president George Davis, was just south of the Sea View property), and Dr. Rossiter Johnson built his first of four summer "cottages" on Bluff Road in 1892. While most of the summer houses remain, this luxurious hotel burned down in 1924.

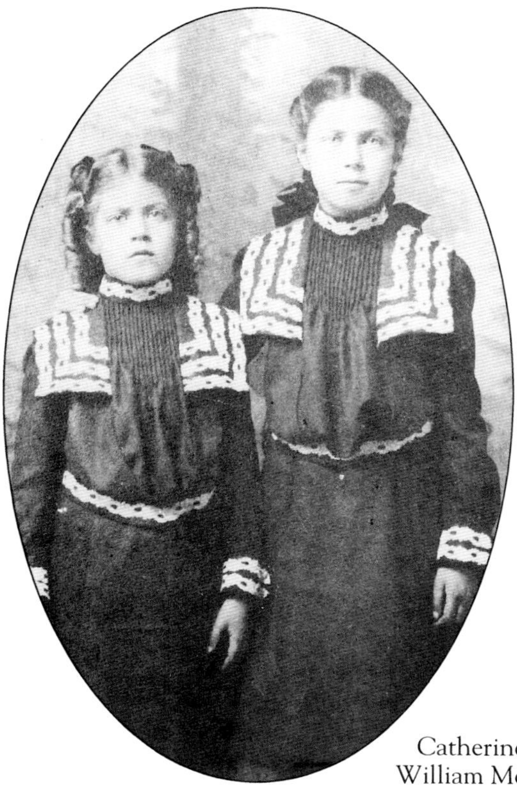

Catherine and Florence Terry were daughters of hotelier William Melvin Terry and his wife Bessie (Hand) Terry.

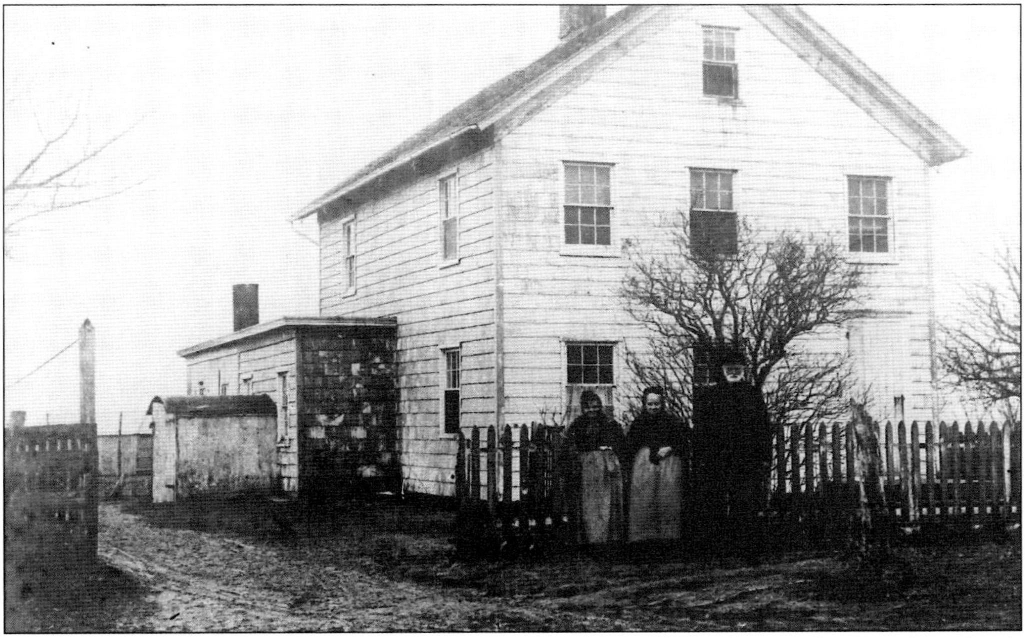

The Jonathan Edwards house on "Old" Montauk Highway is shown here with Mary, Jonathan's daughter; Phebe, his second wife; and Jonathan, a deep-sea whaler. When an unknown photographer came through Amagansett in December 1902, the "resort" community had been developing for generations, the railroad had been here for seven years, and the age of "ragtime" had arrived! Fortunately, many villagers came out to have their pictures taken with their houses, giving us a marvelous record of another transitional time in Amagansett's history.

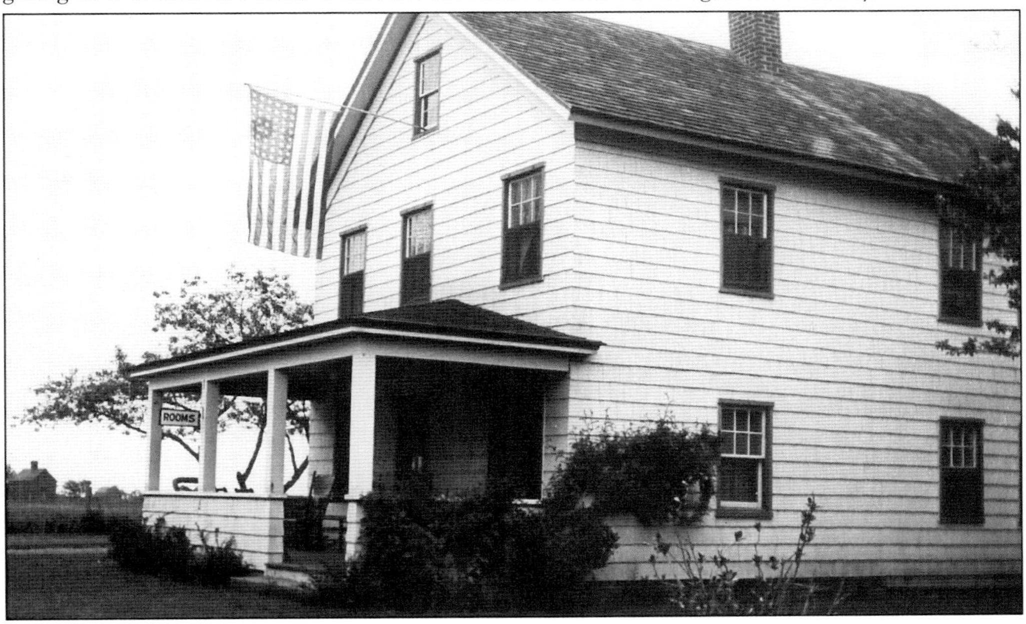

William Kelsey purchased the Jonathan Edwards house—without heat or running water—in 1921, and, with improvements, Emma Bridgens Kelsey ran a rooming house there, from 1927 to 1957.

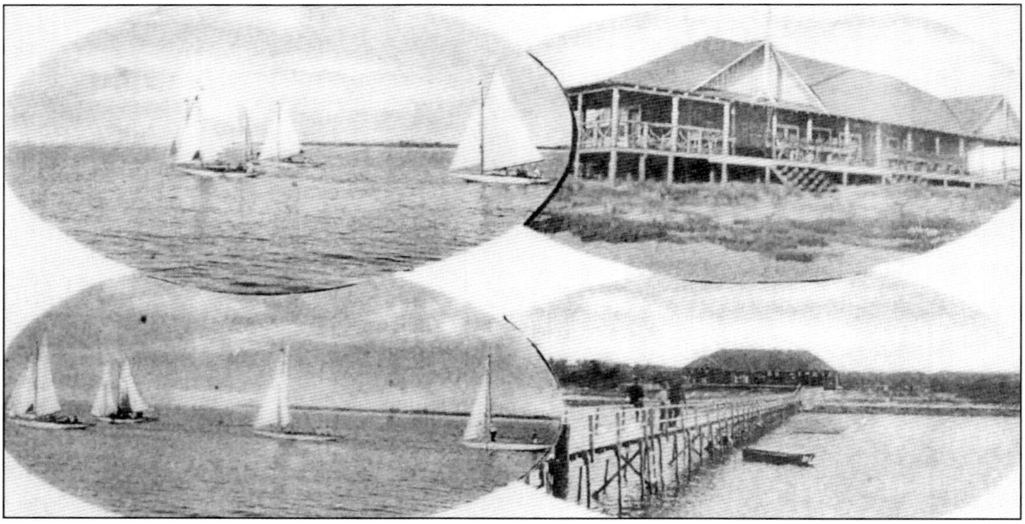

Construction began on the first Devon colony summer houses in December 1908.

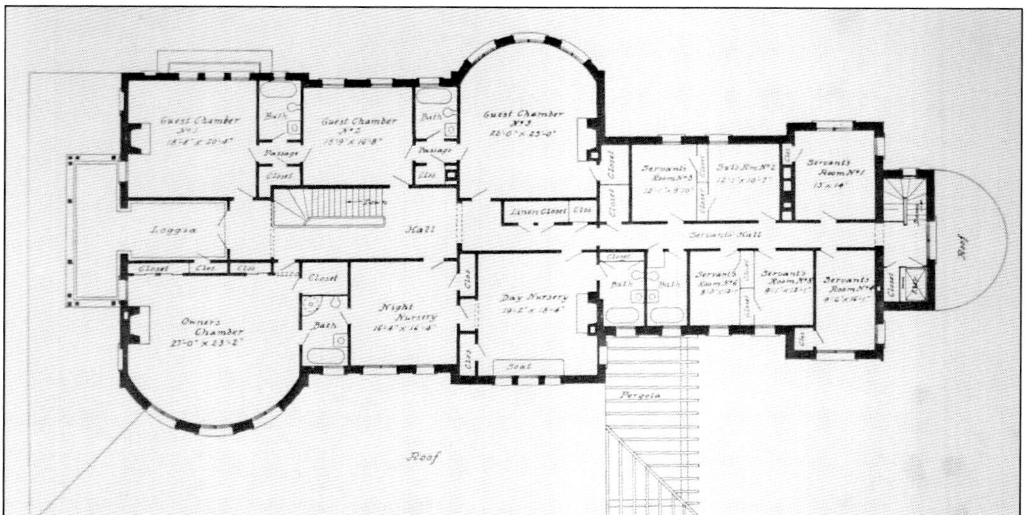

This Devon "cottage" floorplan shows that accommodating guests was also a serious consideration in private summer residences.

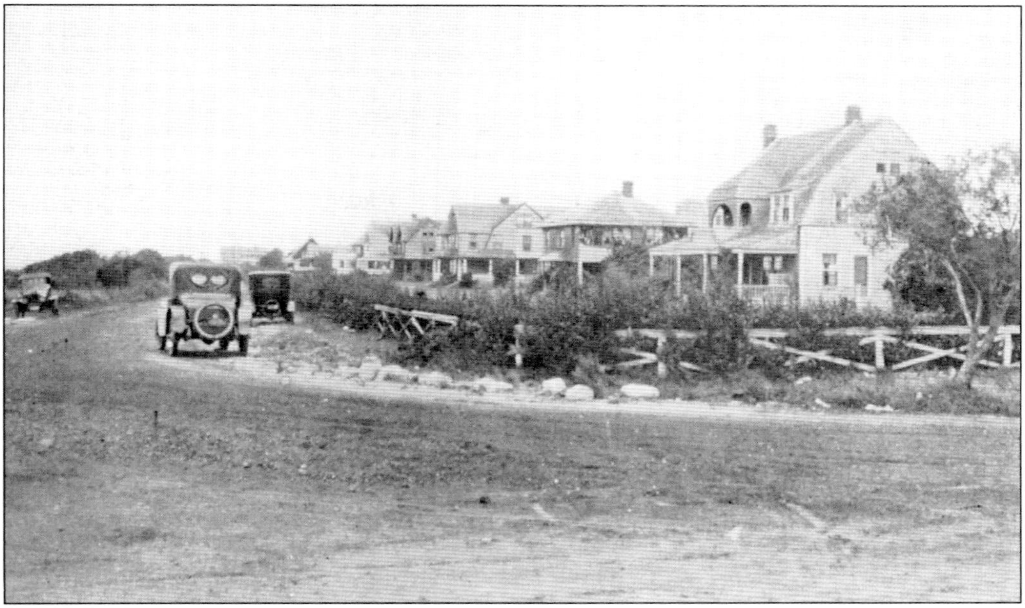

Bluff Road was originally a trail used by the Montauks; this postcard shows "Bluff," "Dune Crest," and other lovingly named summer houses.

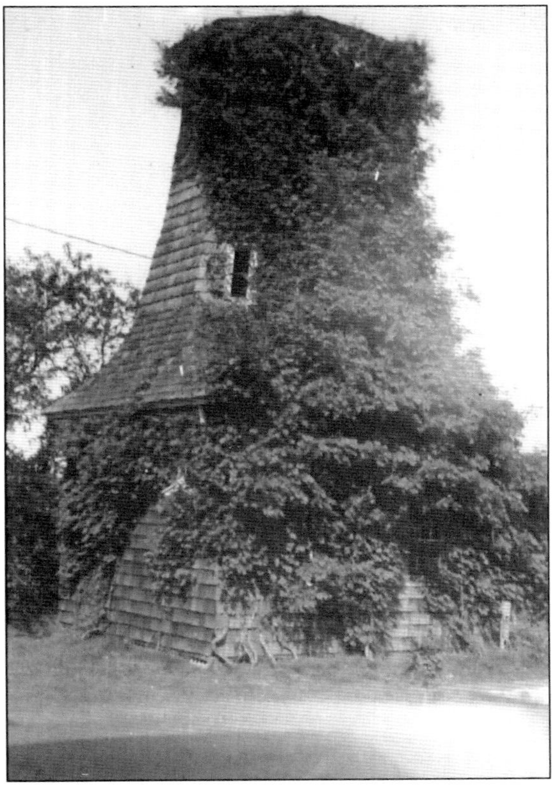

This private water plant on the Rossiter Johnson property was run by a hot-air engine, and housed a large copper tank.

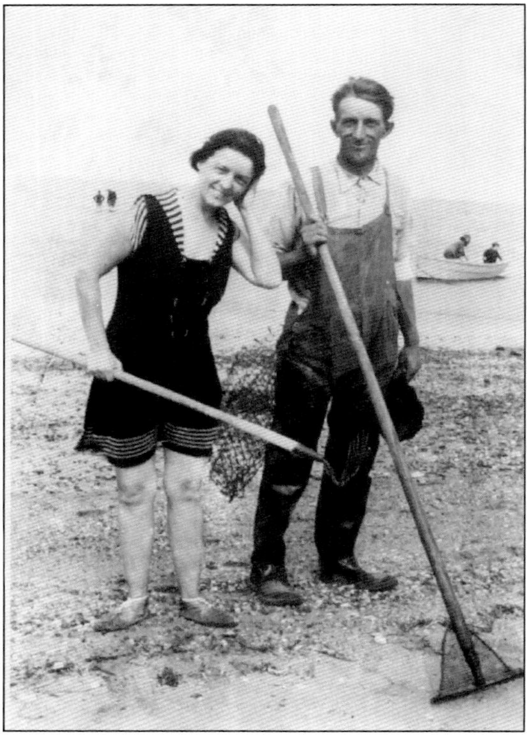

Gertrude (Smith) poses with Charles Lester, son of Captain "Posy" Lester. For local families, the work they had been doing for centuries was not incompatible with summer fun.

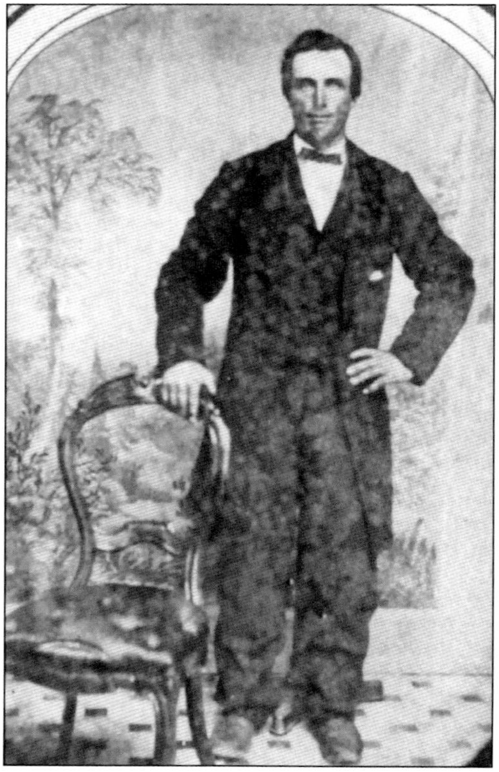

Samuel Selah Lester was the great-uncle of LeRoy (Roy) King Lester, the man for whom the Amagansett Historical Association's Carriage Museum is named. Samuel Selah moved the Amagansett Jonathan Barnes house to the northeast corner of Cedar Street in East Hampton, and even though he is not in the same genealogical "line" as Charles (see previous photograph), the cross-generational resemblance that has evolved in many local families is evident.

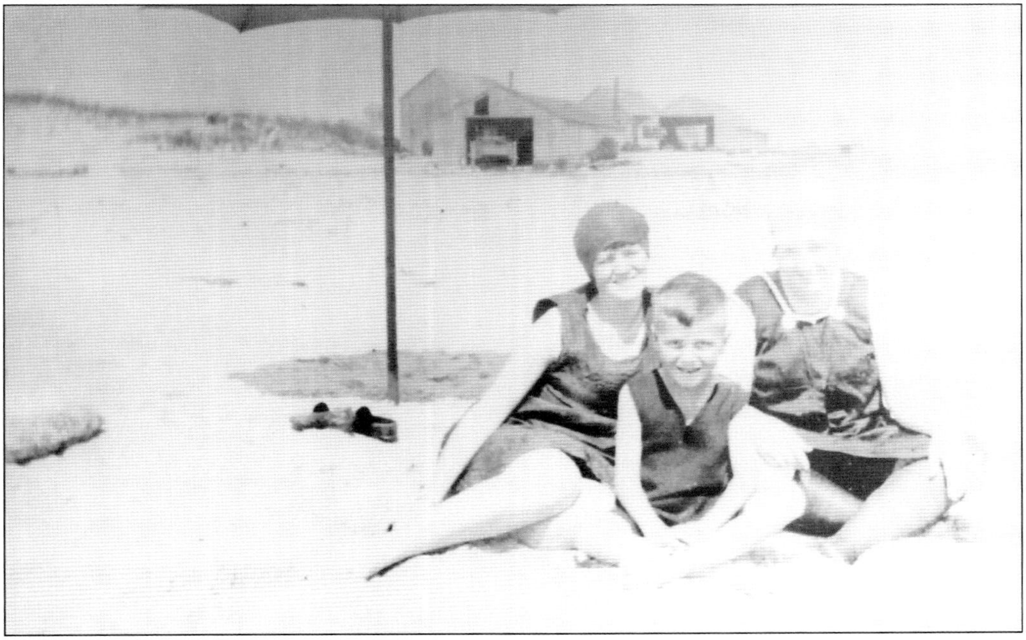

Alice Stuart (later Mrs. Vernon Kelsey), Jane Duryea, and Edwin Tuthill pose on an Amagansett beach, 1920.

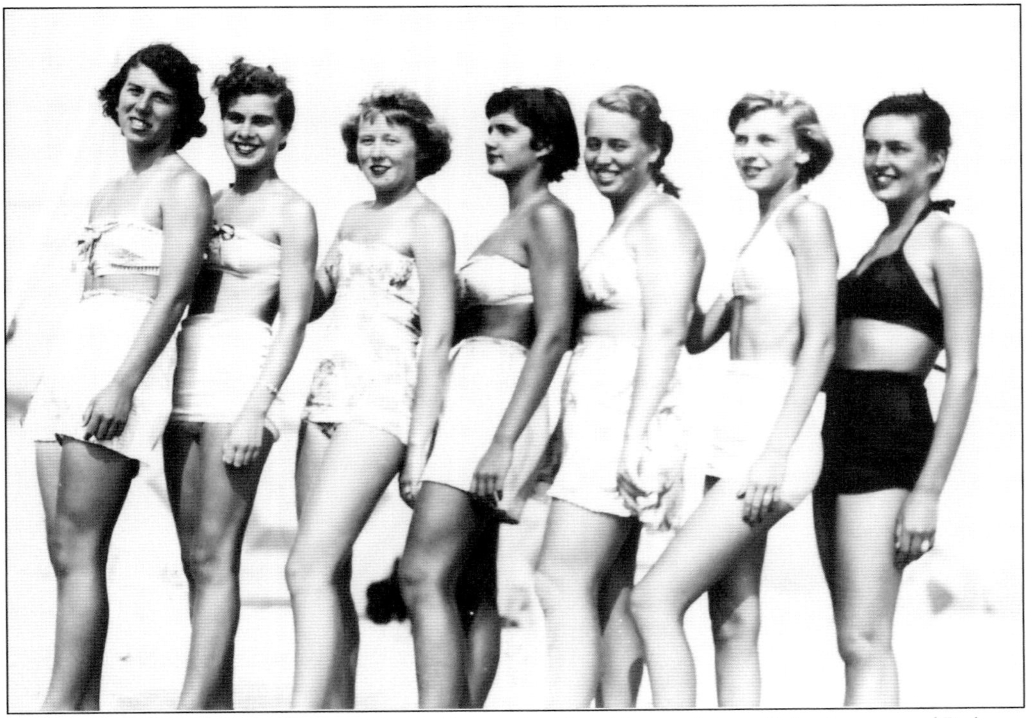

Tina Fernandez, Lillian Stella, Joan Scott , Diane Conklin, Mary Doherty, Helen Loper, and Roberta Gosman in another beach photograph, this time from 1948.

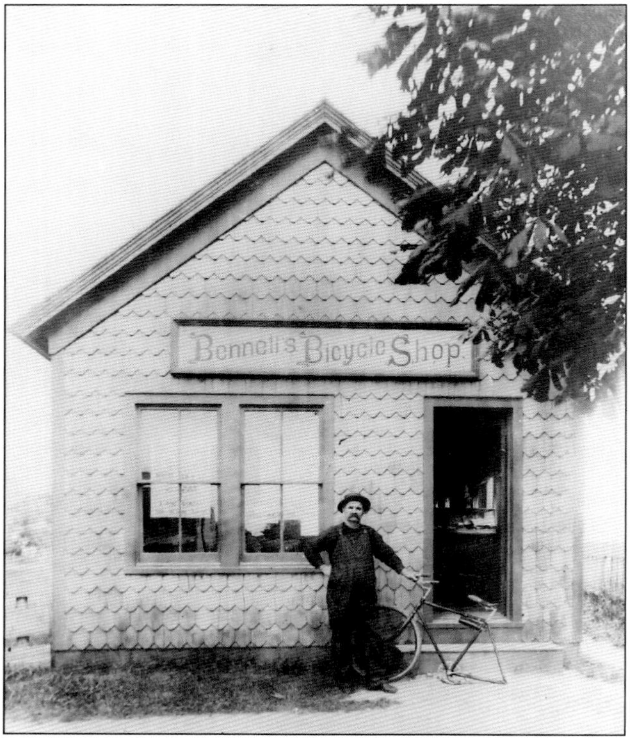

Charles Miller Bennett's thriving bicycle shop was built in 1901.

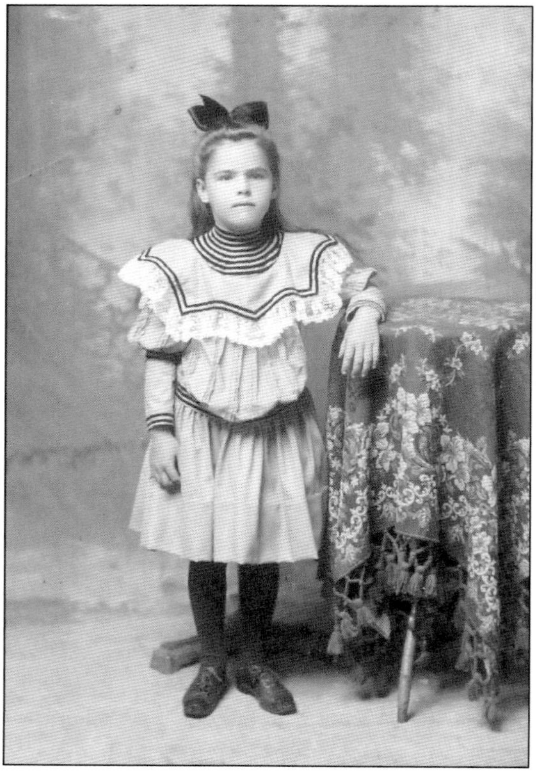

In 1917 Ruth Halsey Bennett, Charles Bennett's daughter, married Amagansett's Ralph Monroe Parsons, a gifted engineer. They lived in Los Angeles.

Three

Here and There

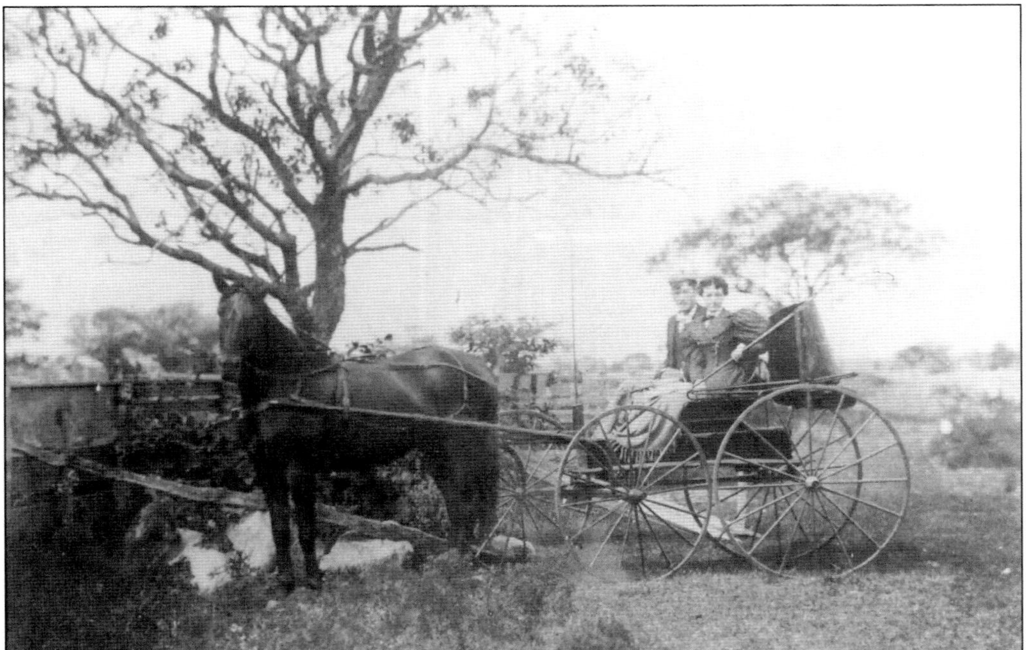

Merrick Hand, a butcher, was the first Amagansett resident to visit the 1893 World's Columbian Exposition. It is not known how many Amagansett residents made the trip to Chicago, but we do know that one man, Frank Griffing, mortgaged his house to raise money for the adventure. A schedule of events from a local scrapbook reveals that there was a recreated glass company, with "200 employees constantly at work," a Bungalow showing how the old Malayan Pirates lived, and an Electric Scenic Theater every half hour. If Merrick got hungry, he could purchase "waffles as big as a grandfather's hat, at five cents apiece." He is shown here with his bride-to-be, Julia Kelsey.

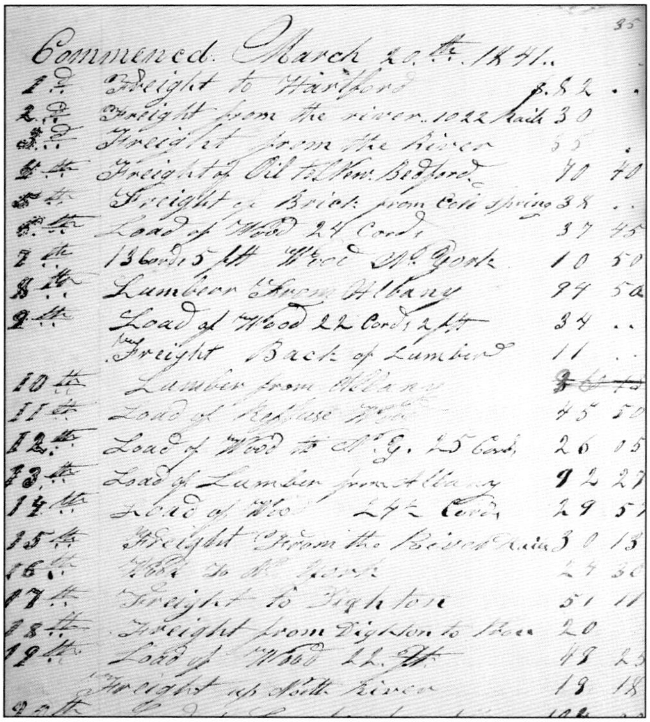

35

Commenced March 20th 1841..

1st	Freight to Hartford	$.82	..
2nd	Freight from the river 1022 [illegible]	30	
3rd	Freight from the River	55	.
4th	Freight of Oil to New Bedford	70	70
5th	Freight of Brick from Cold spring	38	..
6th	Load of Wood 24 Cords	37	45
7th	13 Cords 5 ft Wood N. York	10	50
8th	Lumber from Albany	94	50
9th	Load of Wood 22 Cords 2 ft	34	..
	Freight Back of Lumber	11	..
10th	Lumber from Albany	[illegible]	
11th	Load of Refuse Wood	45	50
12th	Load of Wood to N.Y. 25 Cords	26	05
13th	Load of Lumber from Albany	92	27
14th	Load of Wood 24½ Cords	29	57
15th	Freight from the River [illegible]	30	13
16th	Wood to N. York	24	30
17th	Freight to Dighton	51	11
18th	Freight from Dighton to [illegible]	20	
19th	Load of Wood 22 ft	48	23
	Freight up North River	19	18

This 1841 log, kept by Sineus Edwards (1812–1896) on his sloop *Florian*, gives an idea of the range of shipping traffic from the "landings," and from Sag Harbor. In one month, he made several trips each to Hartford, New Bedford, New York, Albany, and at least one to Providence. The value of the dollar in 1841 was about $35 in present-day (1997) money.

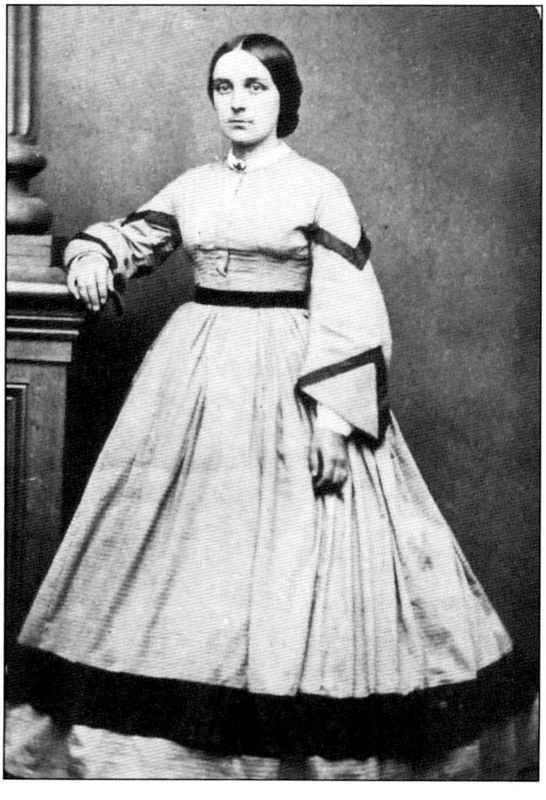

Amanda Edwards (1838–1898), Sineus' niece, married Jeremiah ("Jerry") Baker on October 25, 1860.

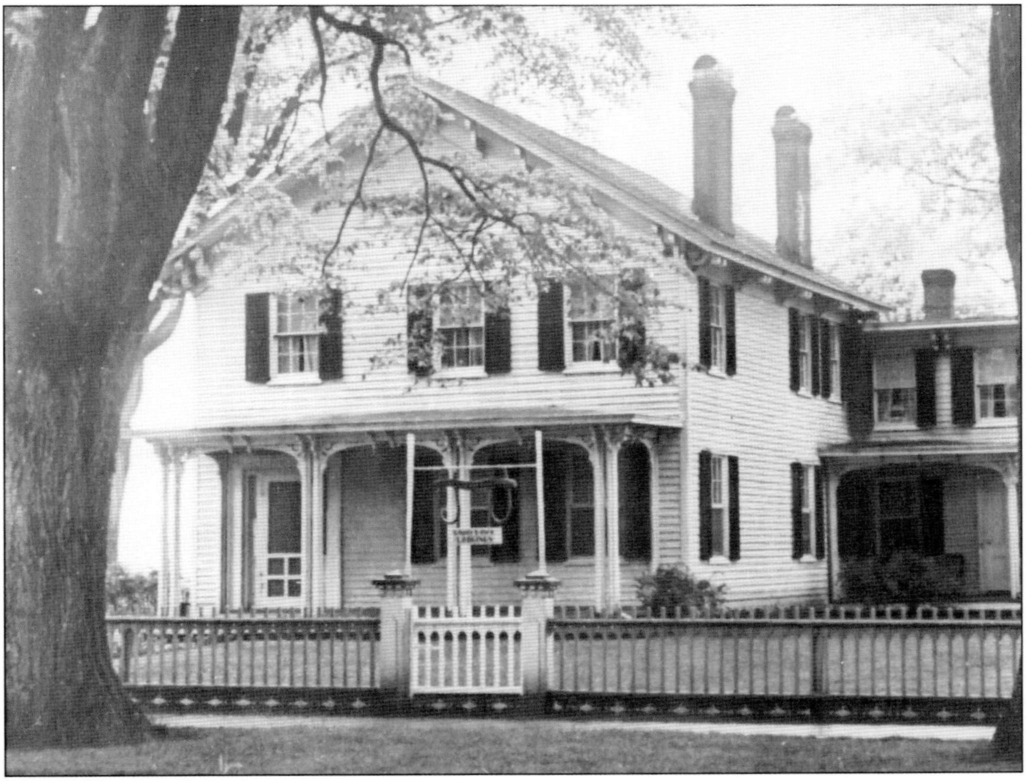

To the right is Jeremiah Baker (1834-1904), who went to California—14,000 miles around Cape Horn!—in search of gold in 1849, with David Barnes of Amagansett. We do not know if he raised enough there to "stake" himself to a stagecoach line, but he began running regular service to Sag Harbor on April 1, 1859. The house above, where he and Amanda lived, still stands on the south side of Main Street.

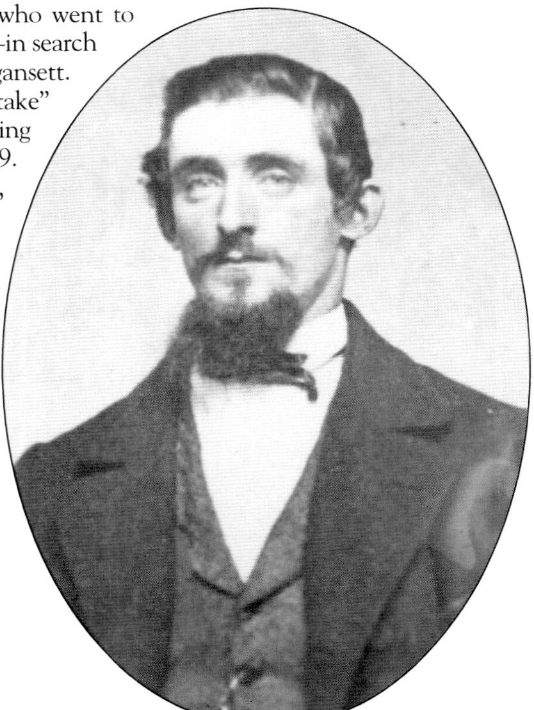

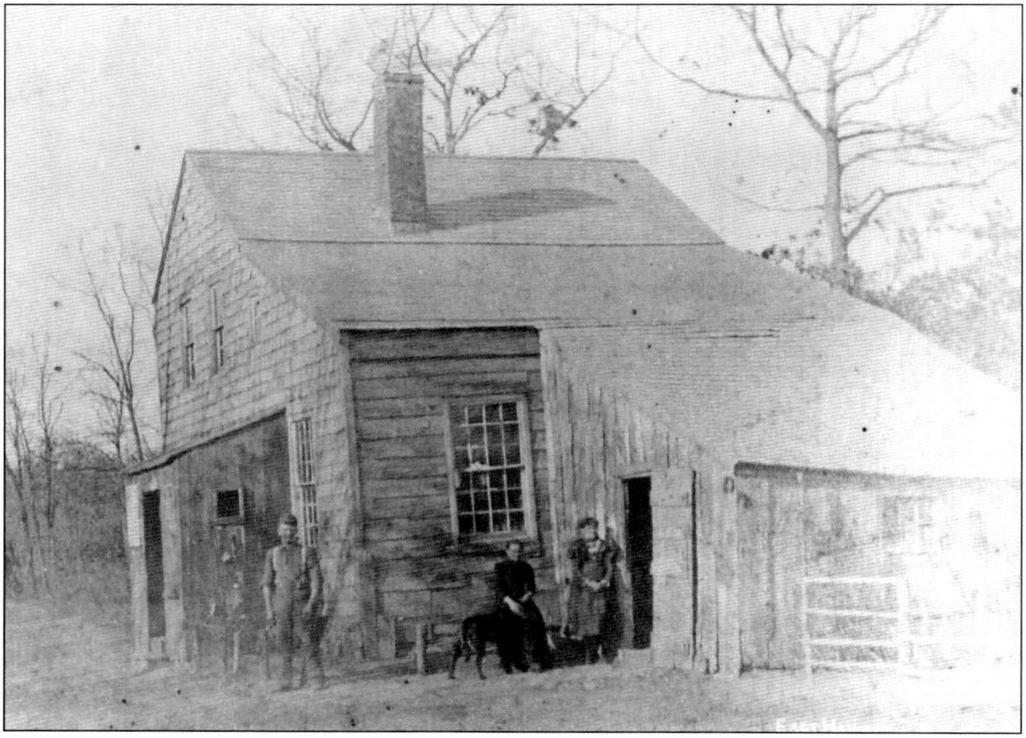

The Sag Harbor tollhouse stood across from the Jewish cemetery on Route 114.

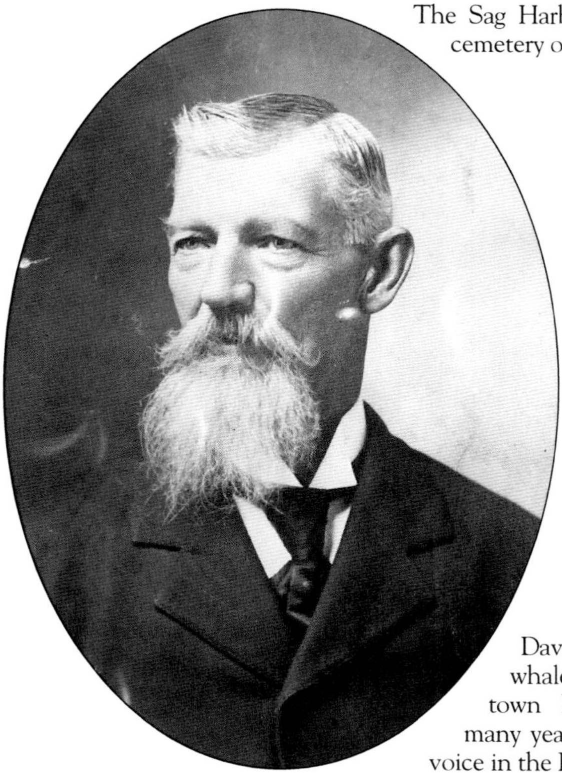

David Barnes, son of Captain Erastus, was a whaler and lifesaving serviceman, and served as town highway commissioner/superintendent for many years. He is also remembered for his deep bass voice in the Presbyterian church choir.

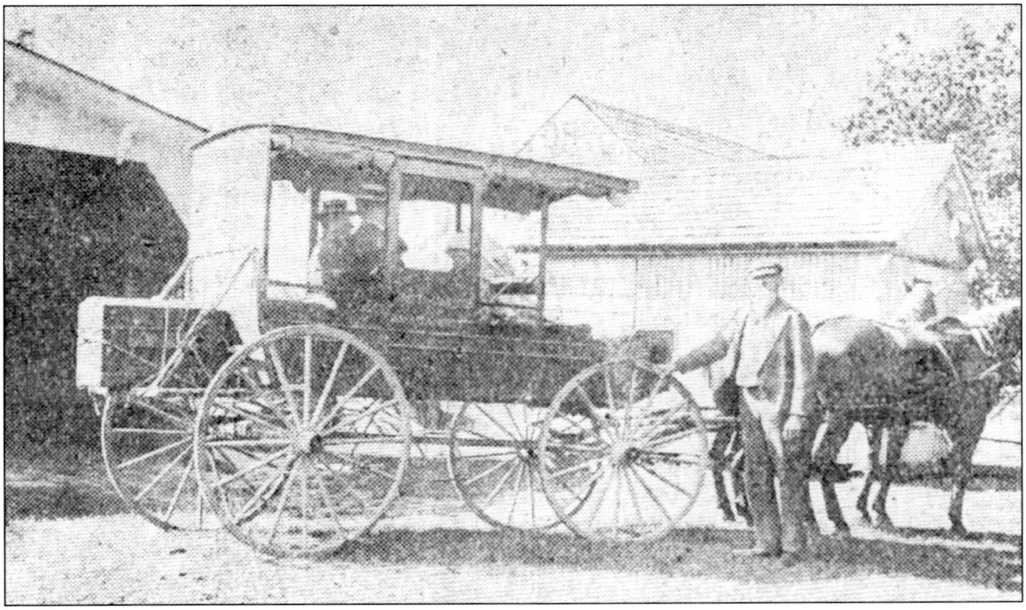

"Jerry" Baker ran this stage, the Sag Harbor "Limited," from 1859 to 1901.

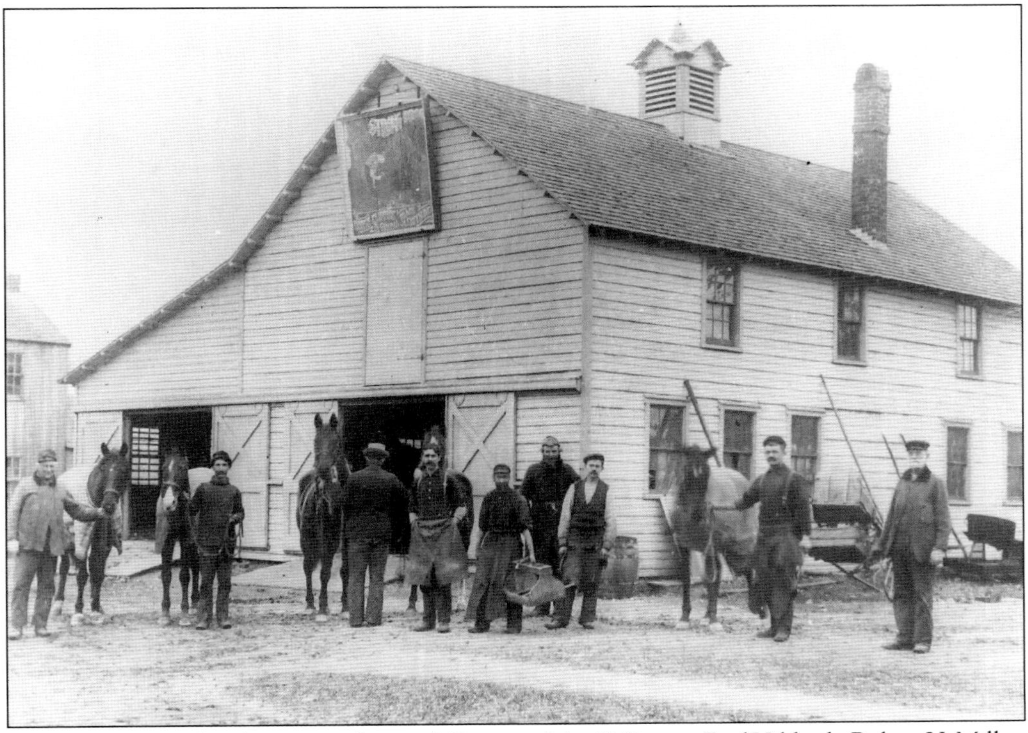

Joseph Osborn, Gilhooly Bennett, Jeremiah Bennett, John Y. Strong, Fred Hildreth, Robert H. Miller, Ed Schumann, James M. Strong, Jr., and James M. Strong pose at the Strong Brothers Blacksmith and Livery Stable. The building on the left is the Worthington Wheelwright Shop. There were three carriage makers in the area, including the aptly named Cartwright of Amagansett.

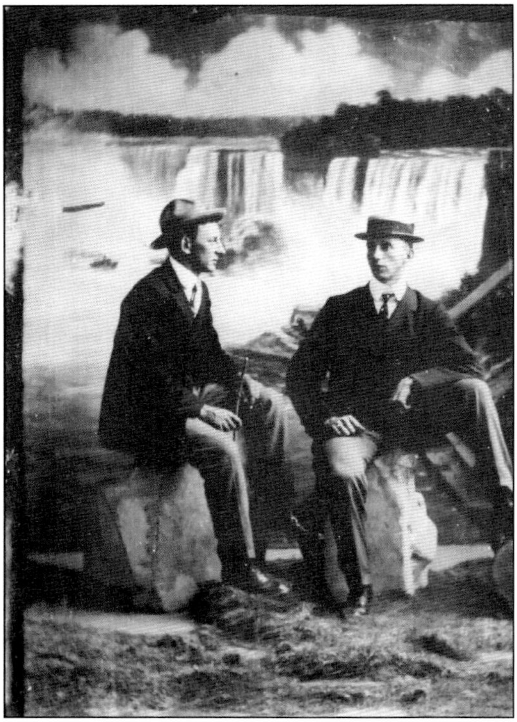

William Cartwright and Lewis Sidney Parsons pose before a "Niagara Falls" backdrop at the 1893 World's Columbian Exposition in Chicago.

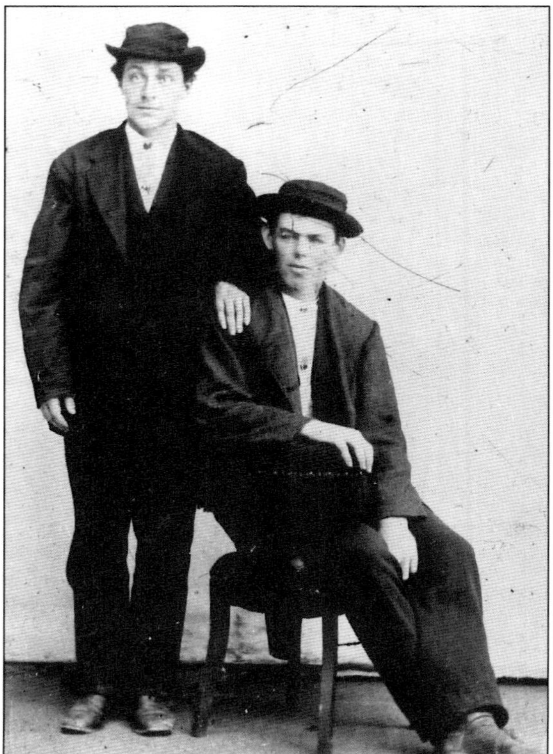

We are not sure where Roy Luther, who ran the Amagansett News Store, and his friend are headed, but they appear to be ready for anything.

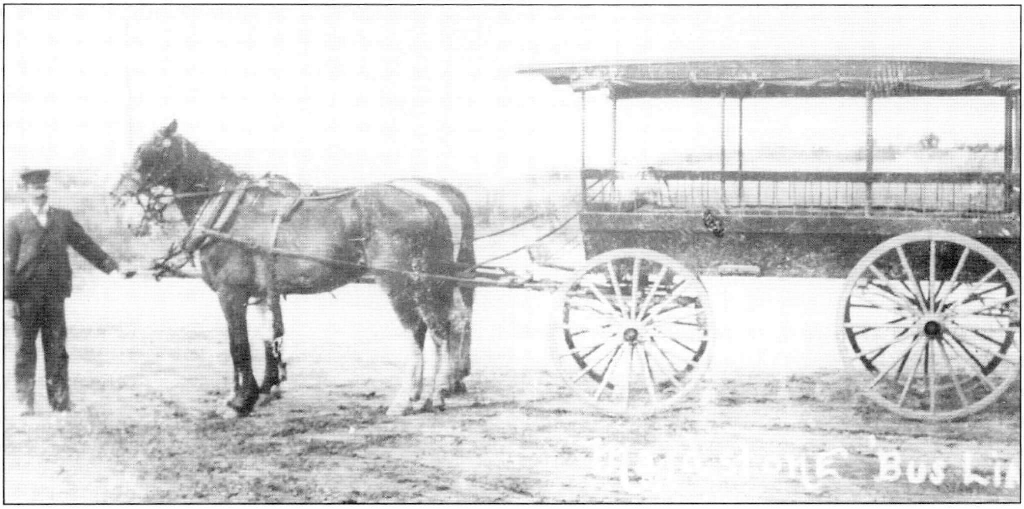

In running his local "bus" line, Floyd Lester was carrying on something of a family tradition—one of the first disbursements by East Hampton Town Trustees was to another Lester "for transportation of men . . . said to be soldiers . . . 17 shillings sixpence."

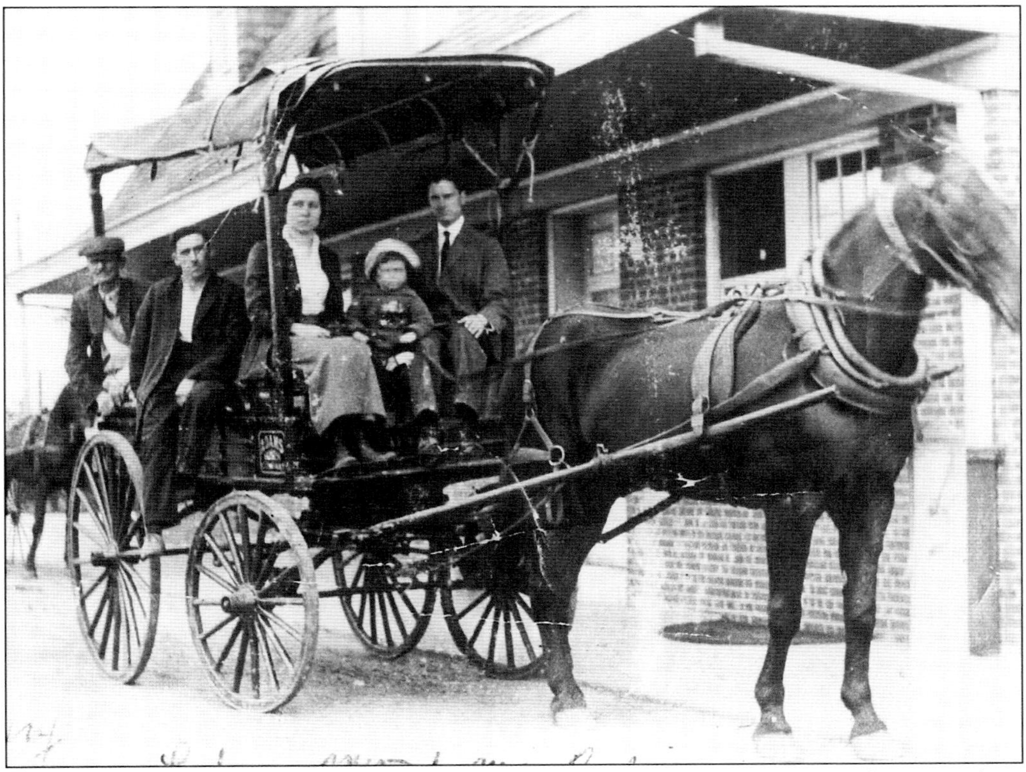

Several express companies served the village, delivering packages sent by train from anywhere from Sag Harbor to San Francisco. Mail was carried by the railroad into the 1950s. George V. Schellinger was the unfortunate victim of a scurrilous stationmaster, who stole George's wedding suit and rings—and then burned the station down "to cover his tracks." He was apprehended when he was seen *wearing* Schellinger's finery.

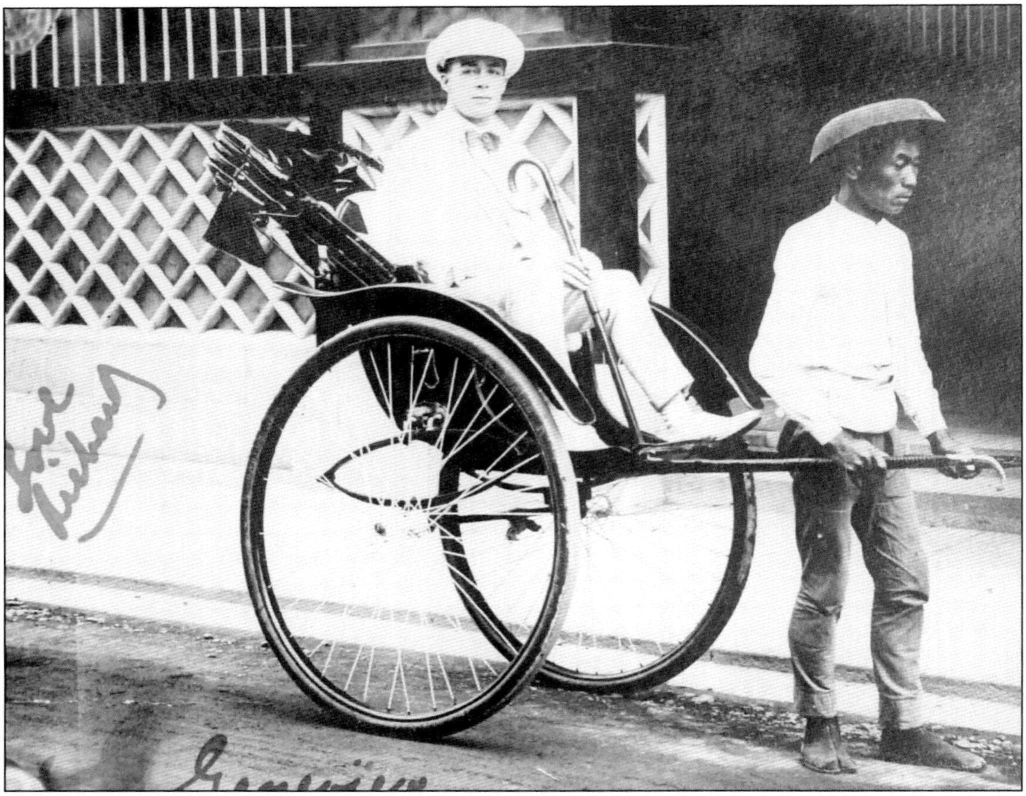

Richard Kelsey is seen here in Yokohama, 1919. Later, he worked as secretary to the territorial governor of Puerto Rico, where he married his wife Genevieve. He spent many years in the import-export business.

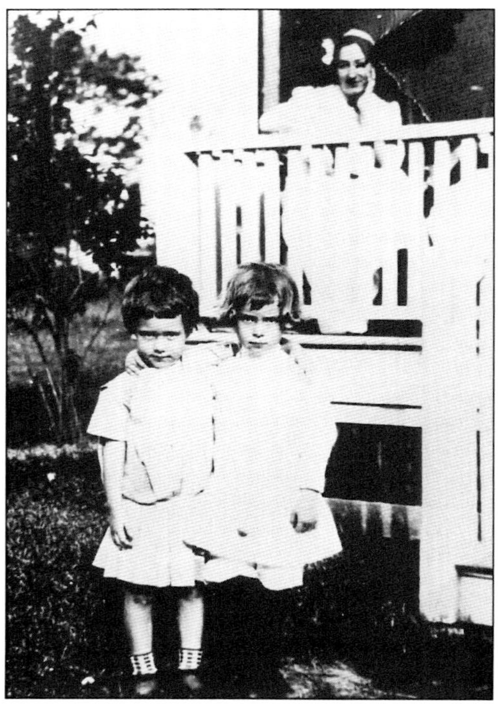

Hettie (Kelsey) Fosset, one of the seven children of Civil War veteran William Kelsey, poses with Adelaide Kelsey and Kendall Osborne. William Kesley's children are representative of the range of Amagansett courtships: Hettie married a man from Maine who came in on a "bunker boat," Julia married Merrick Hand (Amagansett's first visitor to the 1893 Columbian Exposition in Chicago), Libby married an "upstreet" Osborne; Sylvester ("Vess") and his brother William married local Miller daughters; Clarence (Cad) married a woman from Kansas; and Richard married an American woman he met while working in Puerto Rico. William D.'s second marriage was to Lillian Van Horn from Nova Scotia, and his last to Emma Bridgens of Pennsylvania.

Jeannette Edwards, who would later marry Arnold Rattray and buy the *East Hampton Star*, was born in this Barnes house on Atlantic Avenue. Mrs. Rattray traveled widely, writing about her adventures over fifty years in her column, which she signed "One of Ours."

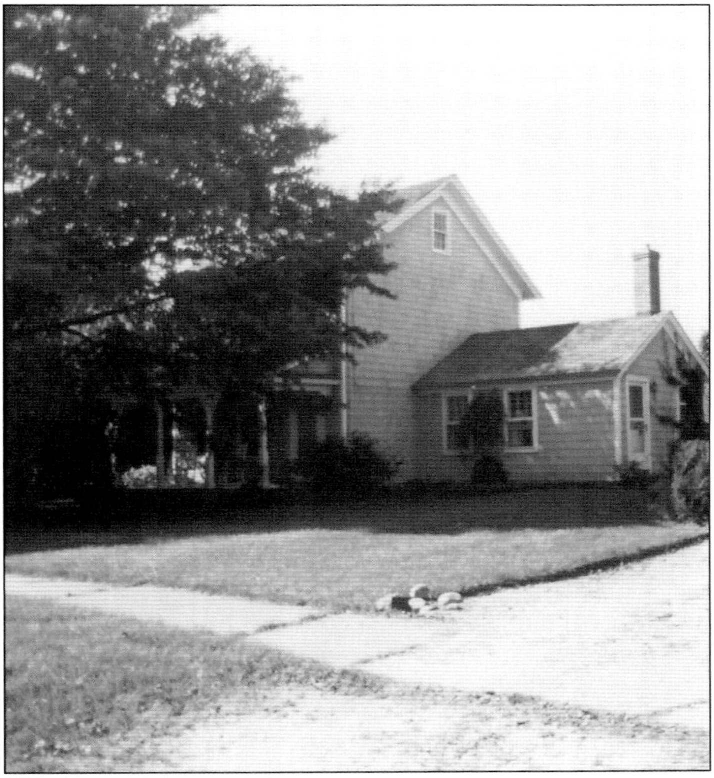

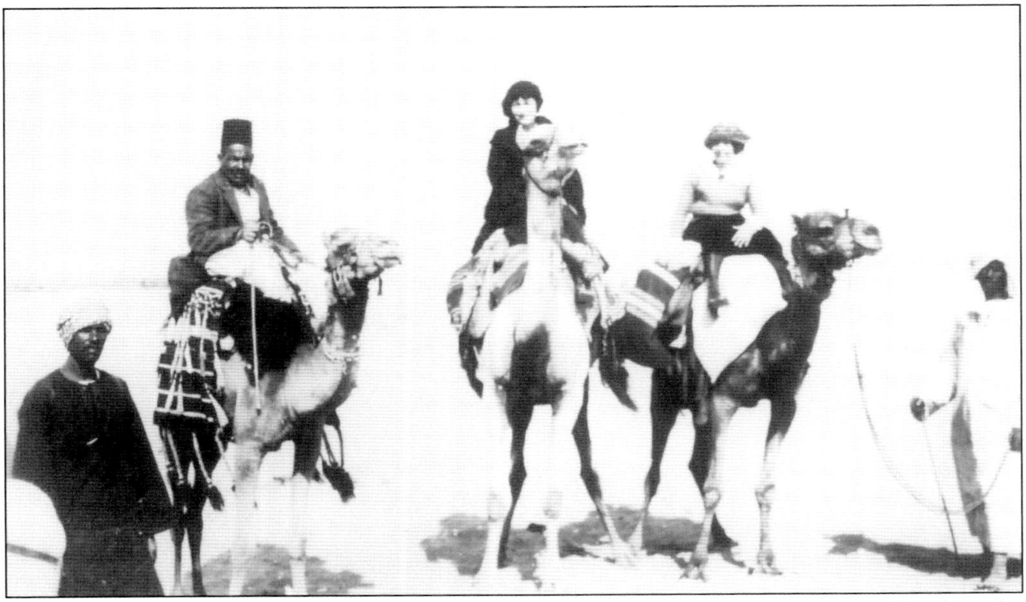

Jeannette Edwards (center) departed on the first of many worldwide adventures in 1920, when she visited her brother Clifford, stationed with the Navy in Constantinople. On that trip, she explored Egypt and Israel with Standard Oil executives' families, and wrote droll letters home.

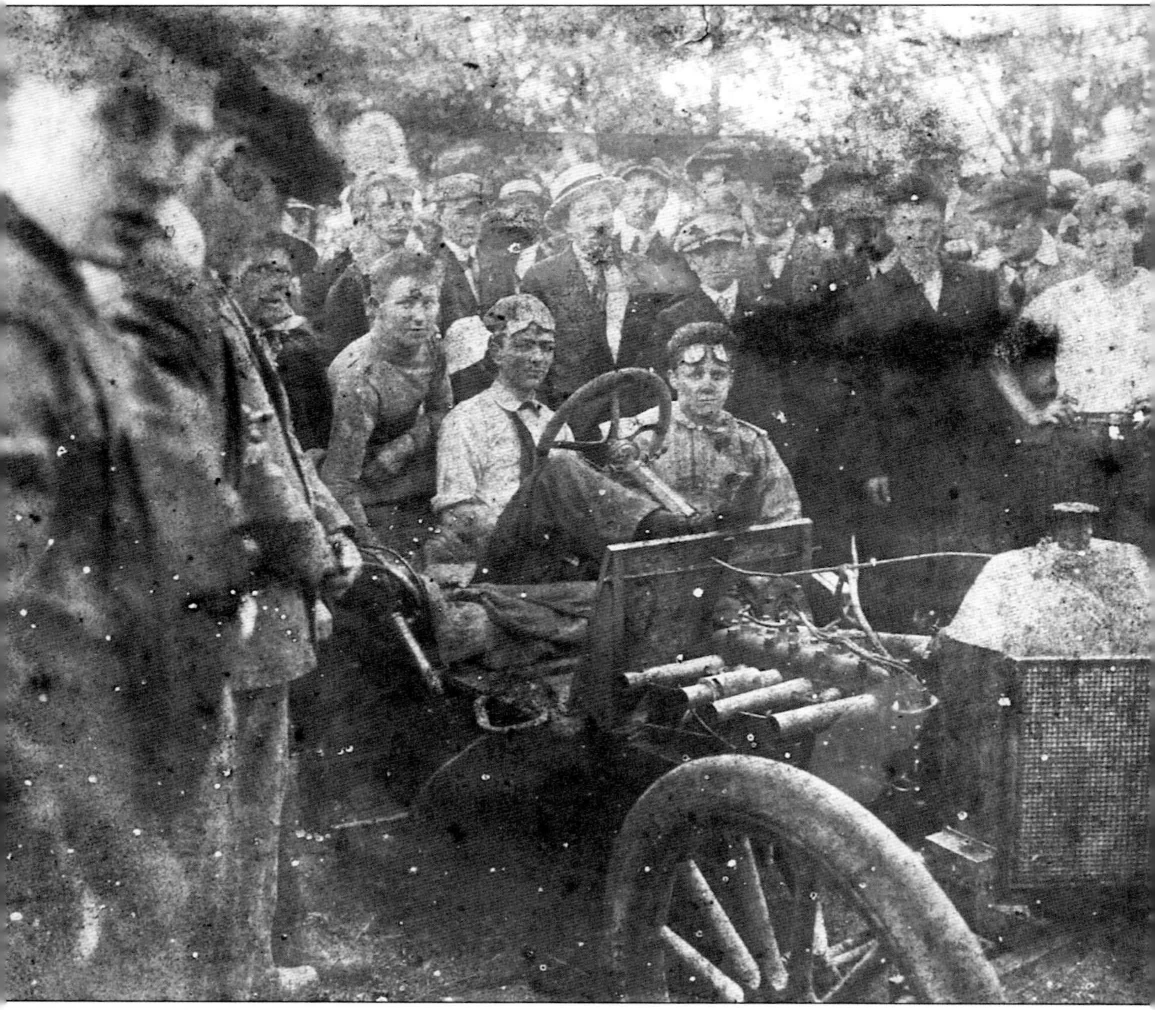

Springs blacksmith and carriage maker Charles Silas Parsons was famous for his ingenuity. The boys who built this car from scrap, with a radiator from the first (1912) Chevrolet, are his nephews. E. Vivian Parsons, at the wheel, became an automobile mechanic. His brother, Ralph Monroe Parsons, studied engineering at the Pratt Institute, and ran a company whose international contracts made him and his wife, Ruth Halsey (Bennett), daughter of the bicycle shop owner, very wealthy.

Four

Warp and Weft

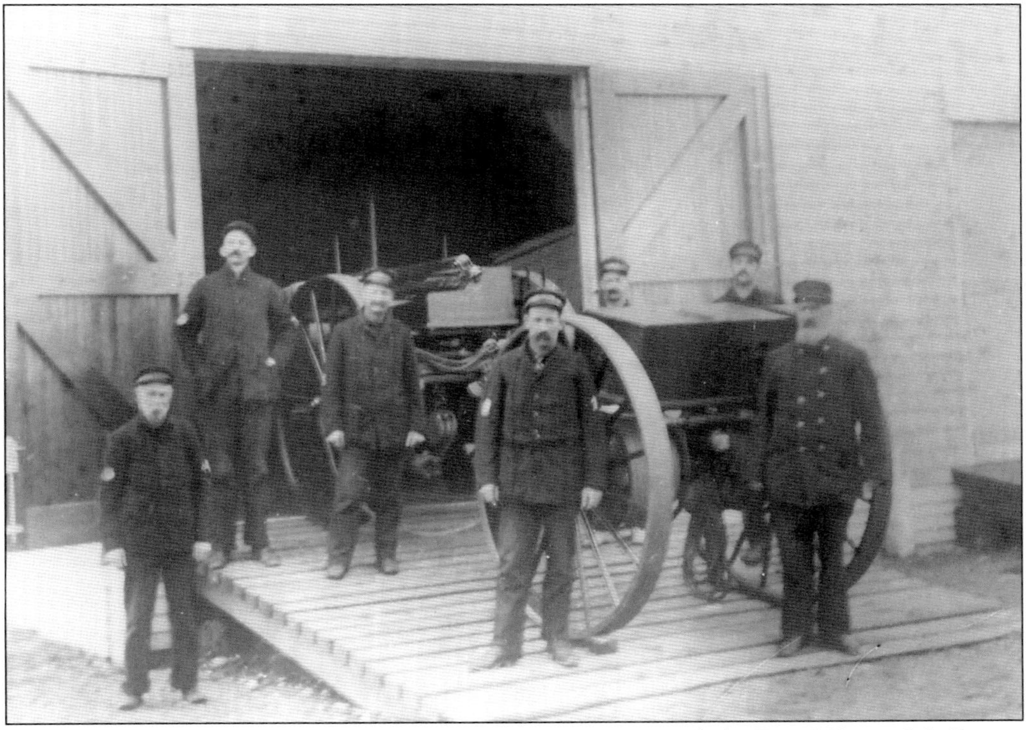

This 1905 photograph of the Amagansett Life Saving Station includes David Henry Schellinger, Charles Edwards, Samuel Lester, Samuel Loper, Frank Miller, George Mulford, and Jesse Edwards, the keeper.

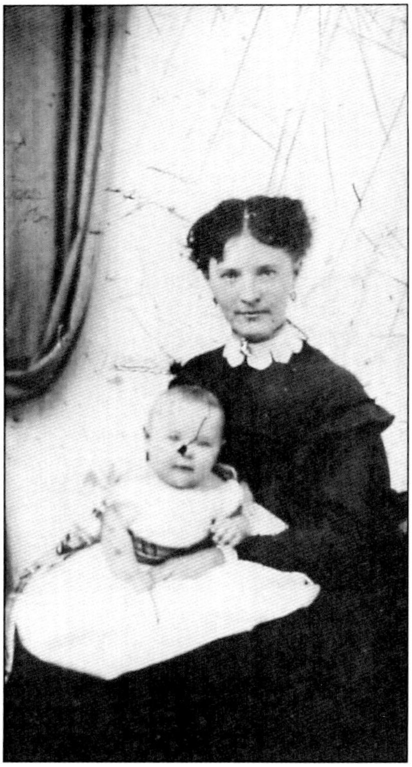

Kate (Bennett) Havens Dominy's parents lived at "Rowdy Hall" in East Hampton. She first married Joseph Havens of Shelter Island, and had Mary Jones ("Minnie") Havens, the infant in this photograph—who became Teunis Barnes' mother-in-law and the great-great-grandmother of one of the authors. Later Kate married Nathaniel Dominy, and they had two sons, John and Erastus.

As you deduce from virtually any one of the chapters in this book, the U.S. Life Saving Service was a great influence on community life, providing jobs for local men and bringing many new families to the area. In 1790, the "Revenue Cutter Service" was established, and unmanned "boathouses" were built in the 1850s. The Life Saving Service started in 1867 and was not taken over by the Coast Guard until 1917. There were five life saving stations in East Hampton Town: at Georgica (shown below), Amagansett, Napeague, Hither Hills, and Ditch Plains. Nathaniel Dominy kept a diary starting when he was fifteen, giving a view of his life in the 1860s—"plenty of farming and fishing chores, with an occasional picnic or clambake, and school rather incidental." He worked as a miller before beginning a long career as the captain of this, the Georgica Station.

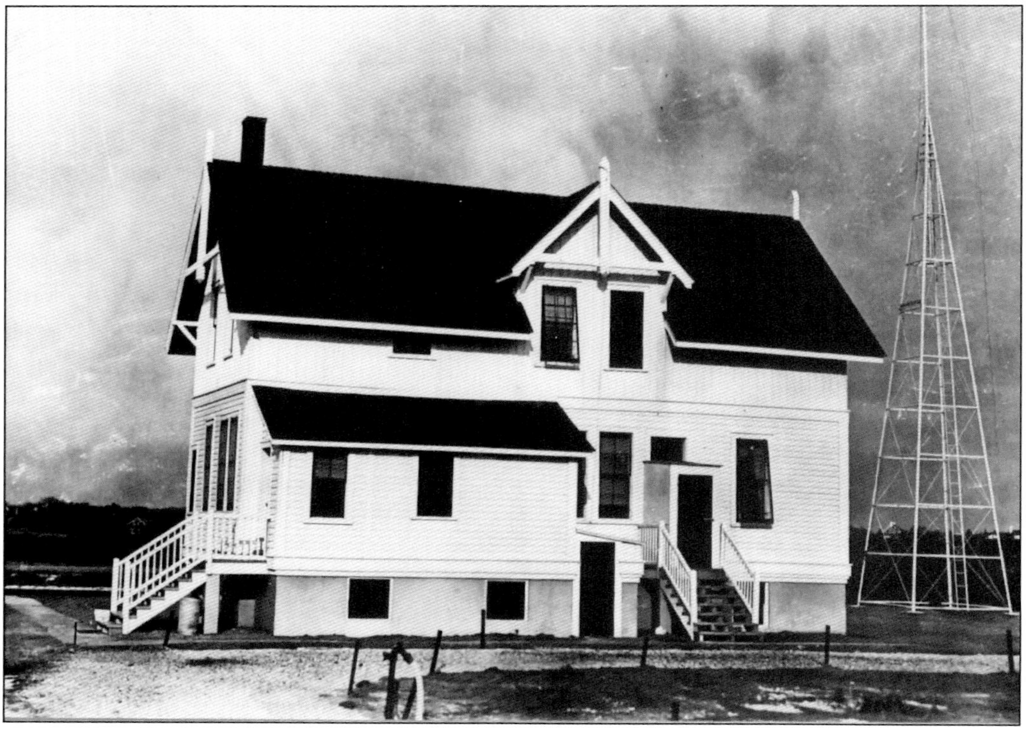

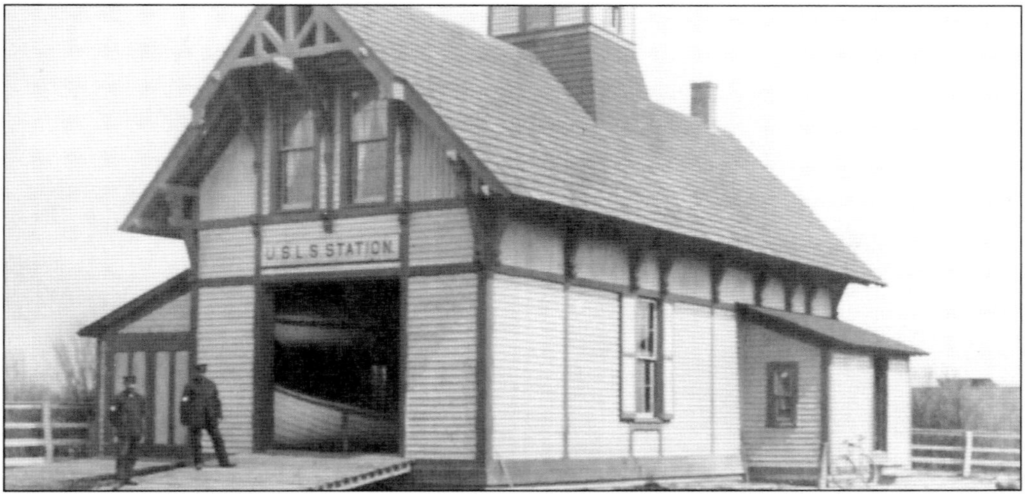

The first life saving station was unmanned—it stood at the end of Atlantic Avenue, and contained lifesaving equipment for volunteer rescue. The second (pictured here) was built in 1880 at the end of Atlantic Avenue. It was moved to Main Street after the 1902 station was constructed and is now LaCarrubba's store. In 1921 the Navy built a "compass" station to receive wireless messages in International Morse Code—a system somewhat different from what Ira Baker used at the railroad station. The compass station was outfitted with a bird-cage aerial which could be turned to ascertain the direction from which the distress signal was coming.

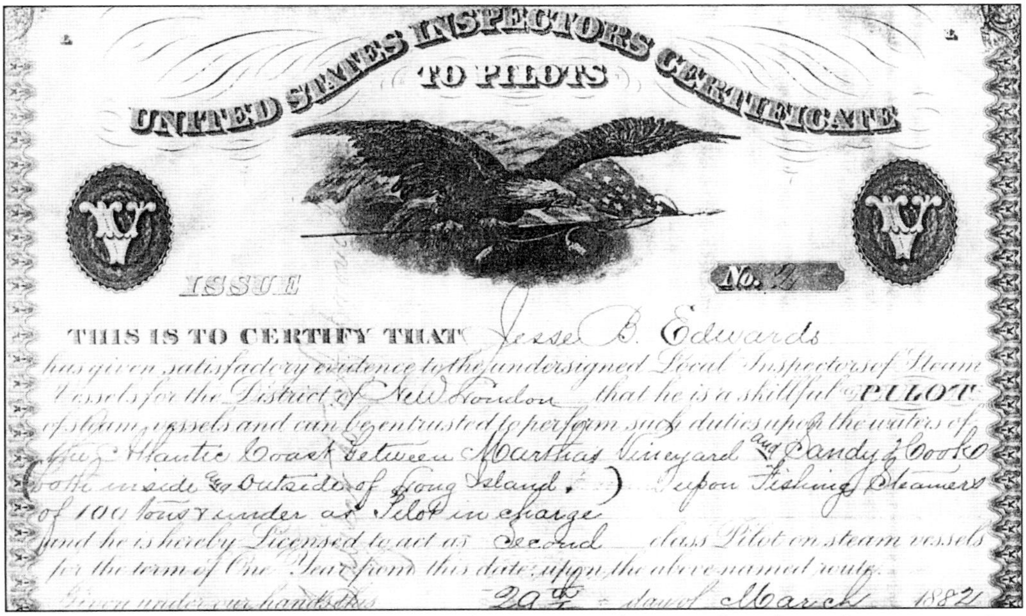

UNITED STATES INSPECTORS CERTIFICATE TO PILOTS

ISSUE

No.

THIS IS TO CERTIFY THAT Jesse B. Edwards has given satisfactory evidence to the undersigned Local Inspectors of Steam Vessels for the District of New London that he is a skillful PILOT of steam vessels and can be entrusted to perform such duties upon the waters of the Atlantic Coast between Marthas Vineyard and Sandy Hook (both inside & outside of Long Island.) & upon Fishing Steamers of 100 tons & under as Pilot in charge and he is hereby Licensed to act as Second class Pilot on steam vessels for the term of One Year from this date, upon the above named route.

Given under our hands this 29th day of March 1882

Jesse Barnes Edwards' pilot's certificate, issued in New London, gave him the authority to conduct fishing steamers of up to 100 tons on the Atlantic Coast between Martha's Vineyard and Sandy Hook, both inside *and* outside of Long Island. His nephew, Samuel Stratton Edwards, was the only Amagansett man to hold an unlimited master's license, on any ship, anywhere—he took a voyage to England after receiving it, and probably also captained ships along the coast of South America.

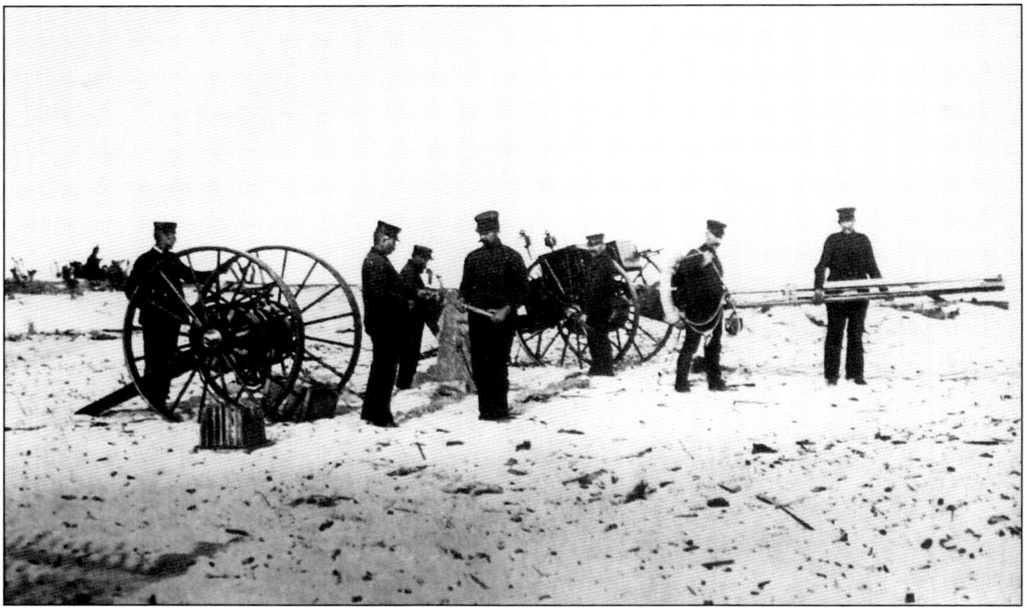

This is an early 1900s postcard view entitled "Life Saving Crew Preparing the Life-Line."

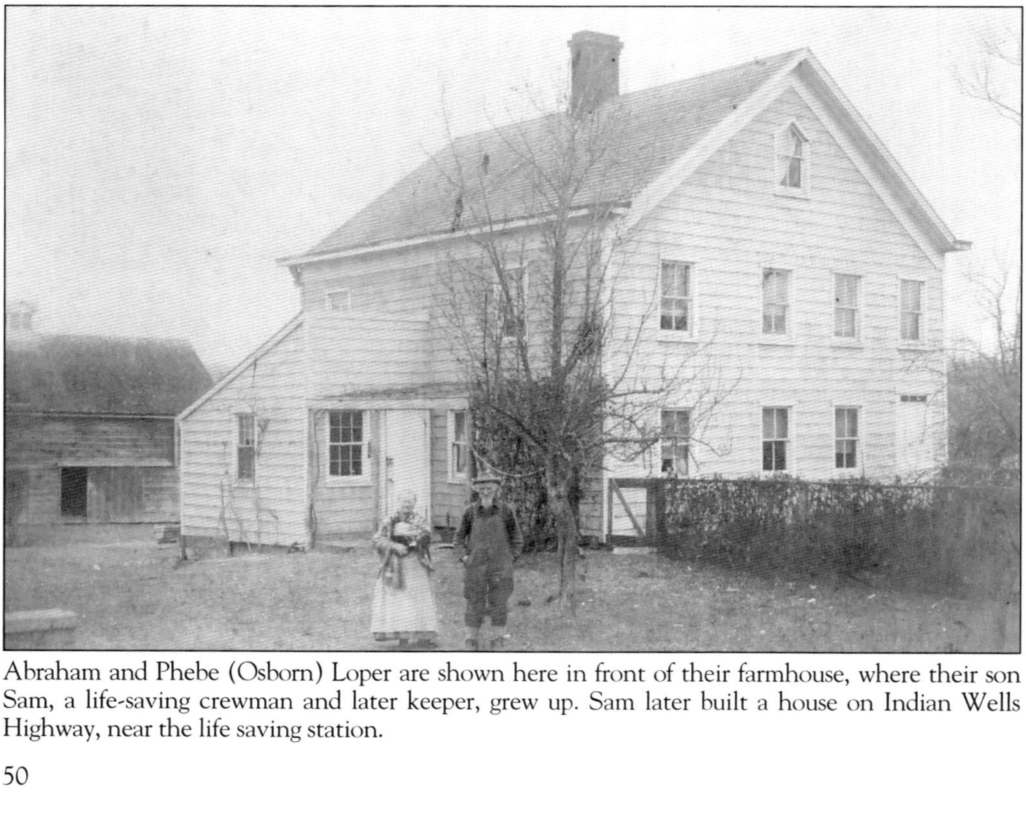

Abraham and Phebe (Osborn) Loper are shown here in front of their farmhouse, where their son Sam, a life-saving crewman and later keeper, grew up. Sam later built a house on Indian Wells Highway, near the life saving station.

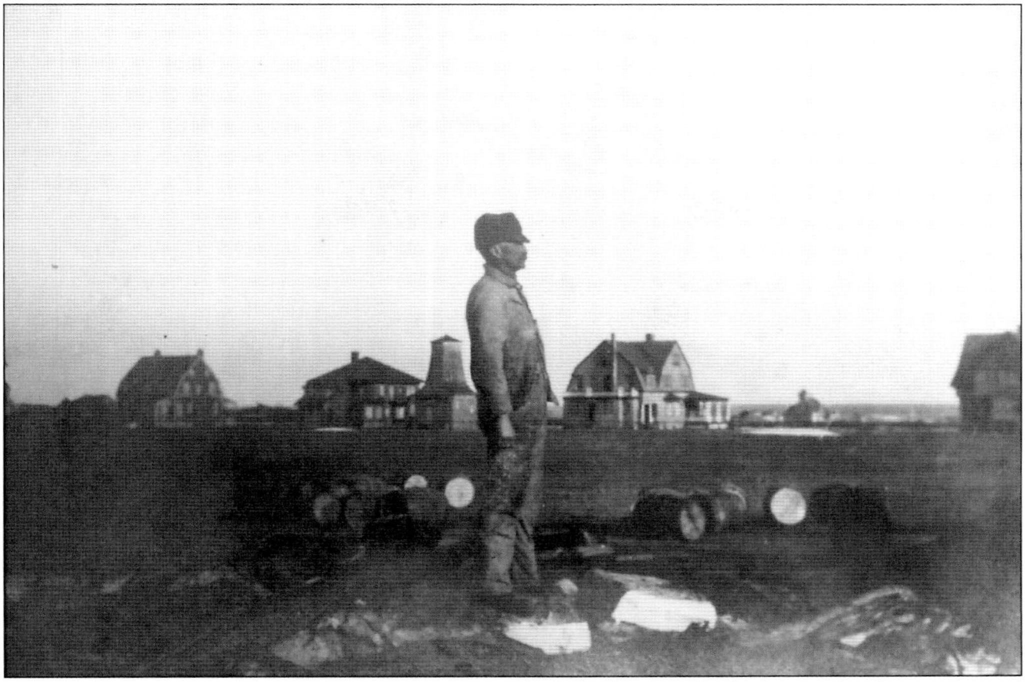

Jesse Edwards' son Clint was a fisherman. He could usually be found gill-netting, haul-seining, and setting lines for cod, but was also a sometime whaler, with his uncles. Here he stands at the try-works for processing whale oil, with the Bluff Road Rossiter Johson summer houses in the background.

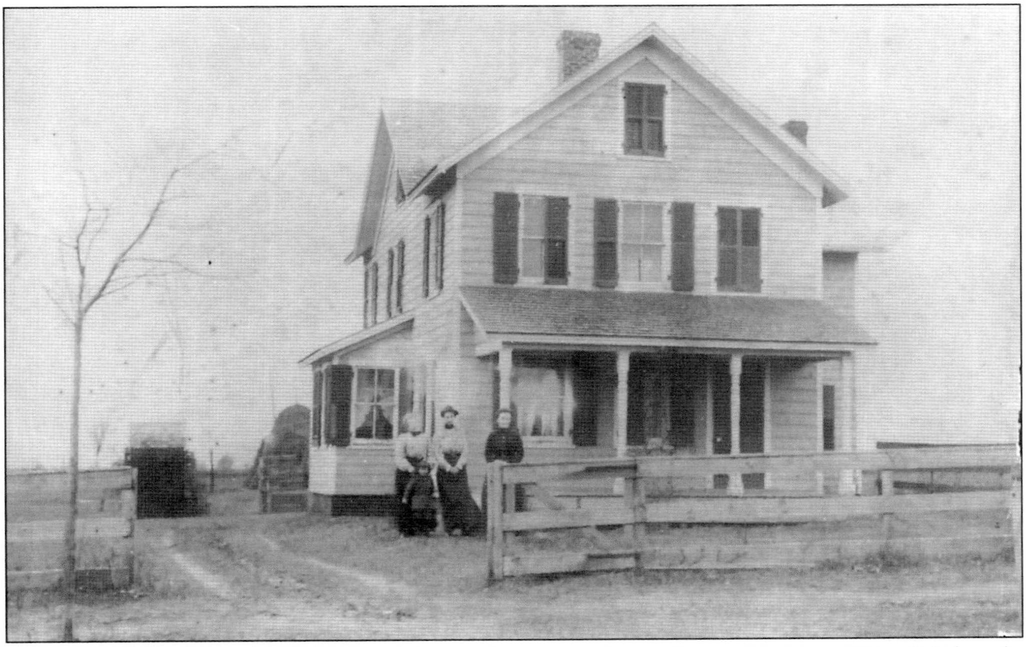

Clinton Havens Edwards' house on Atlantic Avenue is shown here with Mary (Ward) Edwards, daughter Marion, and a "neighbor lady."

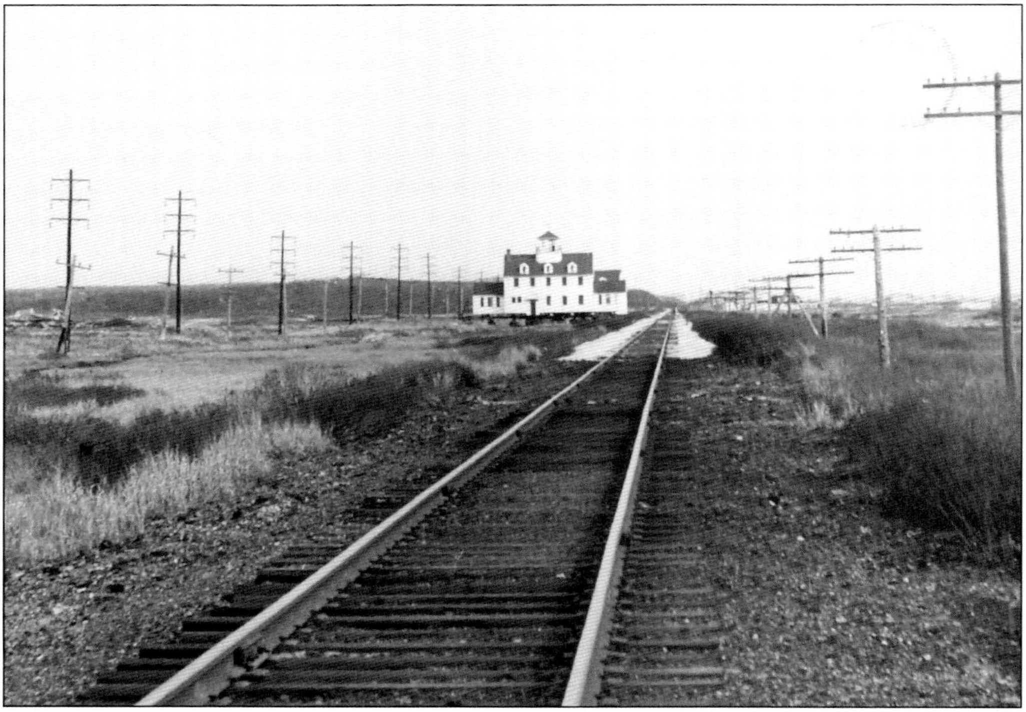

Two wonderful shots show the Napeague Coast Guard Station being moved in 1954. It now stands on Montauk's Star Island, and is the only station still operating in the area.

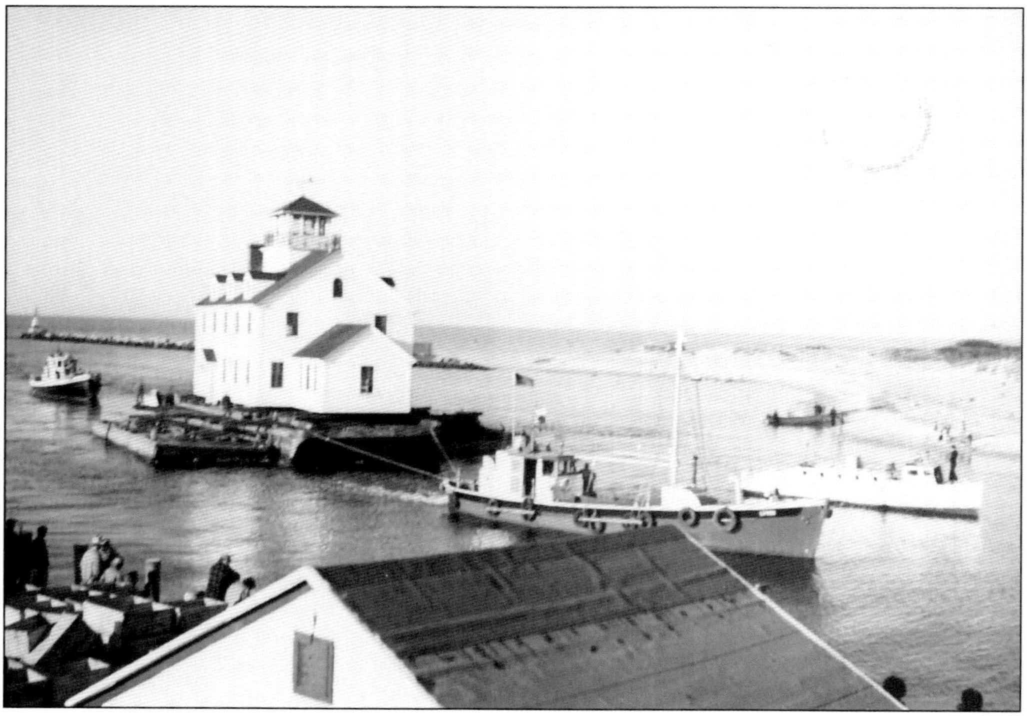

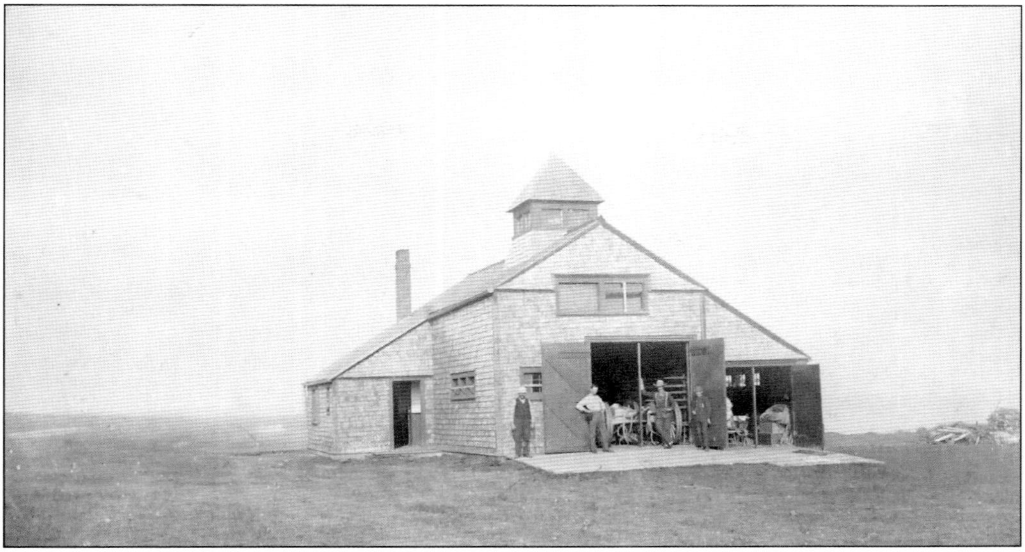

The Hither Hills Life Saving Station was torn down in 1932. In 1873, twenty years before this photograph was taken, Albert Edwards was serving here when his boat capsized and he drowned.

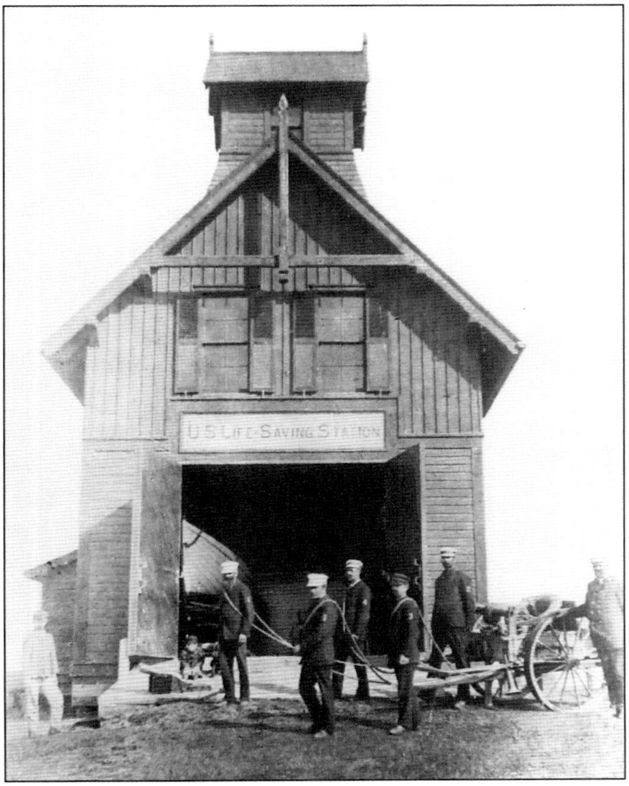

The Ditch Plains Station is shown here *c.* 1902. Stations were placed exactly 3 miles apart on the south shore of Long Island; regular watches required the life-saving crew to walk halfway and meet the man from the next station before returning to base. This, the most easterly of the East Hampton town stations, was where David H. Miller was serving when he "met" his future wife, Ruhamah Bridgens, through a magazine listing and correspondence. They were married in 1893.

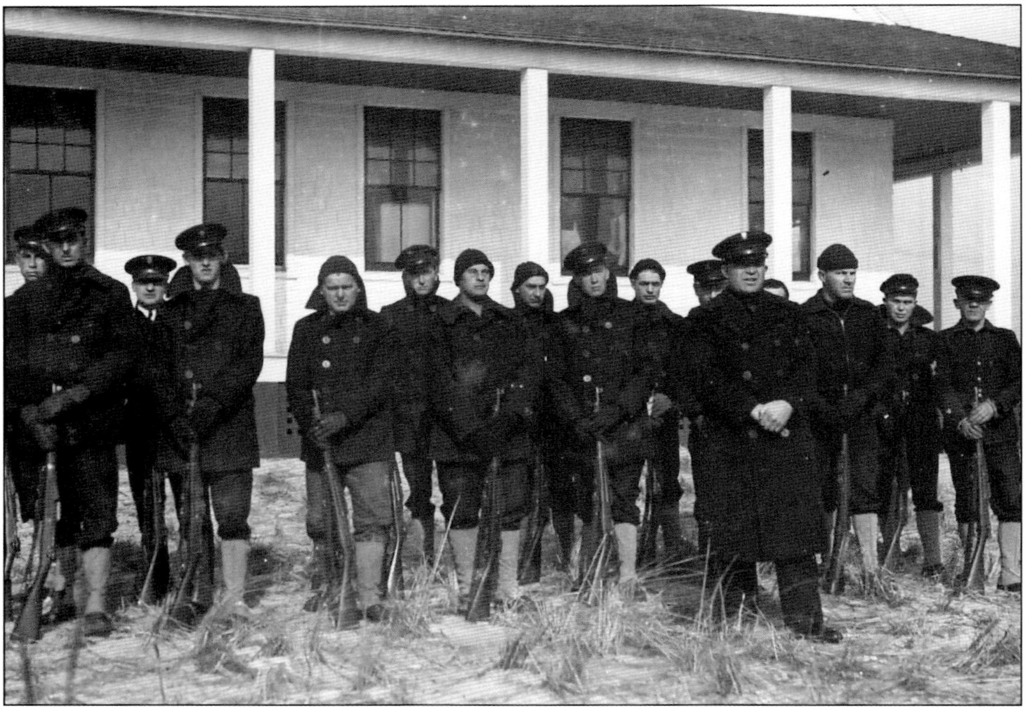

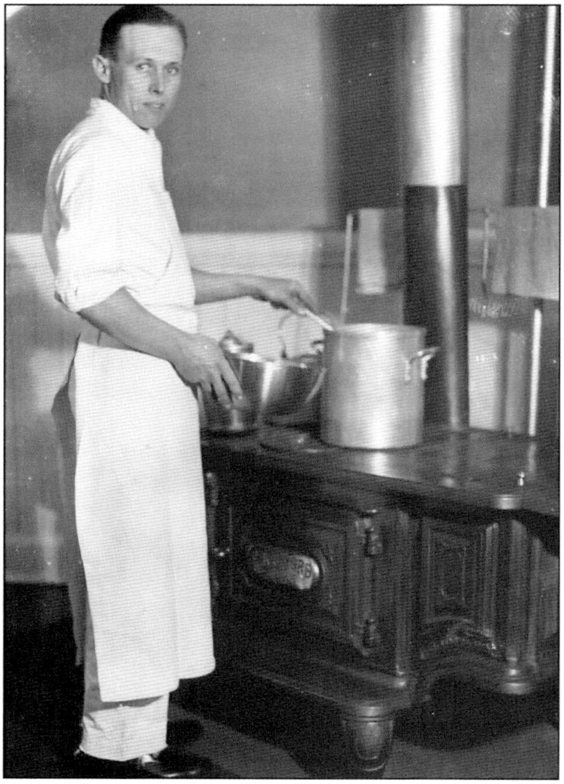

This is Captain Warren Barnes of the Amagansett Coast Guard Station with his crew. The stations closed in 1937, but were reopened, with expanded crews, in 1942. Russell Miller told how, while captaining the Amagansett station during the war and feeling the responsibility for a large barracks, he "tricked" his young charges into attending church on Sunday.

A cook poses briefly for a photograph in the late 1930s at the Amagansett Coast Guard Station.

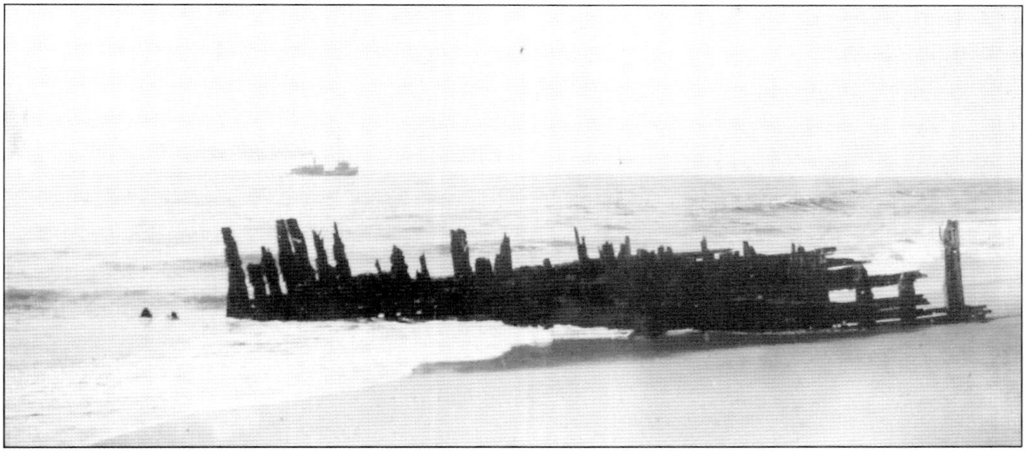

In 1851, a Dublin passenger ship, the *Catherine*, foundered just off the coast of Amagansett, and villagers went down to help the Irish emigrants, all of whom survived and most of whom went on to New York City. One woman, however, was adopted by John Strong and married (Lyman) Beecher Bennett. Another survivor, Patrick Lynch, bound for the California gold fields, was offered a job as soon as he reached the shore and remained here. The local Lynches, including one who fought in the Civil War, are his descendants. Catholic Mass was said in Patrick Lynch's home until the first Catholic church, St. Philomena's (now Most Holy Trinity), was built in 1894. One of the area's most prominent Catholics was Julia (Gardiner) Tyler, wife of President Tyler. Bits of the *Catherine* wreck can still be seen on the Amagansett beach when the tides are right.

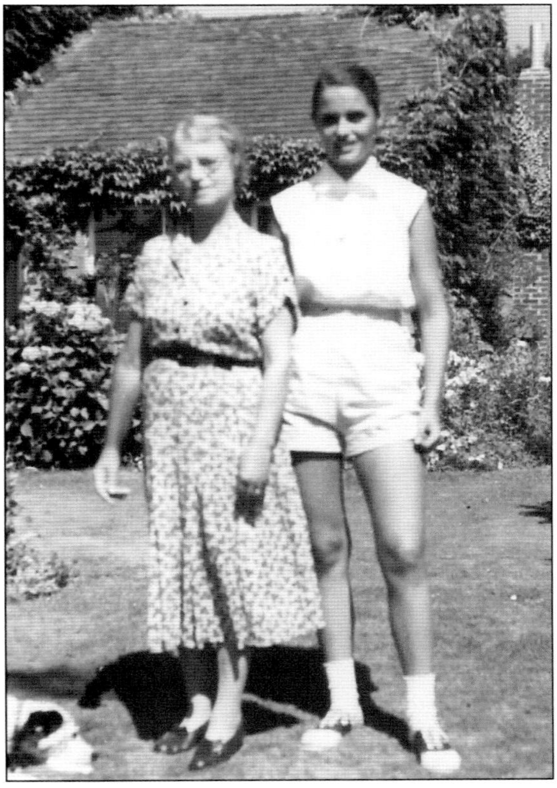

It didn't take long for the Irish to have an effect on the area. In 1868 Juliet Hand wrote in her diary, ". . . St. Patrick's Day the Irish were out in full force. The men & boys marched in procession with drums beating and flags and banners flying. They had a supper and a lecture in the evening." The November 5, 1920 *Star* reports that a group of businessmen, perhaps thinking of the Celtic homeland, were going to attempt to transform Long Island peat into gasoline. In between, many Irish girls came to Amagansett as cooks and housekeepers in the large summer houses, and several, like Florence Smith, pictured here with her daughter Annie, stayed on to marry local men.

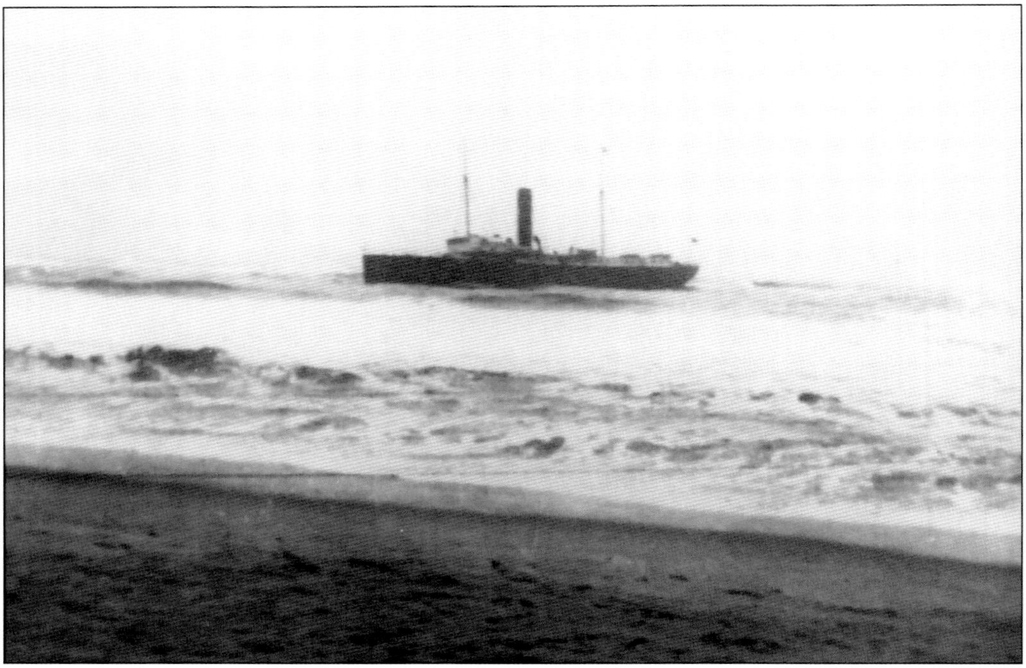

The *Kershaw* ran aground off Ocean Avenue in March 1917, but was towed back to sea.

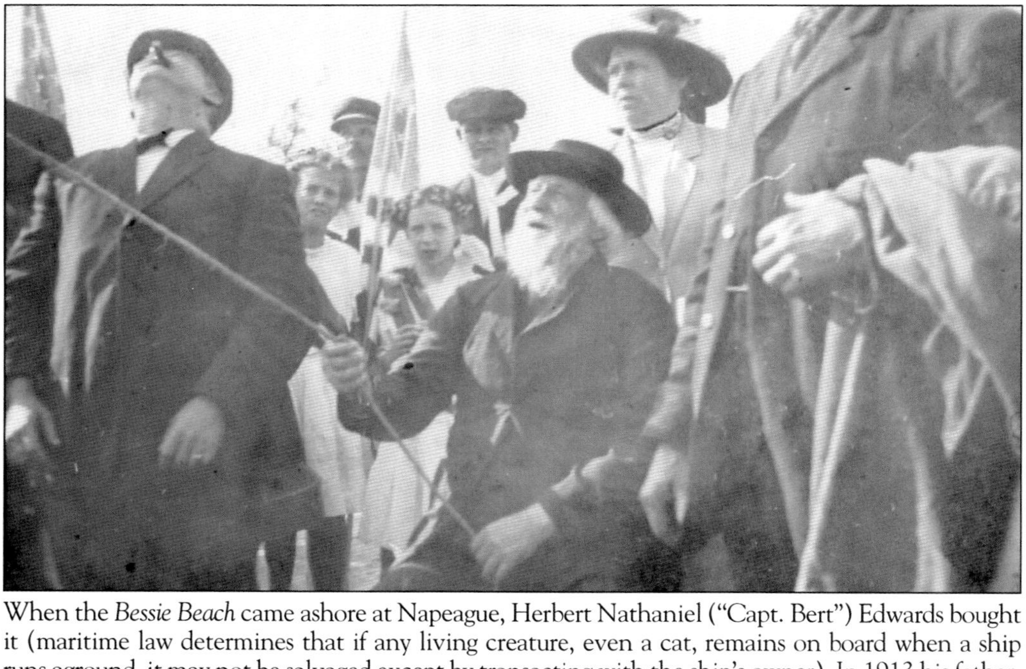

When the *Bessie Beach* came ashore at Napeague, Herbert Nathaniel ("Capt. Bert") Edwards bought it (maritime law determines that if any living creature, even a cat, remains on board when a ship runs aground, it may not be salvaged except by transacting with the ship's owner). In 1913 his father, "Capt. Josh," commemorated the *Bessie Beach*'s mast as the village flagpole. Rosa Belle (Edwards) Mulford stands behind her father.

Five

Land and Water

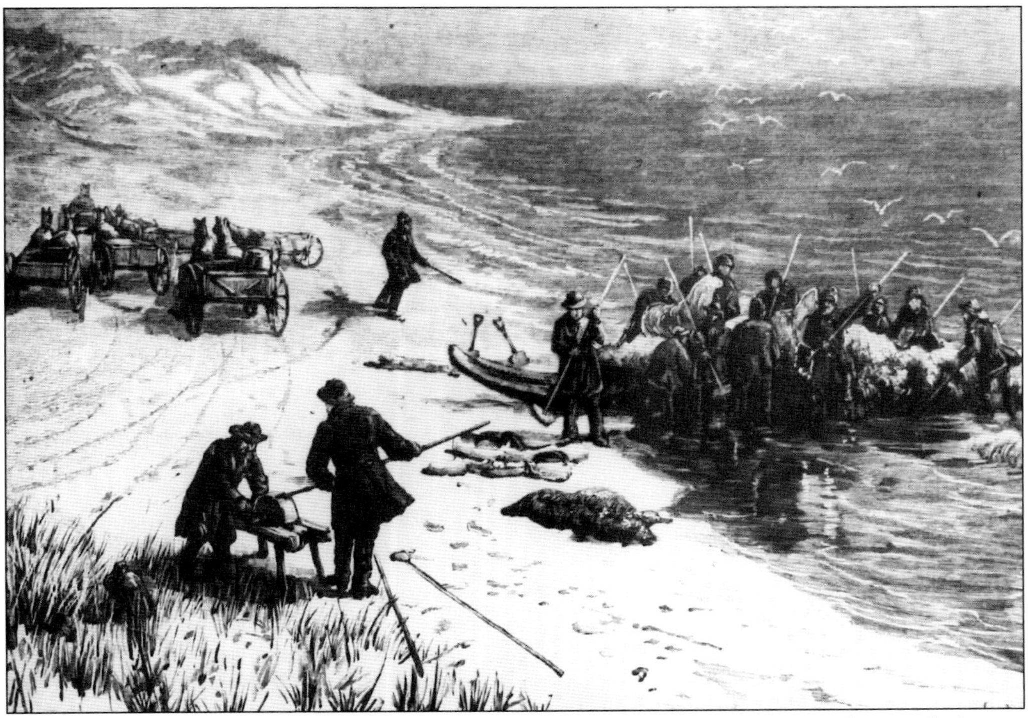

This 1870 lithograph from *Harper's Weekly* shows the "cutting in" stage after a whale was taken offshore.

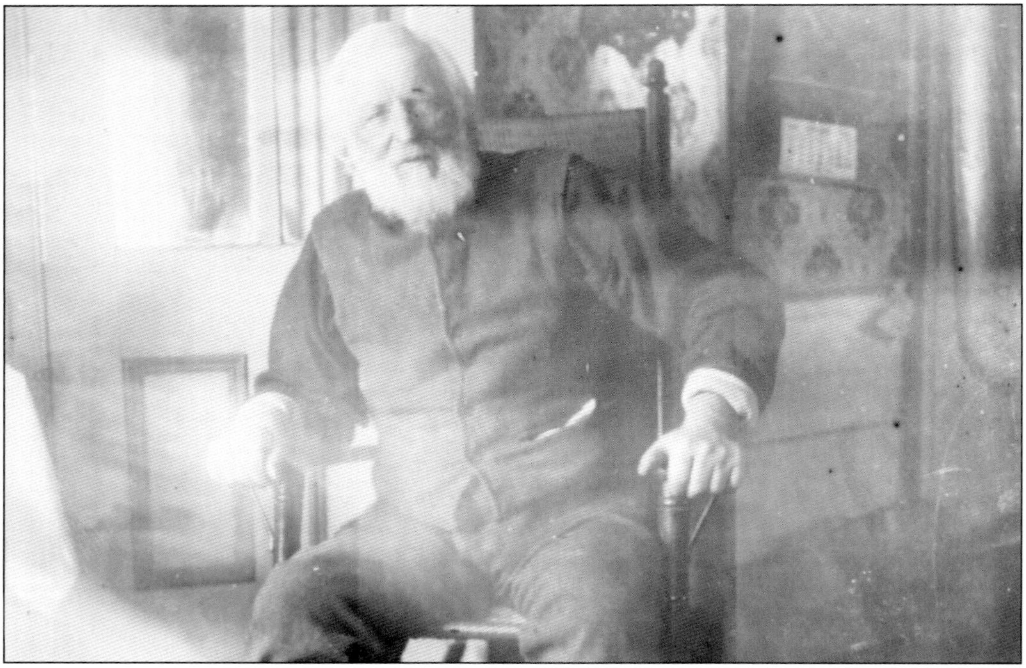

"Captain Josh" Edwards was the patriarch of a family who were not only famous deep-sea whalers, but ran a number of thriving businesses. Juliet Hand's diary tells us that Adelia Conklin and Joshua Edwards were married on the morning of September 30, 1868. The same morning several Amagansett people who were headed off to the Suffolk County Agricultural Society Fair learned that the excursion boat *Water Lily* was aground near Riverhead, and returned home.

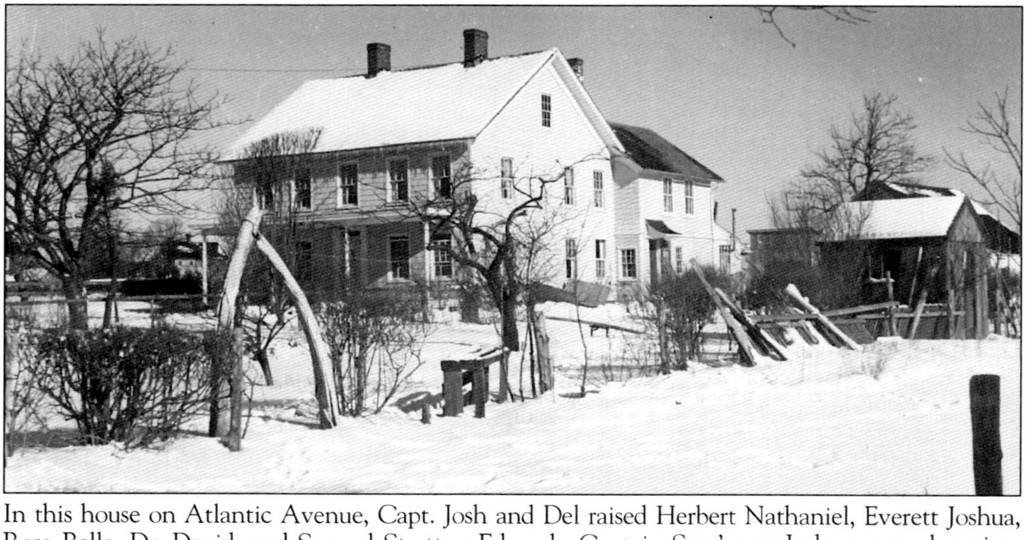

In this house on Atlantic Avenue, Capt. Josh and Del raised Herbert Nathaniel, Everett Joshua, Rosa Belle, Dr. David, and Samuel Stratton Edwards. Captain Sam's son Joshua was a longtime captain of bunker boats, and of the Cross Sound Ferry from Orient Point to New London.

Albert Edwards drowned while stationed with the Life Saving Service at Hither Hills.

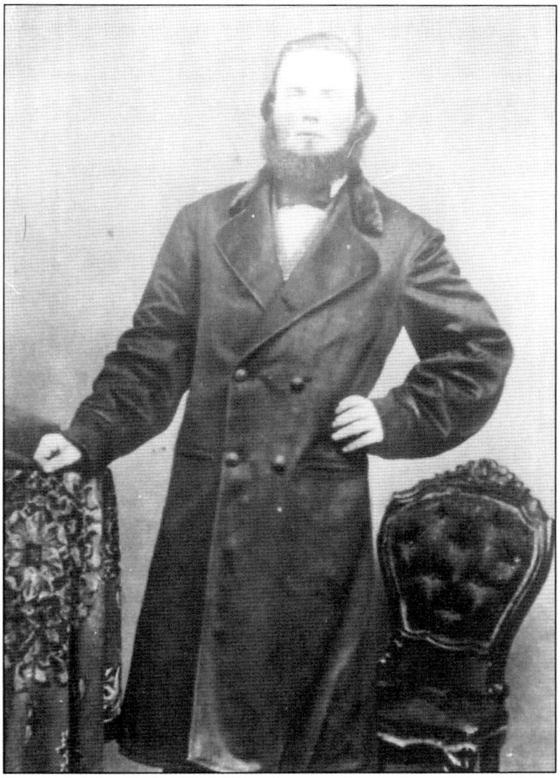

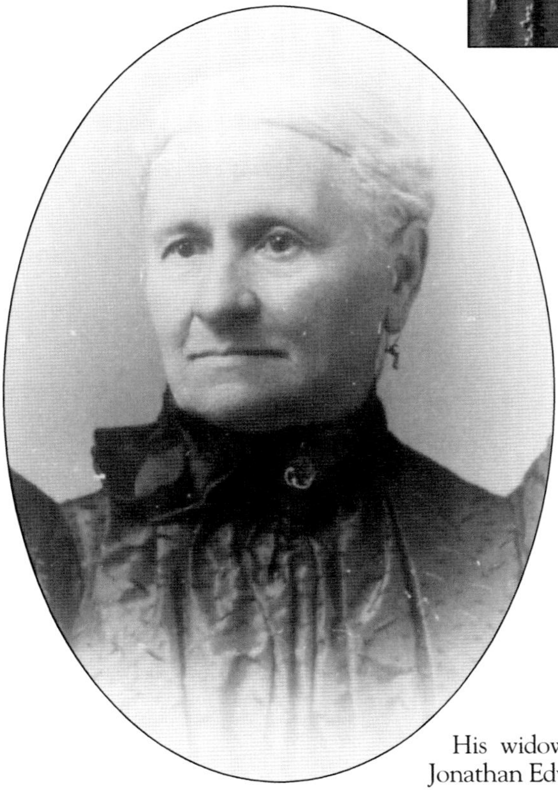

His widow, Phebe, later married his uncle, Captain Jonathan Edwards.

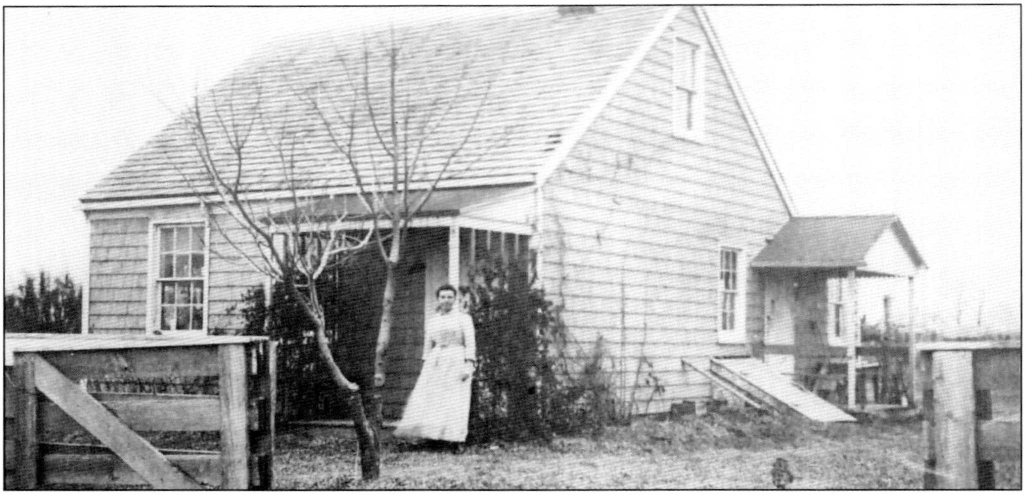

Albert Edwards' house was passed on to Charles Sanford Edwards, his son. The woman standing in front is Edith (Leek), Charles' wife.

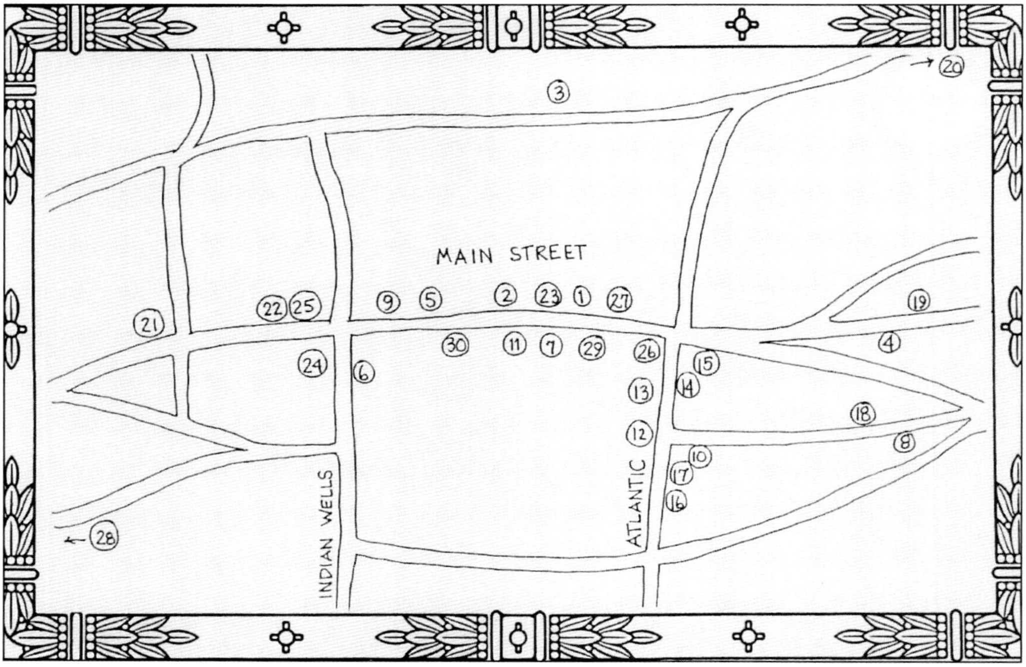

This map shows thirty houses which are featured in this book. Only family residences, and those which are still standing, are numbered, according to their order of appearance: 1) Zebulon Conklin; 2) Nathaniel Baker (Main Street); 3) Nathaniel Baker (Stony Hill); 4) Talmage Barnes; 5) Erastus Barnes; 6) Matthew Barnes; 7) Jonathan Baker; 8) Madison King; 9) Schellinger "Red House"; 10) Jonathan Edwards; 11) Jeremiah Baker; 12) Jonathan Barnes (Atlantic Ave.); 13) Clinton Edwards; 14) Joshua Edwards; 15) Albert Edwards; 16) Nathaniel Edwards; 17) Elijah Bennett; 18) Egbert King; 19) Silas Sherman; 20) Joseph Miller; 21) Nathan Miller; 22) David Miller; 23) Jeremiah Conklin; 24) Lorenzo Leek; 25) J. Knowles Smith; 26) Nathan Hand; 27) Nathaniel Hand; 28) Edwards/Hand; 29) Theodore Hand; 30) Osborne-Hedges.

Nathaniel Edwards (1826–1890) married Betsey Schellinger on New Year's Day, 1861. They were the first couple to wed in the new Presbyterian church.

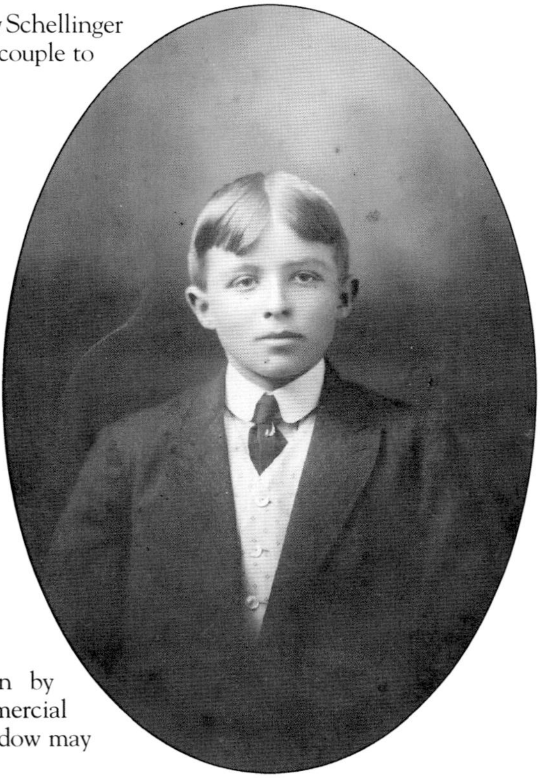

This photograph of their house was taken by Fred Parsons—Amagansett's first commercial photographer. The woman in the upstairs window may be Juliette (Schellinger) Strong, Betsey's sister.

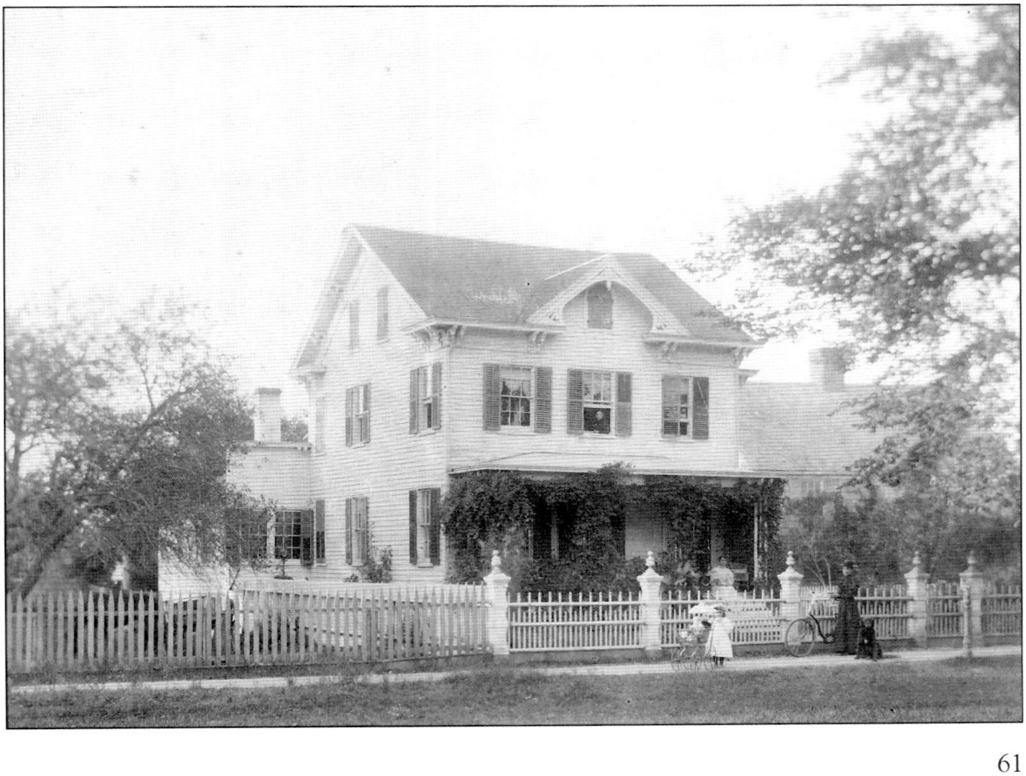

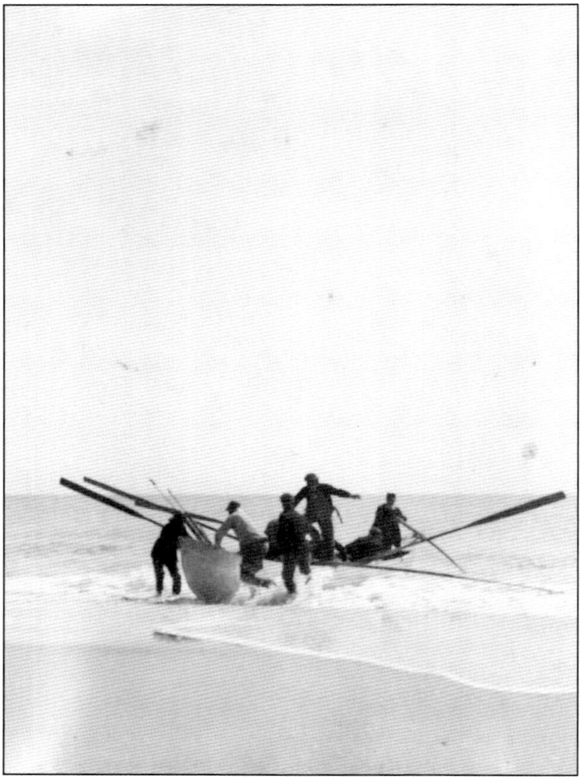

This is one of a series of postcards made of the capture of a right whale off Amagansett, February 22, 1907. This view depicts the launching of the whaleboat.

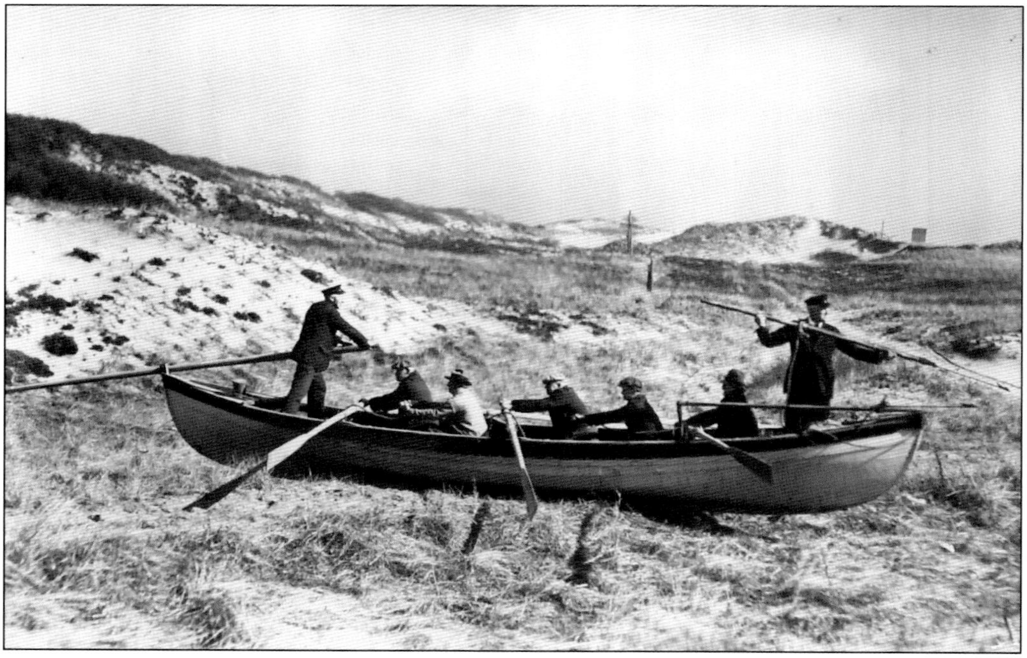

Everett J. Edwards is leading a whaleboat re-enactment on the beach, with Felix Dominy, Charles Baker, Forest Hulse, and Wines Hulse.

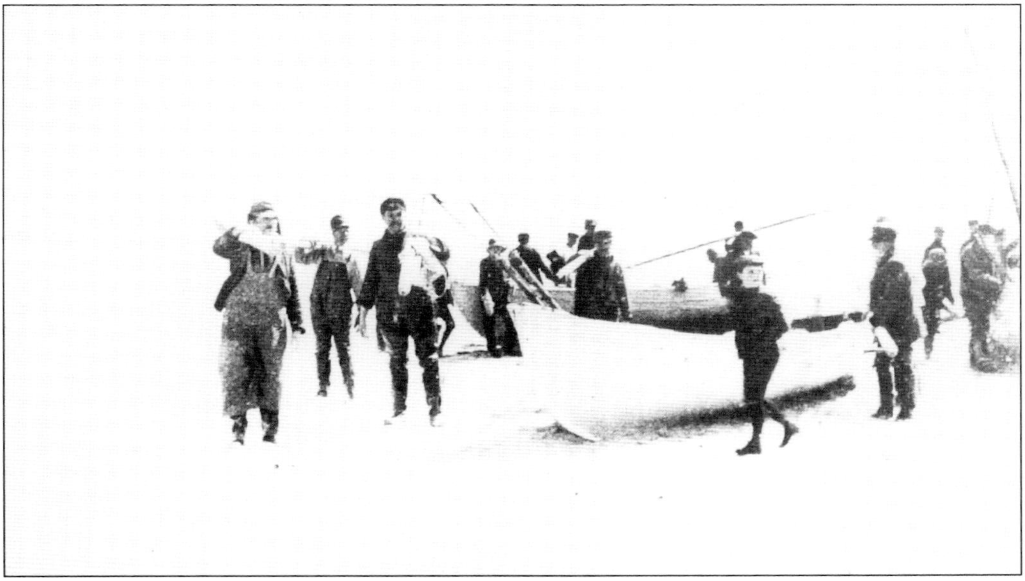

"Whalemen Landing" is another of the postcard series.

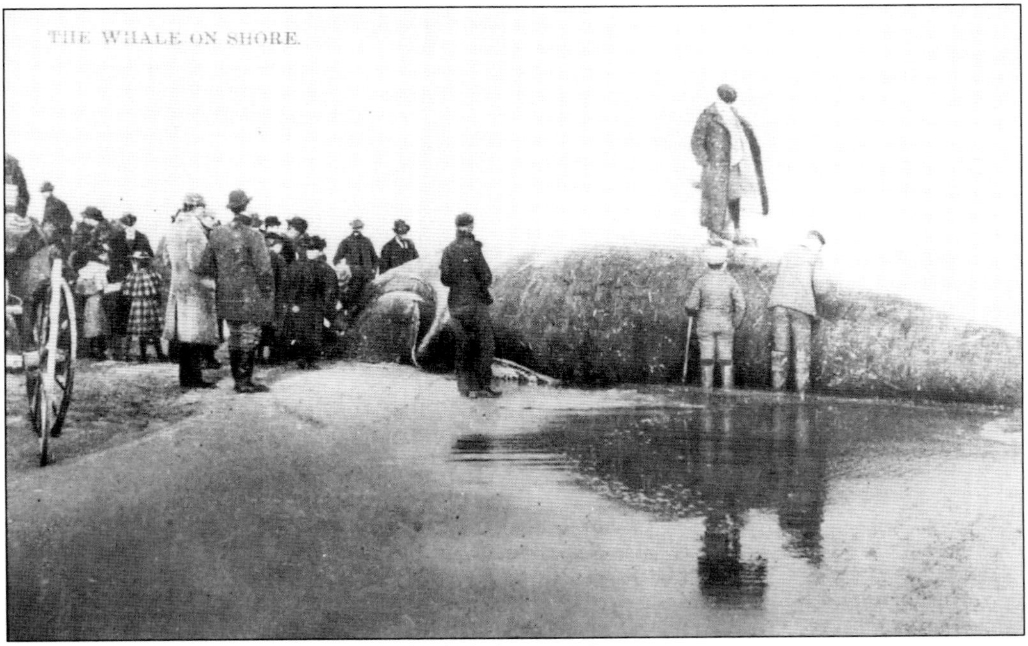

Villagers gathered to examine this beached whale in 1897.

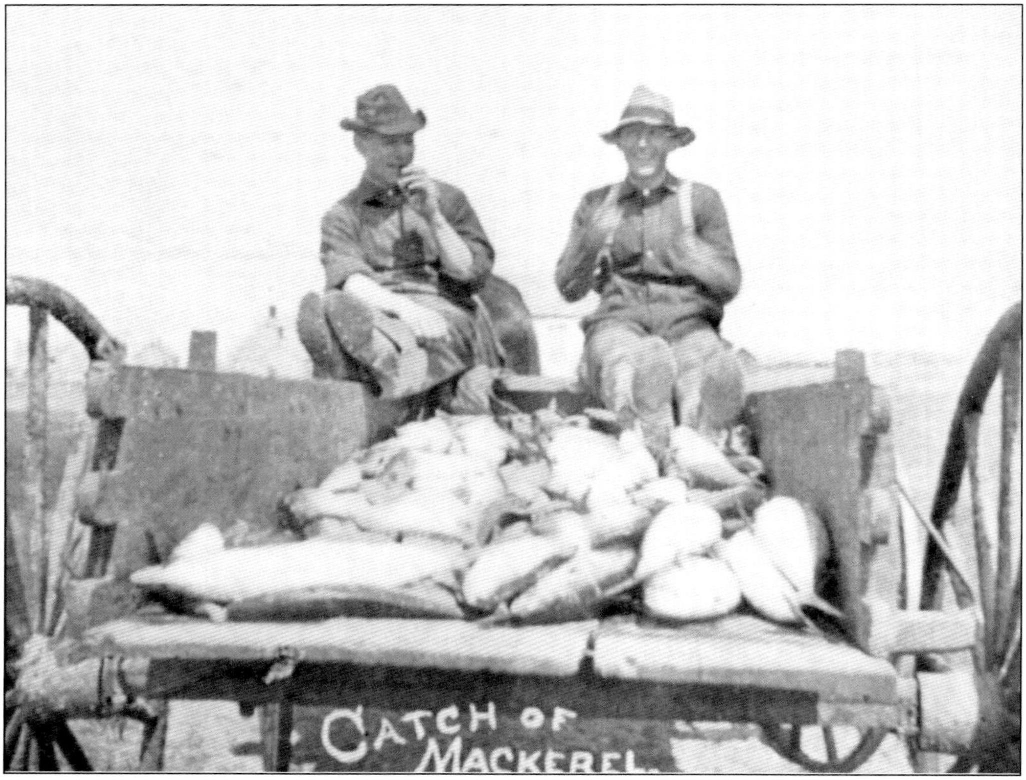

This turn-of-the-century postcard and photograph of fishermen "taking their ease" belie not only the importance of commercial fishing to the local economy, but the intricate methods (for both harvesting and marketing) that have been employed by even the smallest independent crews.

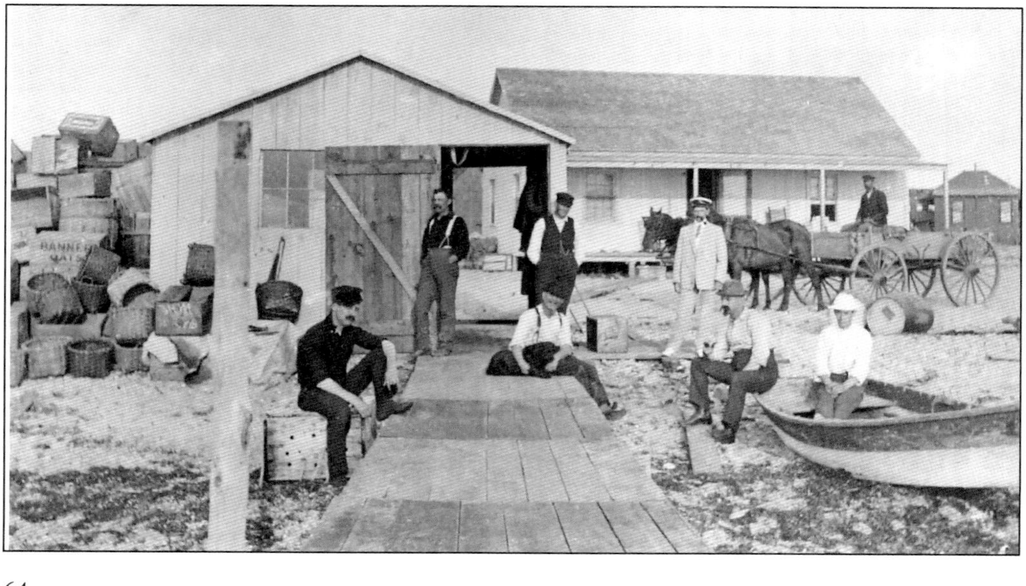

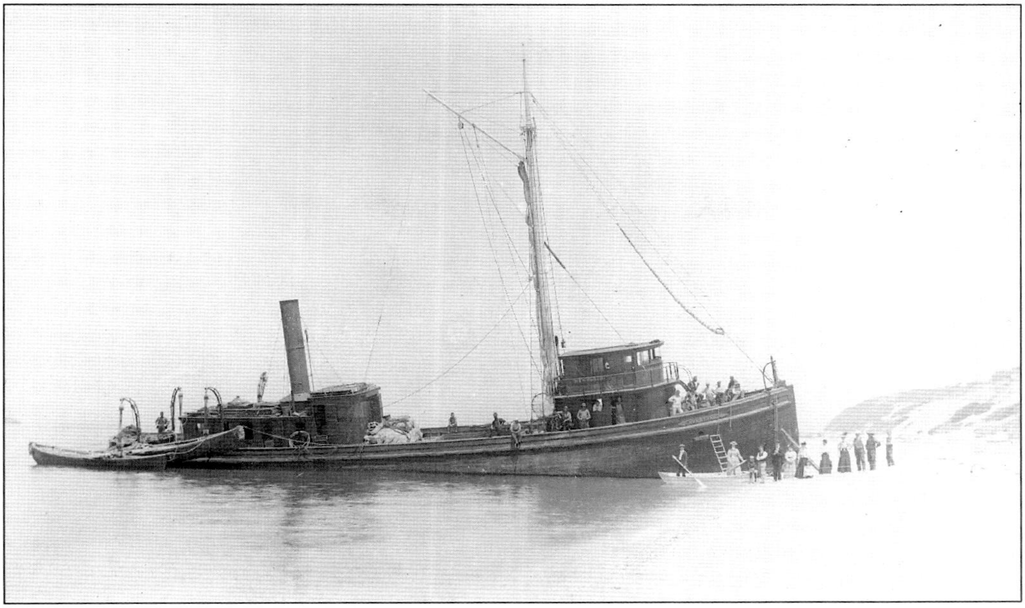

The bunker steamer *Sterling*, captained by Gabriel Edwards, is seen after it ran aground at Rocky Point.

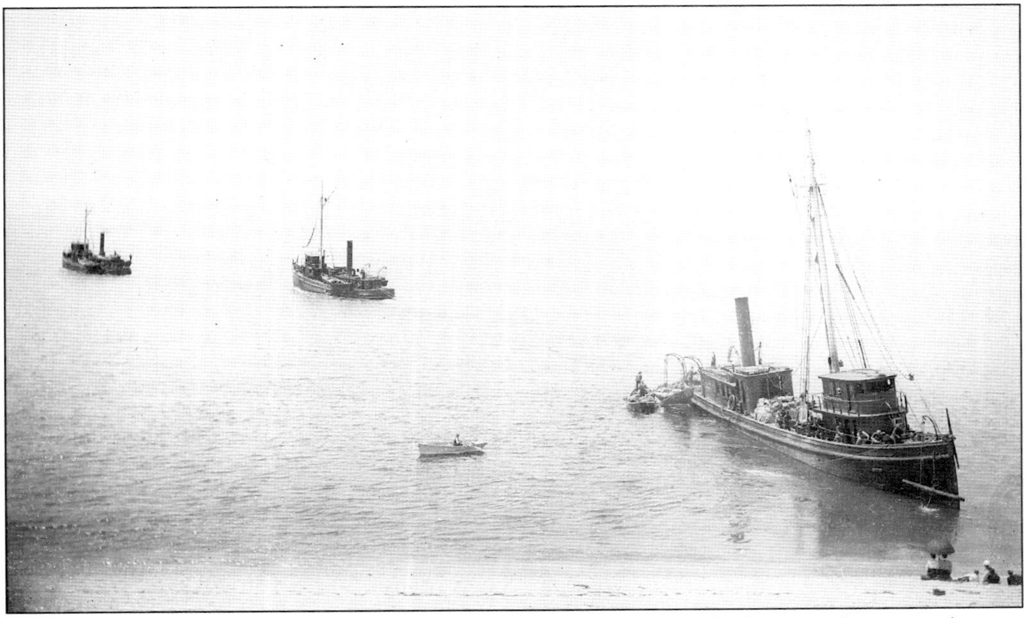

The steamers *Lawrence* and *Price* haul the *Sterling* back to sea. Both photographs were taken on July 8, 1898.

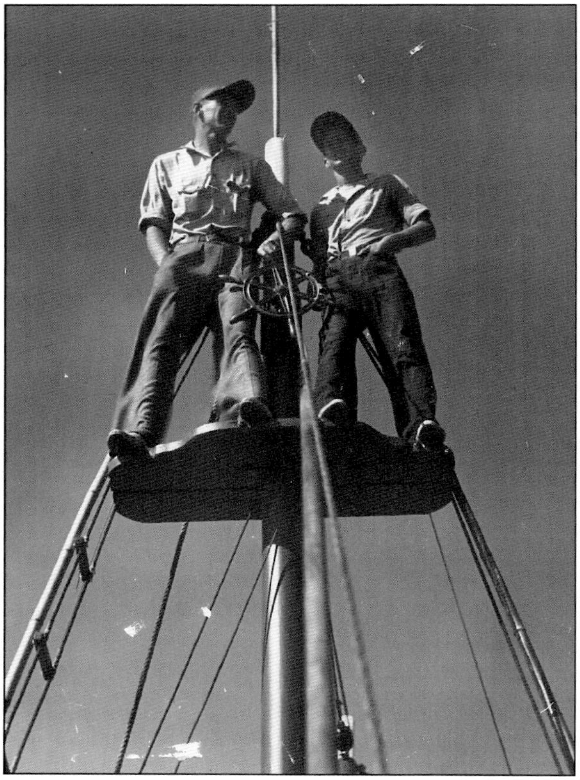

Carl Erikson and David Miller, framed against a background of sky, search for schools of fish.

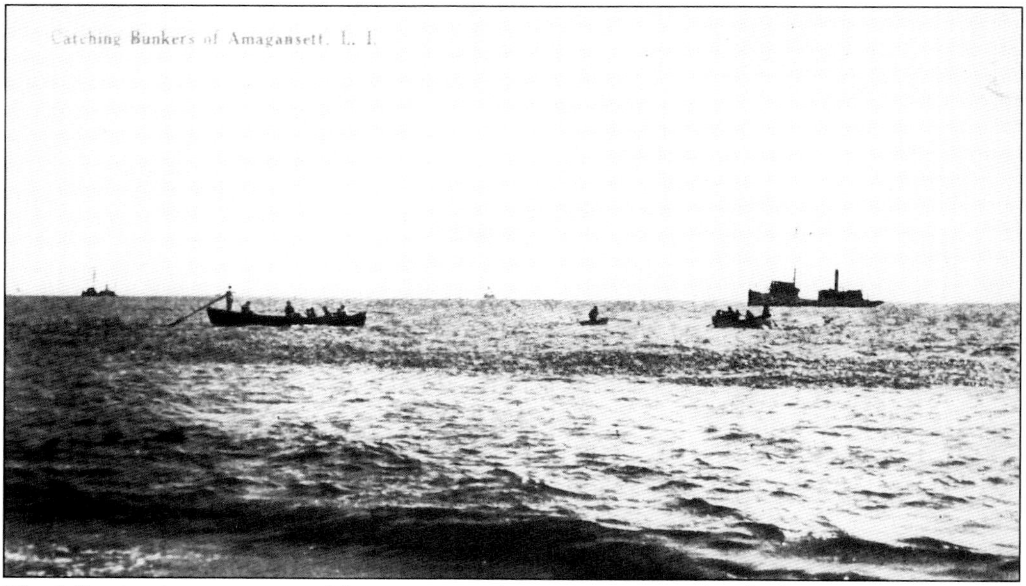

The following is a summary of the steps in making a "set" on a school of menhaden, or bunker fish. When the lookout sights a school of fish, the seine-setter uses a "striker" boat to follow the fish, indicate their position, and support the corkline after the crews set the net.

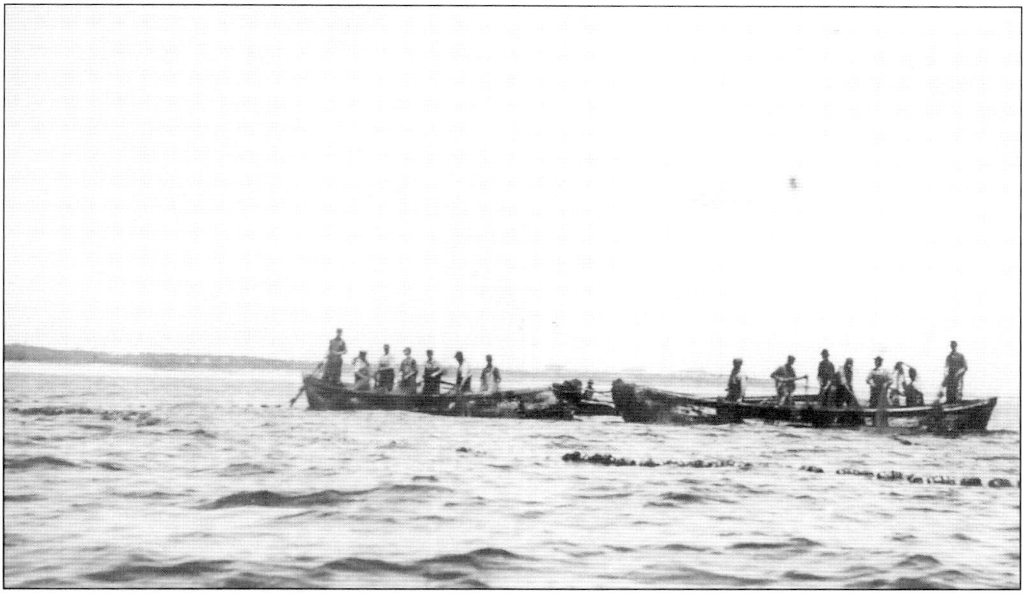

The purse boats and crews then head for the front of the school, separate, and quickly release the seine, encircle the school, and bring the ends of the net together . . .

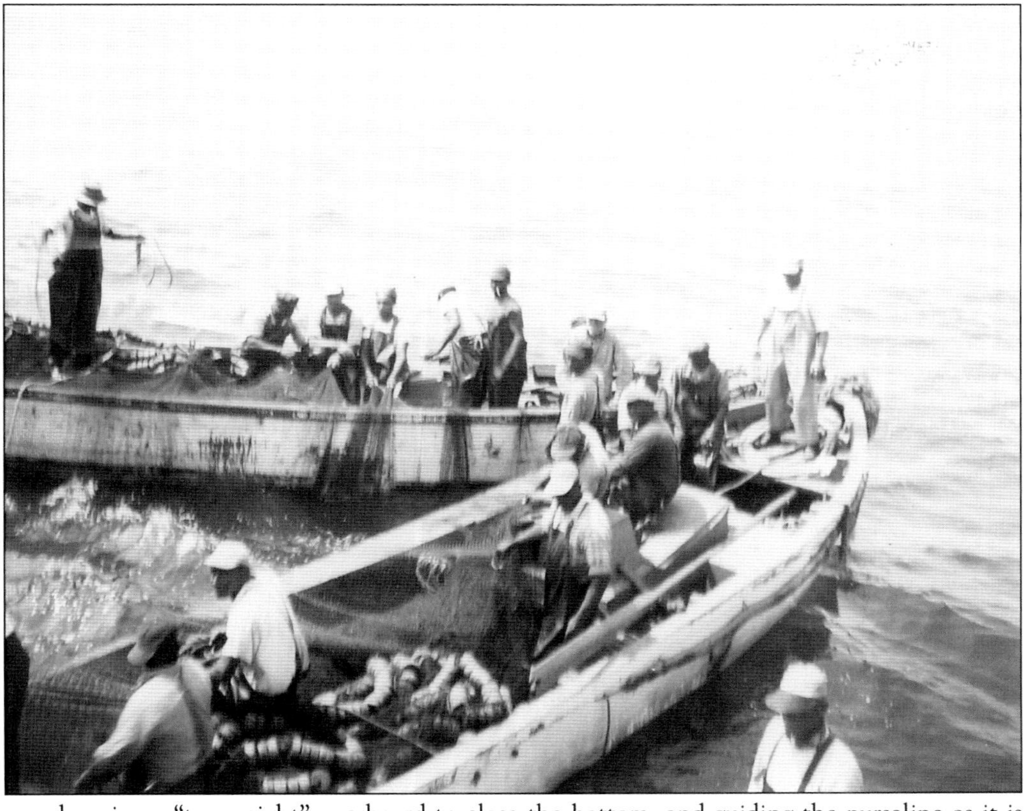

. . . heaving a "tomweight" overboard to close the bottom, and guiding the purseline as it is hauled in to purse the net.

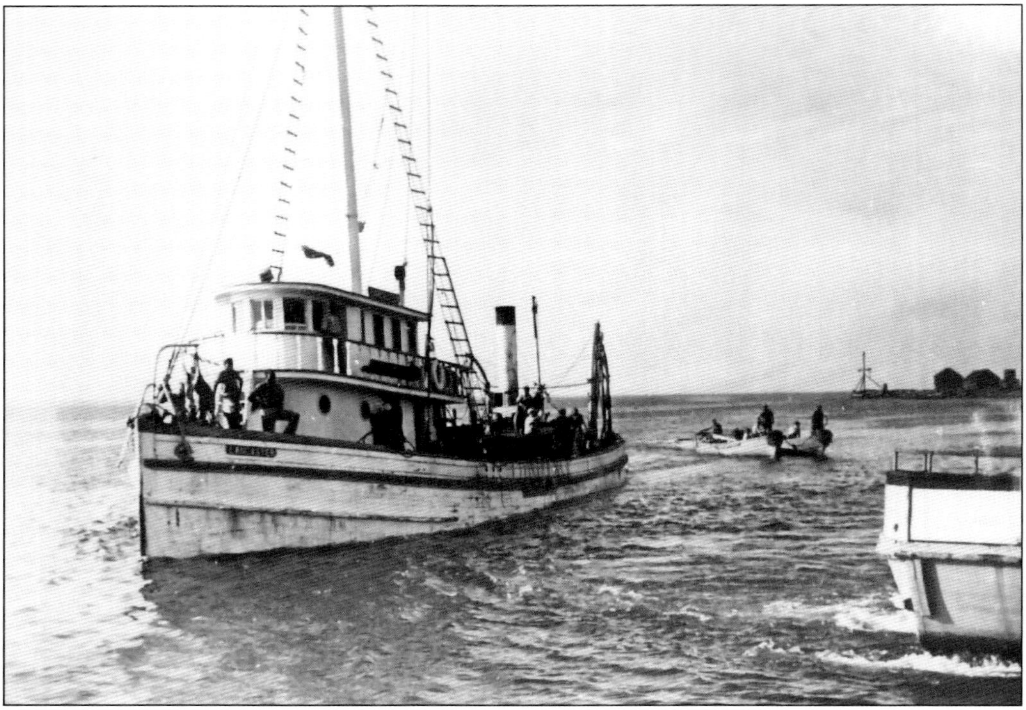

Jeannette (Edwards) Rattray wrote in her *East Hampton Star* column,". . . although our nose has to remain in firm grip of a large handkerchief during the entire visit, we never miss a chance to go to Promised Land and see the bunker steamers come in, and a good many other 'land lubbers' seem to feel the sameway about it." The Edwards Brothers' Basin at Promised Land and the two "fish factories" operated into the mid-1920s, when the bunker fish disappeared from local waters. When they reappeared in the early 1930s, the industry thrived—and reeked—once more, until the 1960s, when the development of synthetic fertilizers coincided with another bunker vanishing act.

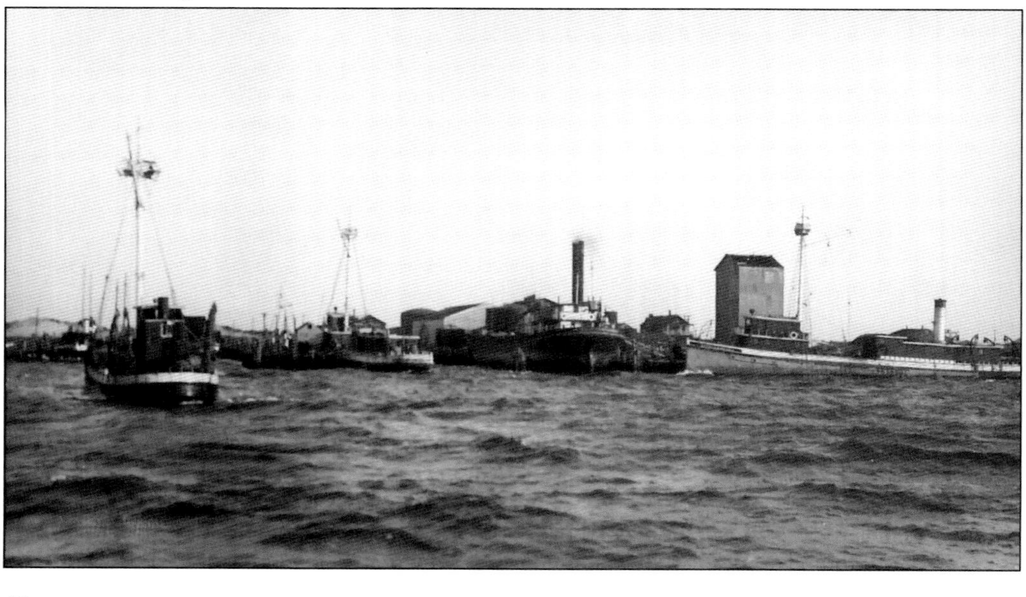

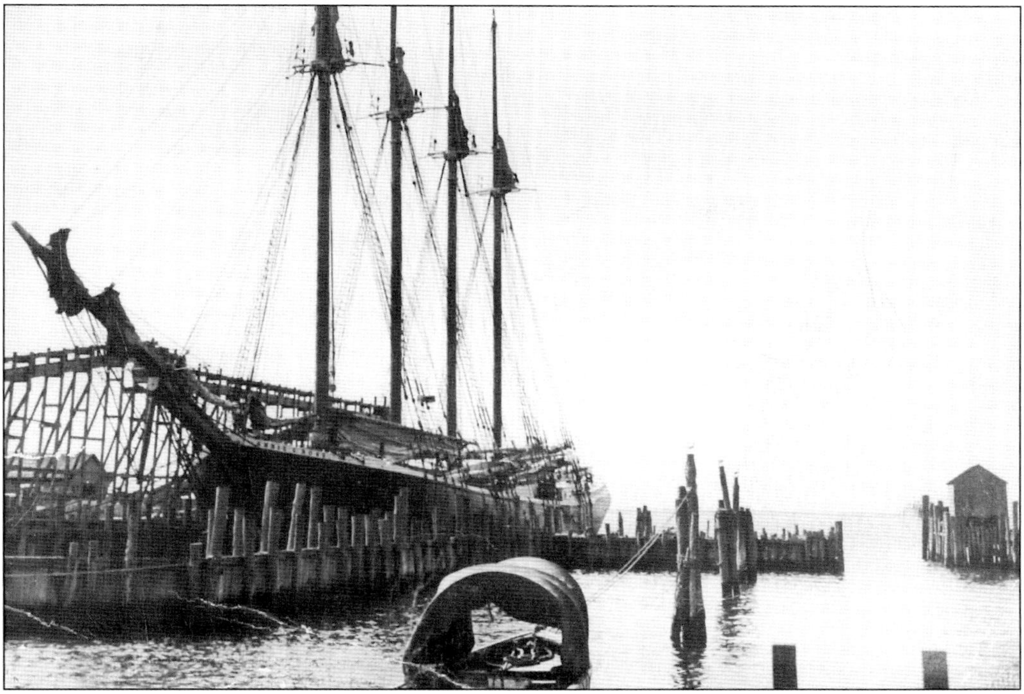

A schooner at Promised Land picks up scrap in 1940. Not only were there a variety of vessels at Promised Land, but there were a variety of people from around the world. One 1920s issue of the *Star* mentions the arrival of sixty Mexicans to work in the factories; at other times in the industry's history, large numbers of Canadians and Nova Scotians, and Southerners, black and white, worked on the fishing crews and in the plants.

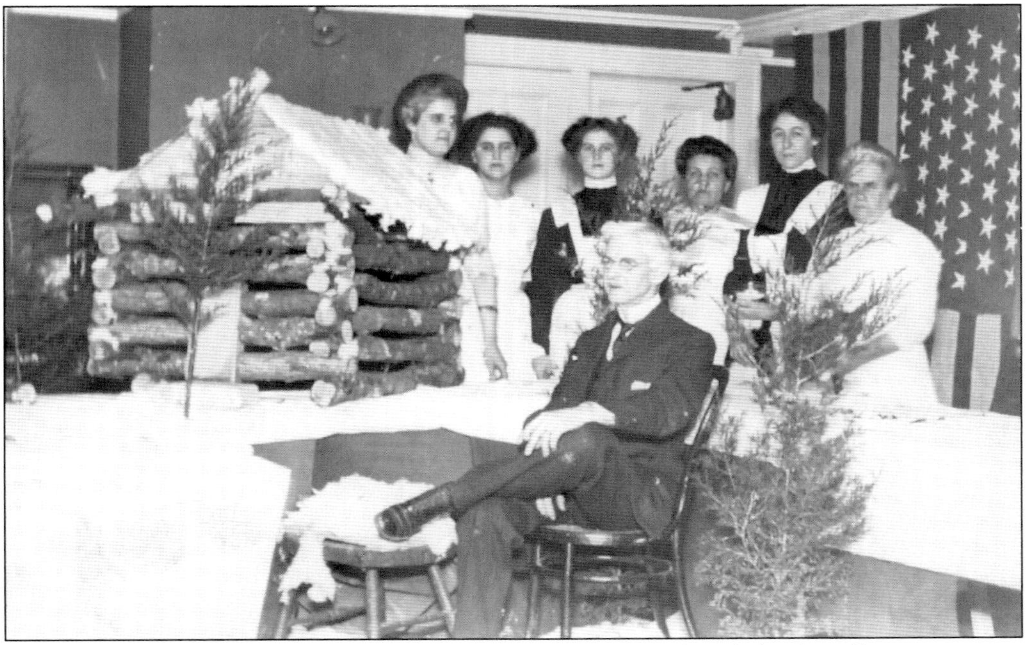

This early 1900s photograph of a "Canada" party is from the Edwards family collection.

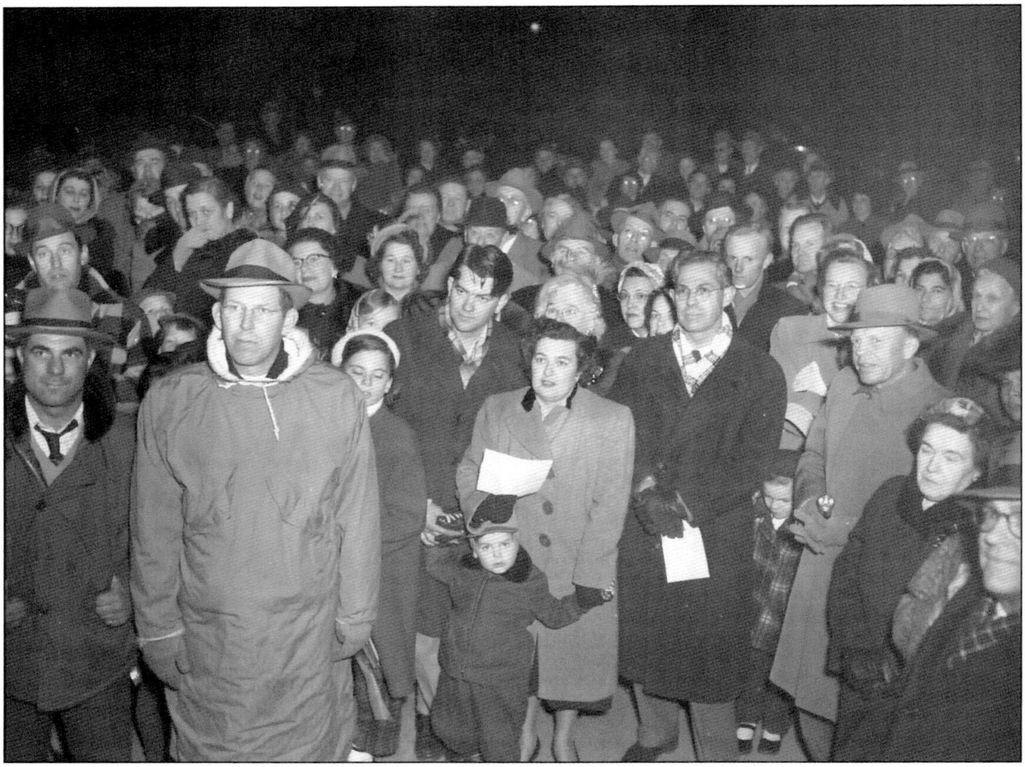

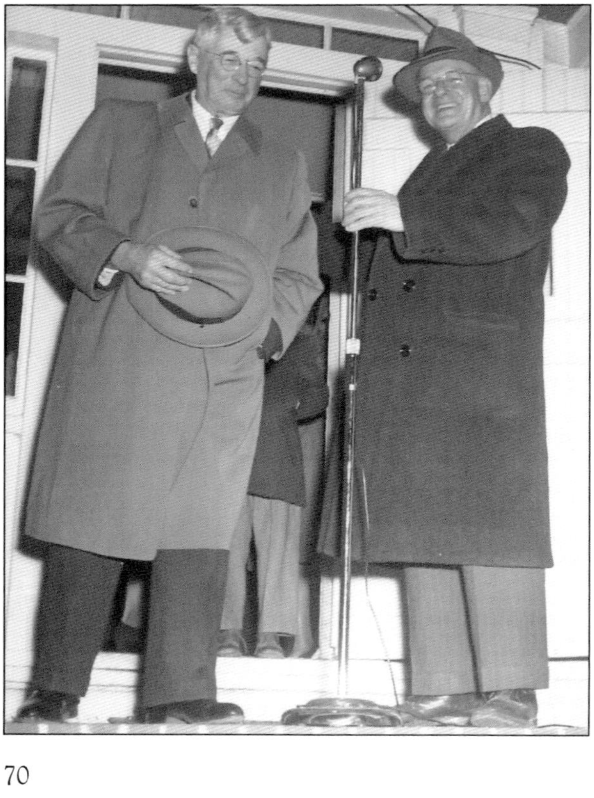

ABOVE: Dr. "Dave" Edwards practiced medicine for fifty years and, as this photograph of well-wishers at his 1952 "retirement party" shows, he was well-loved. LEFT: Dr. Edwards is standing with Judson Bannister, who came to Amagansett as a steamfitter for the Devon Colony homes and opened a steam laundry on Race Lane in East Hampton, now the popular "Laundry" restaurant.

Six

Roots and Scions

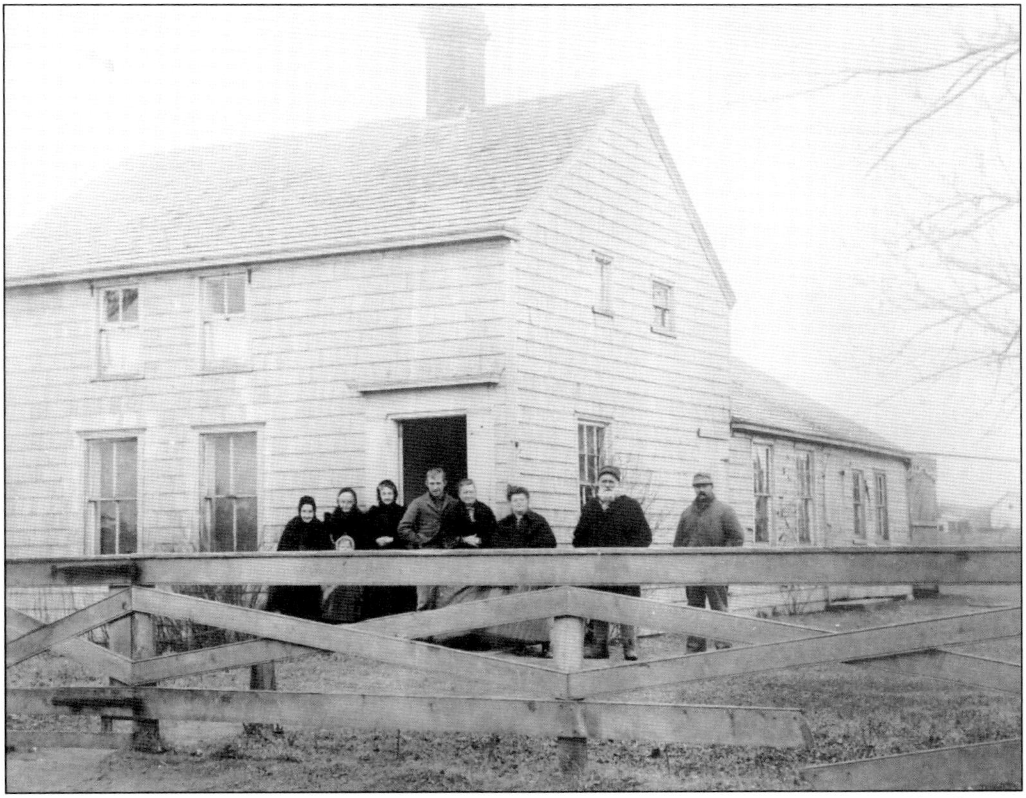

Elijah Bennett, life saving captain, died in 1887. When this photograph was taken of his house, his wife Sarah, son Frank, and daughter-in-law Lottie (King) lived there. From left to right are Sarah (Conklin) Bennett, Asenath (Conklin) Sherman, Esther (Conklin) (Mrs. Abner) Bennett, Harold King, Iantha Capitola (Bennett) King, Bertha Case Miller, Abner Bennett, Frank Bennett, and, in front, Edna Bennett (Frank and Lottie's daughter). Sarah's sister Esther married Elijah's brother Abner. This house has been moved to a hummock of Old Stone Highway.

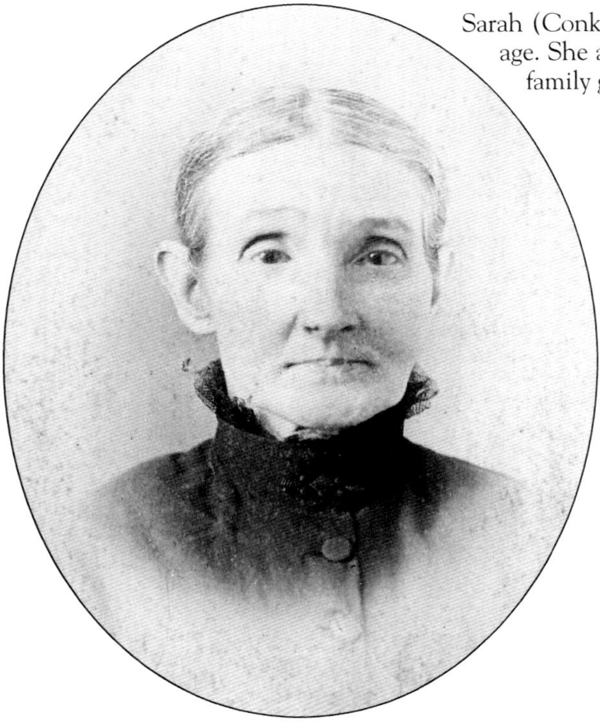

Sarah (Conklin) Bennett is shown here at an older age. She also appears in the Elijah Bennett house family group.

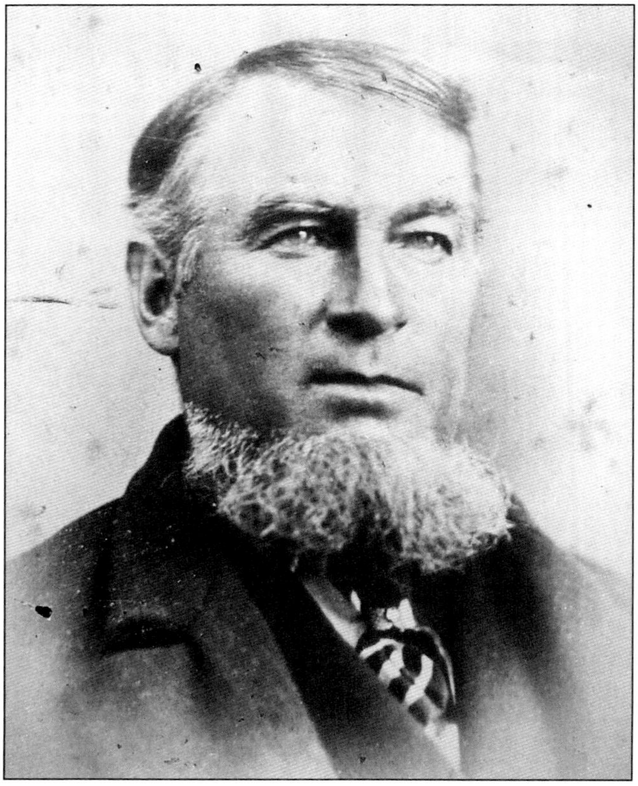

Captain Elijah Bennett, a lifesaving captain at Napeague and a carpenter, married Sarah Conklin in 1850. They had five children, four of whom lived to adulthood. Their two daughters were Isadora, who married Madison King, and Iantha Capitola, who married Madison's brother Egbert.

The oldest photograph in the Kelsey collection, this 1853 image shows Sarah (Conklin) Bennett with her daughter Isadora.

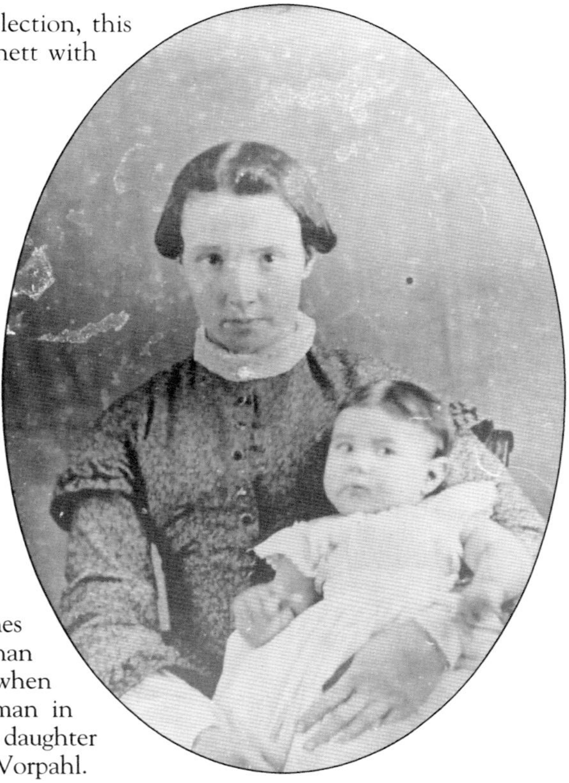

This house, which stood in the Barnes Landing area, was built by a whaler, Jonathan Bennett, and was probably torn down when the Bell Estate was developed. The woman in the photograph is Jonathan's youngest daughter Blendena (Deenie), who married William Vorpahl.

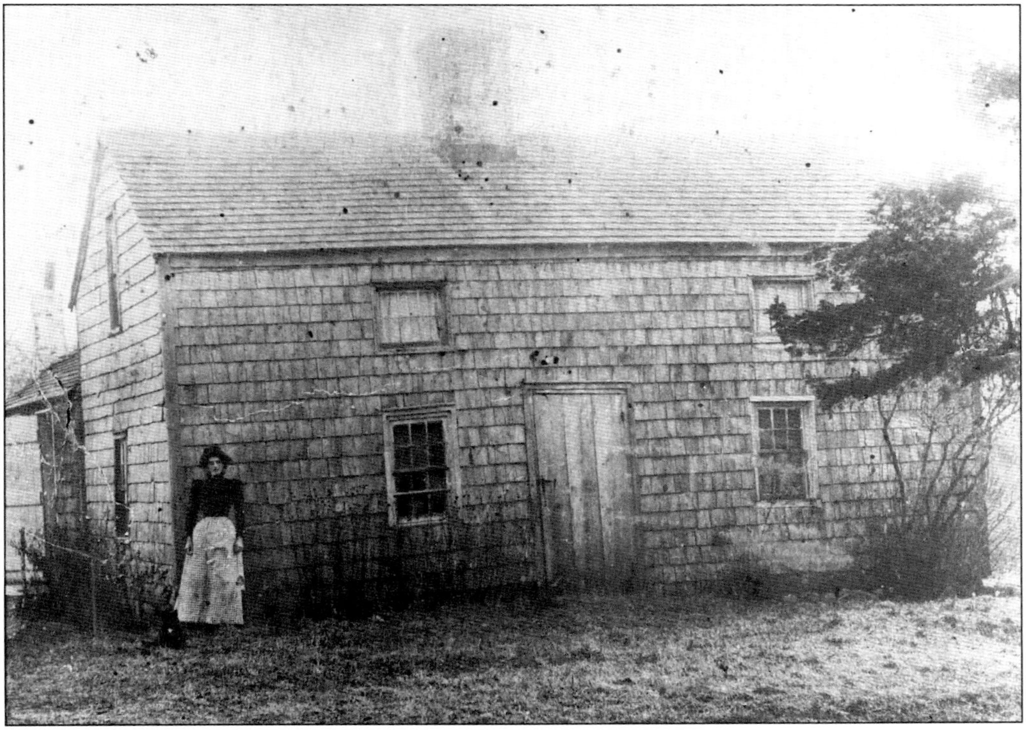

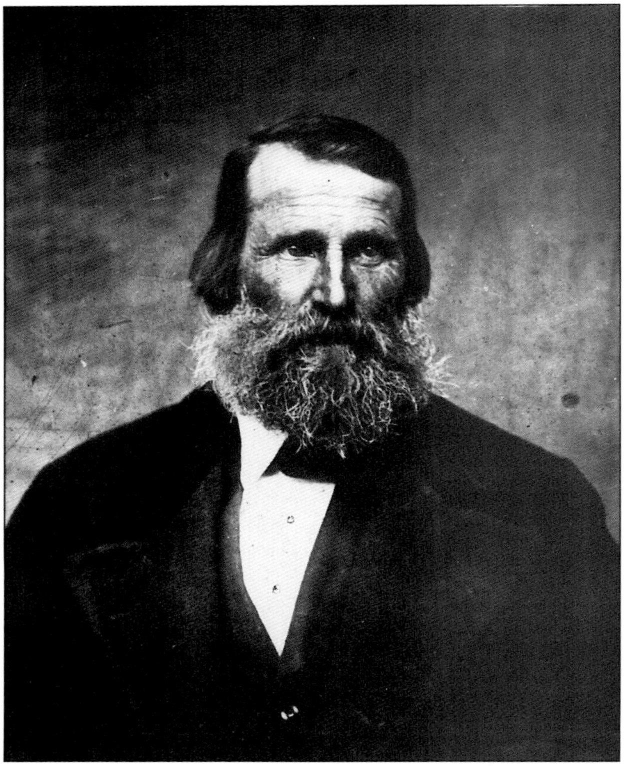

Elijah Bennett's brother Augustus and his wife Electra (Bush) lived at Fresh Pond, where his enterprises included the cutting of ice from the pond. It is not certain that he shipped ice to distant ports, but it is possible. Providing ice to markets as far south as the Caribbean augmented local families' incomes.

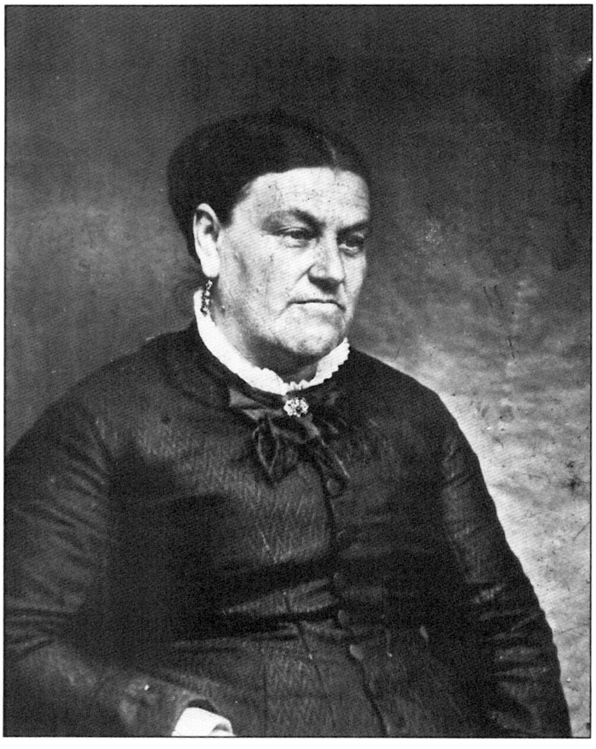

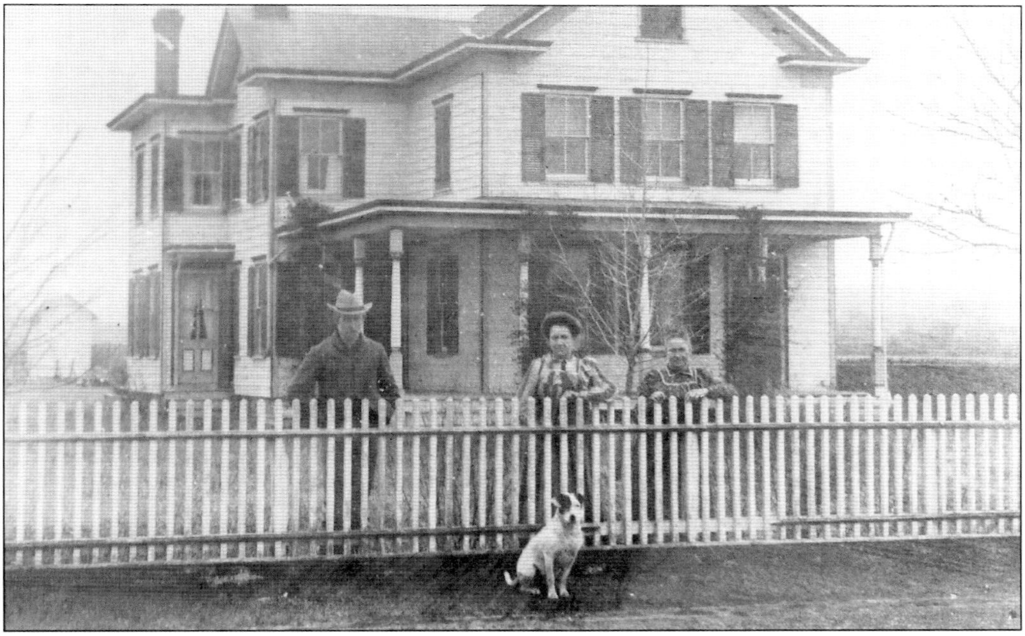

Harold King, Eva (King) Edwards, and Iantha Capitola (Bennett) King are shown here; not shown are Iantha Capitola and Egbert's third child, Abner Morton. "Mort" was married to Marietta (Abrams), who, to distinguish her from a village full of Marys, was called "Mary Mort." Affixing a husband's first name, or nickname, to his wife's for purposes of accurate identification in conversation is a long-standing Amagansett custom.

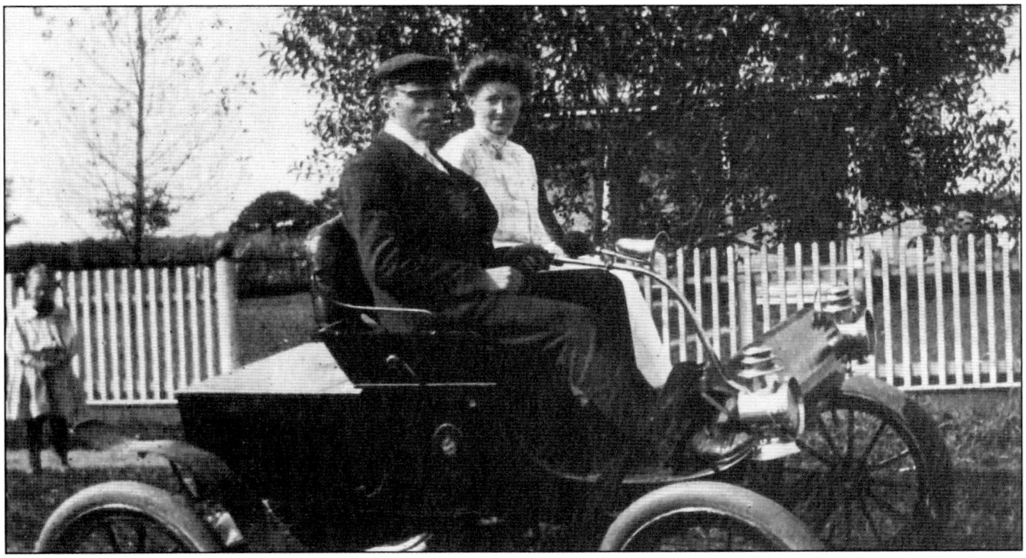

The daughter of Egbert and Iantha Capitola (Bennett) King, Eva (King) Edwards had one of the more basic King names. One genealogist wrote, "The King family has not been so difficult to trace as some because King parents showed more inventiveness in [naming] their offspring . . . Some King babies' names, especially in the nineteenth century, have been real flights of fancy." Barzilla King is one of the more memorable. Here Eva is seen with her husband, "Capt. Sam" Edwards, in their curved-dash Oldsmobile.

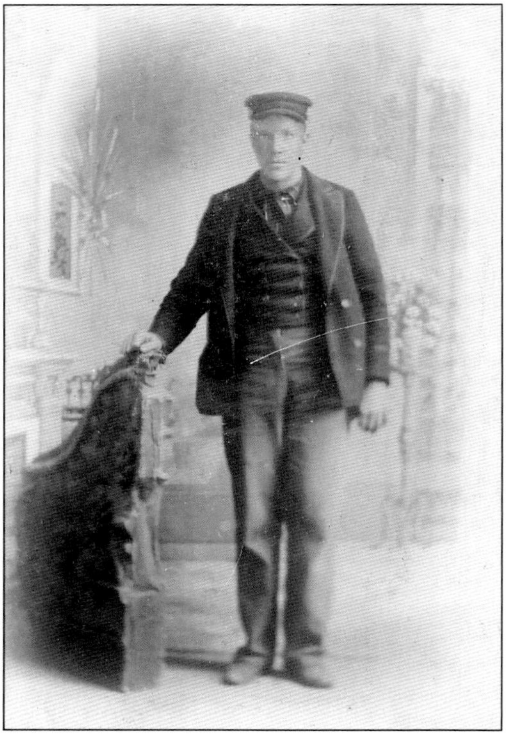

Ellis King, son of Madison and Isadora (Bennett) King, died at age nineteen, leaving a widow, Bernice, and a daughter, Mariellis. His sister Esther, married to Charles Barnes Edwards, had a son shortly after Ellis' death, and she named him Ellis King Edwards.

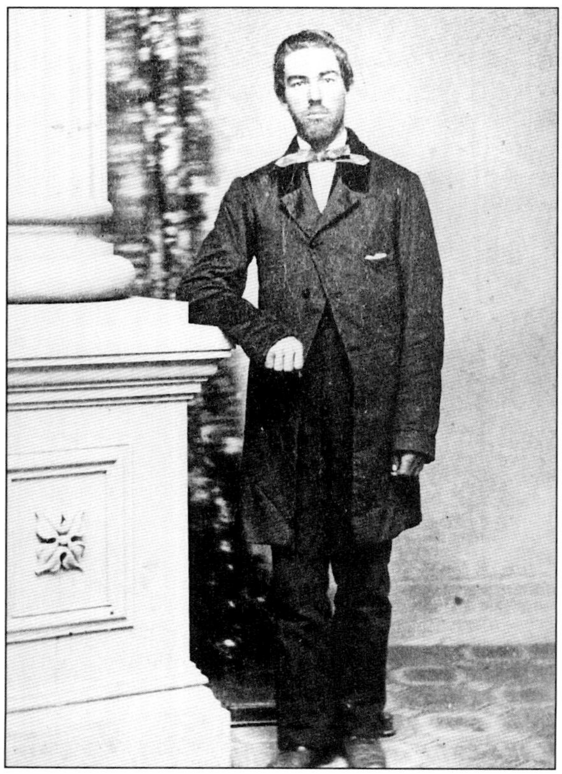

Albert Bennett (1806–1843), left, had this photograph taken, perhaps for his wife-to-be Fanny Edwards, and probably with a bittersweet sense of how important such mementoes were to those awaiting "the sailor's return." Two of his relatives had drowned in Gardiner's Bay, and his half-brother Joshua, first mate on a Dutch whaleship, died in Rotterdam after sailing from Madagascar. Albert made it home to Amagansett, but did not live long enough to know his great-nephew, Ellis King (1876–1895), the only son of Madison King and Albert's niece, Isadora Bennett. Acquired at two very different times from different sources, these are two of very few formal portraits of young Amagansett men in our collection, and it is typical of Amagansett's heritage that these men are directly related.

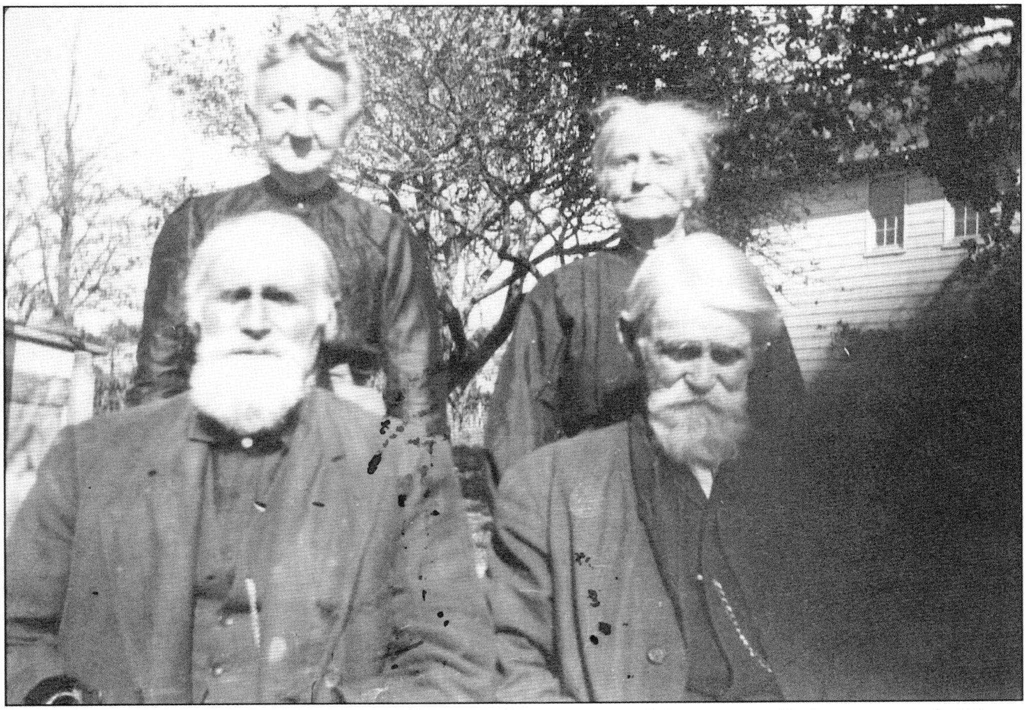

Asenath ("Seenie") Conklin married Jason Sherman, and her sister Esther married Abner Bennett. Both couples are shown here.

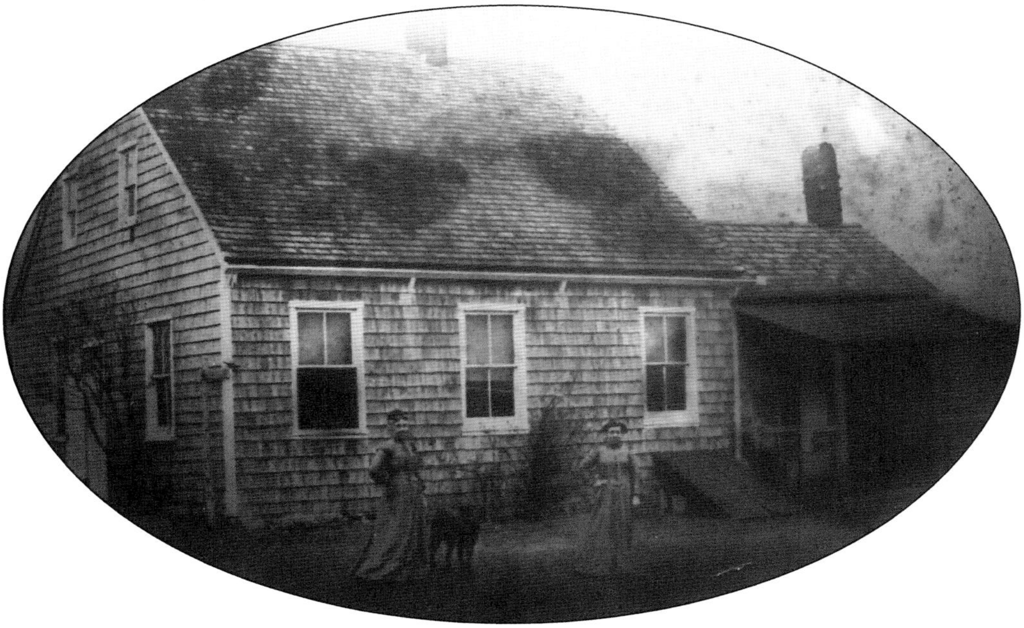

The Silas Sherman house, which was once an early East Hampton store owned by Madison Huntting, was moved to Fresh Pond. You may see where the front, with the center door for customers, has been turned to the east. Mrs. Nathan Brown and her daughter, pictured while living in the house purchased by Wathan Brown of the Life Saving Service, froze to death here one winter.

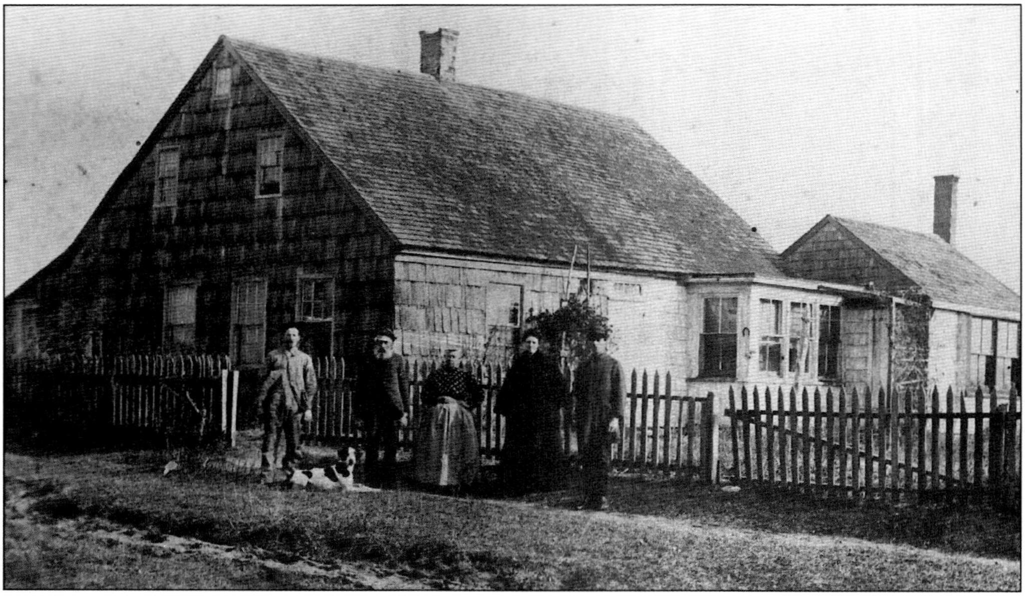

Two Miller brothers, Joseph and George, settled in this area originally; Miller is the most prevalent East End name. In 1936, when the movie *Ah Wilderness* (about a "typical" American family named Miller) was screened in East Hampton, any man or woman bearing the name was admitted free—provided they brought a non-Miller along! This East Side photograph shows "Aunt Gloriana" Miller's second husband (who ostensibly died of a chicken scratch) between Gloriana and their son. Newlyweds Ida and Frank Miller are on the right.

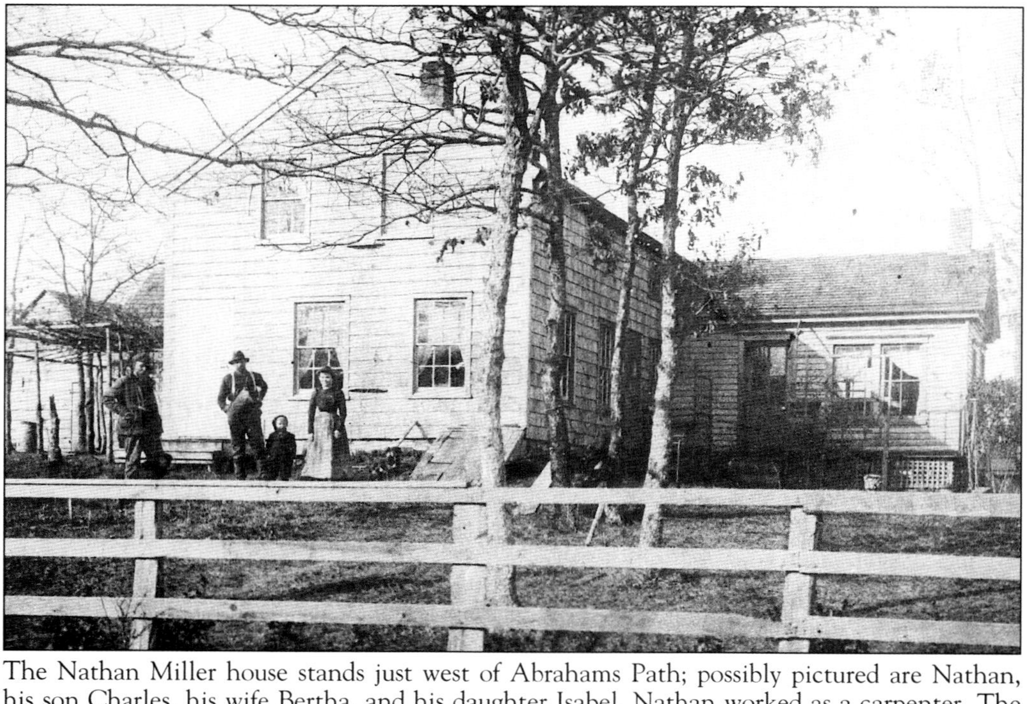

The Nathan Miller house stands just west of Abrahams Path; possibly pictured are Nathan, his son Charles, his wife Bertha, and his daughter Isabel. Nathan worked as a carpenter. The addition, at the right, came from a summer house in East Hampton.

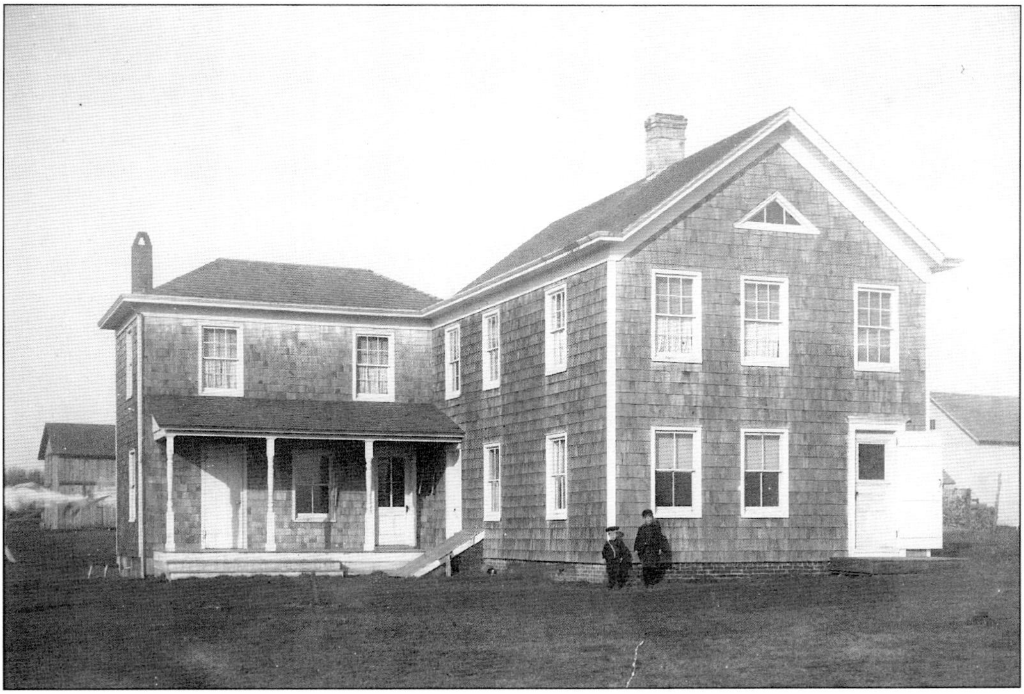

This photograph of the David Huntting Miller house on Main Street shows the addition Mr. Miller built so that Ruhamah could have her pump indoors.

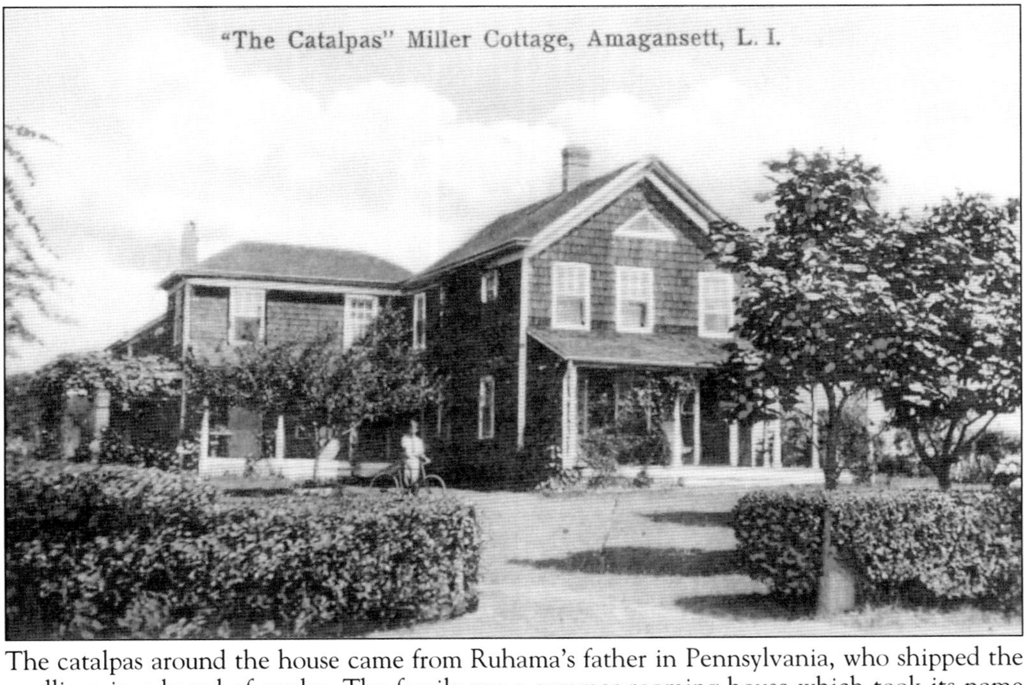

The catalpas around the house came from Ruhama's father in Pennsylvania, who shipped the seedlings in a barrel of apples. The family ran a summer rooming house which took its name from these trees.

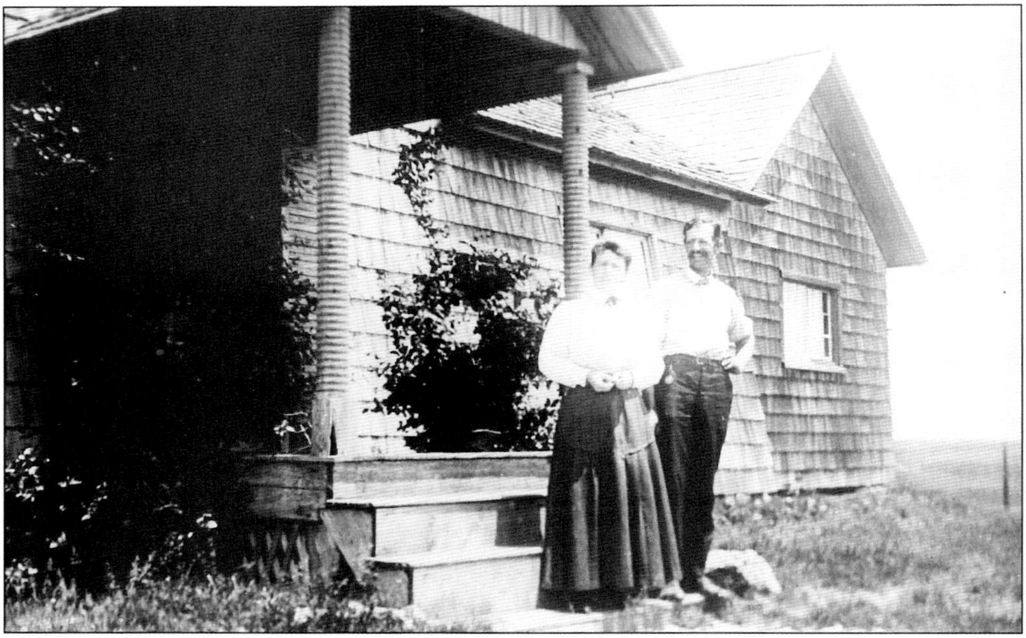

Hiram, brother of David Huntting Miller, and his wife Emma (Edwards) were caretakers on Gardiners Island.

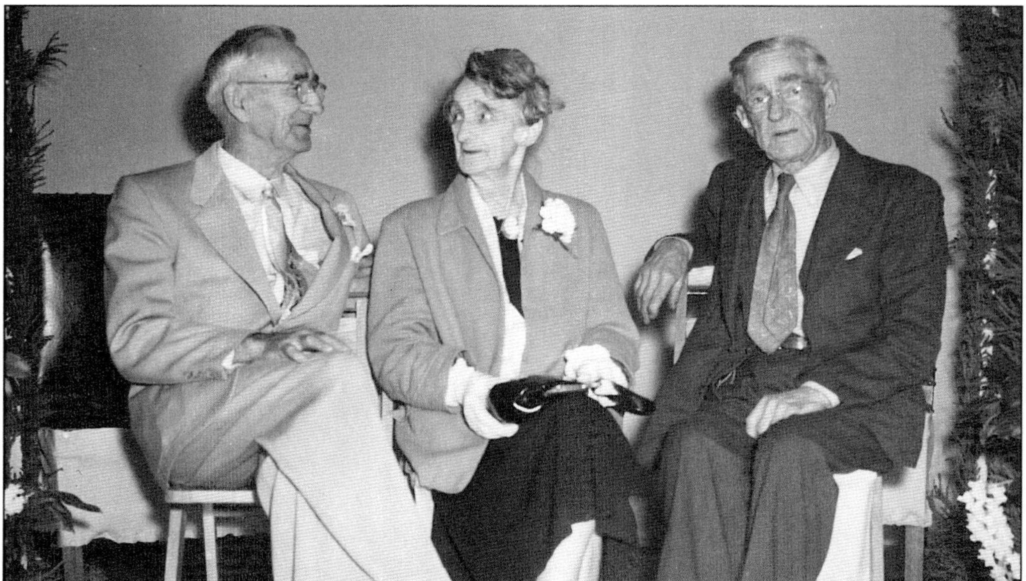

Samuel Russell Garfield Miller and Mary Elizabeth (Miller) celebrated their 50th wedding anniversary, on May 3, 1952. Seated at the party are brothers and sister Thomas, Mary Elizabeth, and Russell Miller. Their father, Jonathan Allen Miller, was keeper of the Montauk Lighthouse: he had lost a hand to a cannonball while serving in the U.S. Navy during the Civil War. Mary Elizabeth recalled that when she lived at "the Light" as a child, Stephen Pharaoh ("Stephen Talkhouse") jounced her on his knee, and treated her to his famous acrobatic "war whoop," on his frequent visits to the lighthouse keeper's family.

Seven

Thought and Action

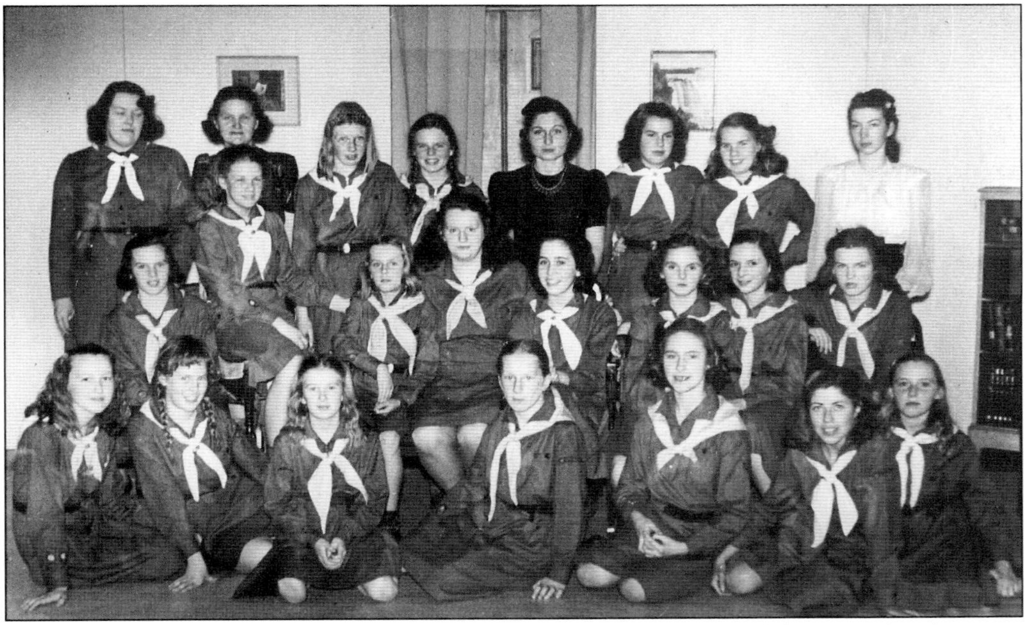

The Girl Scouts met first at the Amagansett School, and later acquired their own headquarters on Main Street. It has since been moved, and is now private guest quarters on a Skimhampton property. Given today's real estate values, it is remarkable that, well into the 1960s, a lot on Main Street could be used for a humble "clubhouse." Amagansett's Girl Scout Troop in 1938 consisted of the following, from left to right: (front row) Betty White, Patsy Griffing, Ruth Anderson, Caroline King, Jacqueline Kuykendall, Marion Scoville, and Ruth Kessen; (middle row) Mae Daniels, Dorothy Miller, Helen McGrath, Agnes Clint, Harriet Oxenham, Lois Sweeting, June Finch, and Faith Edwards; (back row) Gladys Robinson, Rosalie Hadel, Adelaide Mundell, Judy Talmage, Beverly Baker, Janet Schellinger, and Jean Cozzens. One of these scouts wrote, "I recall that we engaged in a great many activities, among them a hike to the [Stony Hill] fire tower and an all day picnic at Hither Hills." While we do not picture any Boy Scout troops, they were equally active; a 1918 newspaper reports that the "busy" Amagansett Boy Scouts had collected a quantity of good serviceable clothing for Belgian Relief.

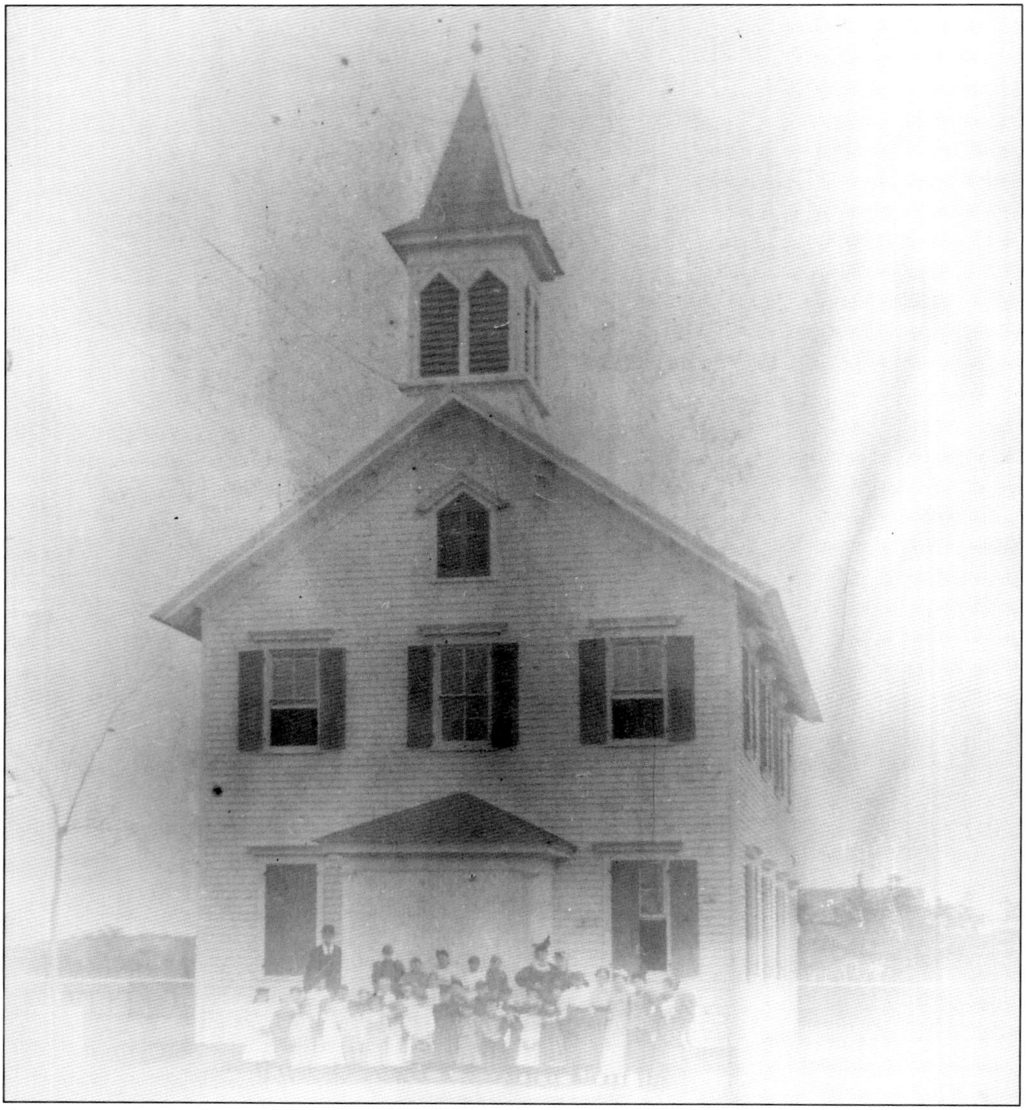

Amagansett's intellectual life has ever been integral and varied, reflecting its prosperity and global outlook. Prior to 1802, when Samuel Schellinger built a one-room schoolhouse in the middle of what is now Montauk Highway, children were home-schooled, or, when parents could afford it, educated at East Hampton's Clinton Academy. Their school year was often determined by the cycles of land and sea harvests. Sylvester Schellinger, brother of the one-room schoolhouse's builder, wrote that he taught "30 scholars and expect more. They give me $2 to $2.50 per scholar. I pay $20 per year for house and garden. Cheap enough." Sylvester Miller, son and namesake of the notable Amagansett whaling captain whose whaling logs are in the Mystic Seaport archives, taught in the "middle of the road" school in the 1850s. Edgar Mulford, later "a very able MD," taught there in the 1860s. An 1870s schoolteacher related that "one day 95 pupils were crowded into a room hardly large enough for 40," but "the people at length woke up to a sense of duty, and a large and beautiful school building (this one) was erected, . . . a credit to the village," in 1881. A contemporary trustees' account shows 1880s teachers' wages ranging from $182 to $225 per year.

A record of scholars attending the village's first schoolhouse in 1858 includes Juliet Lucilla and her father, Marcus Bolivar Hand. They are just two of many Amagansett people whose names derived from erudition in classic literature and interest in world news of the day, as well as family heritage. Marcus' middle name honors Simón Bolivar (1783–1830), "El Liberatador" of what are now Bolivia, Colombia, Ecuador, Peru, and Venezuela. Other examples of "current events" names are the several Pulaski Bennetts, namesakes of the Polish patriot and U.S. colonial army officer.

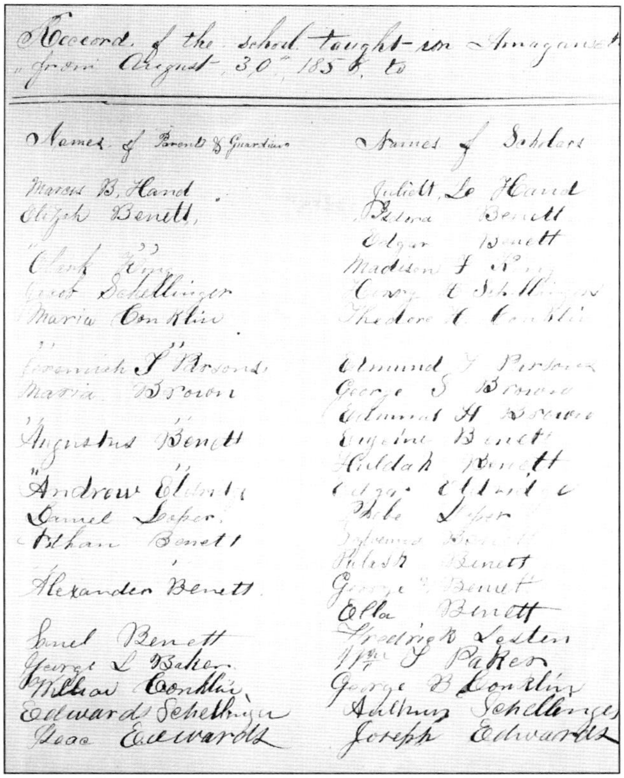

Record of the school taught in Amagansett from August 30th 1858 to

Names of Parents & Guardians	Names of Scholars
Marcus B. Hand	Juliett L. Hand
Elijah Benett	[illegible] Benett
"	Edgar Benett
Clark King	Madison [illegible] King
Geo. Schellinger	[illegible] Schellinger
Maria Conklin	Theodore [illegible] Conklin
Jeremiah [illegible] Parsons	Edmund [illegible] Parsons
Maria Brown	George S. Brown
"	Edmund H. Brown
Augustus Benett	Eugene Benett
"	Huldah Benett
Andrew Eldredge	Edgar Eldredge
Daniel Leper	Phebe Leper
Ethan Benett	[illegible] Benett
"	Pulaski Benett
Alexander Benett	George [illegible] Benett
	Ella Benett
[illegible] Benett	Fredrick Lester
George L Baker	Wm S Baker
William Conklin	George B Conklin
Edward Schellinger	Anthony Schellinger
Isaac Edwards	Joseph Edwards

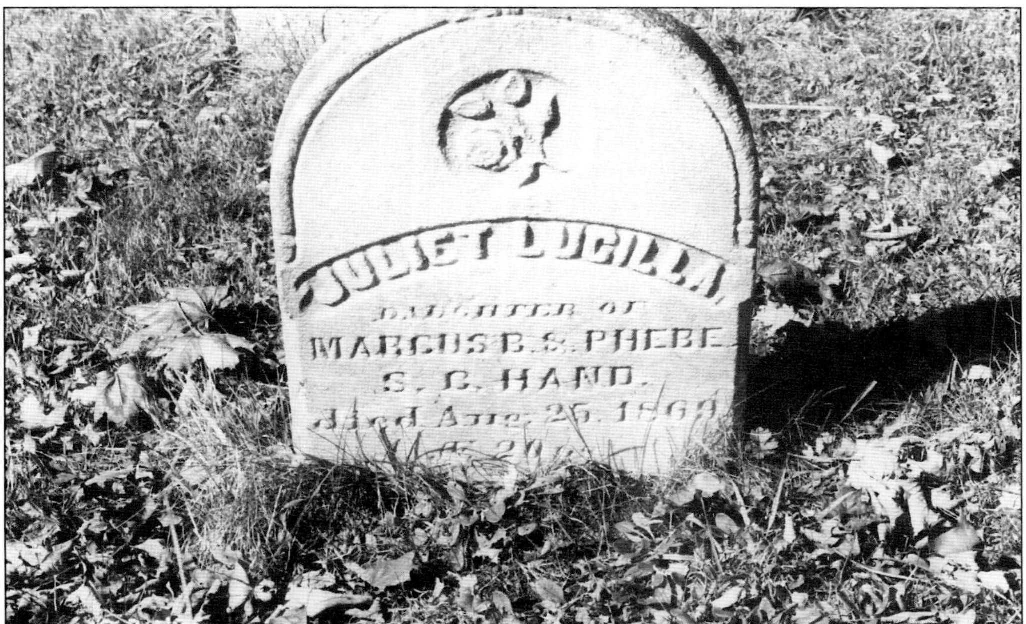

Juliet kept a "very sweet and cultured and touching" diary, the only existing written record of a nineteenth-century girl's life in Amagansett, until her death at age twenty. Its last entry records the driving of the "golden spike" on the transcontinental railroad. Her tombstone is shown here.

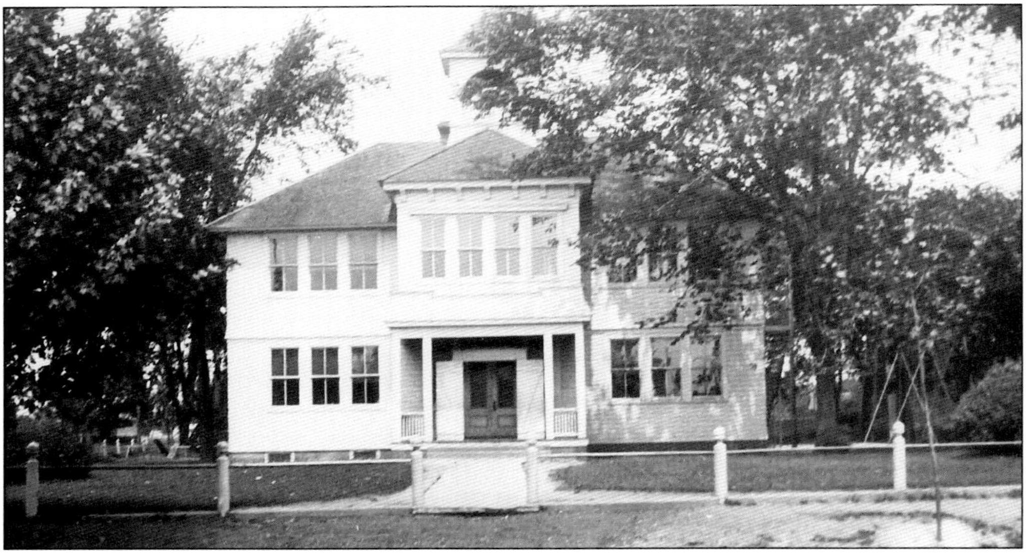

Twenty-five years after the second "elegant" schoolhouse was built and furnished for $2,253, four rooms were added by Everett W. Babcock—a grandson of Samuel Schellinger's—at a cost of $4,900. By this time, David Edgar Parsons had sent elm saplings from Monroe County, and the schoolyard benefited from the ambitious landscaping of Main Street. Although this building was torn down in 1937, the original 1881 cupola survived as a shed on Oak Lane.

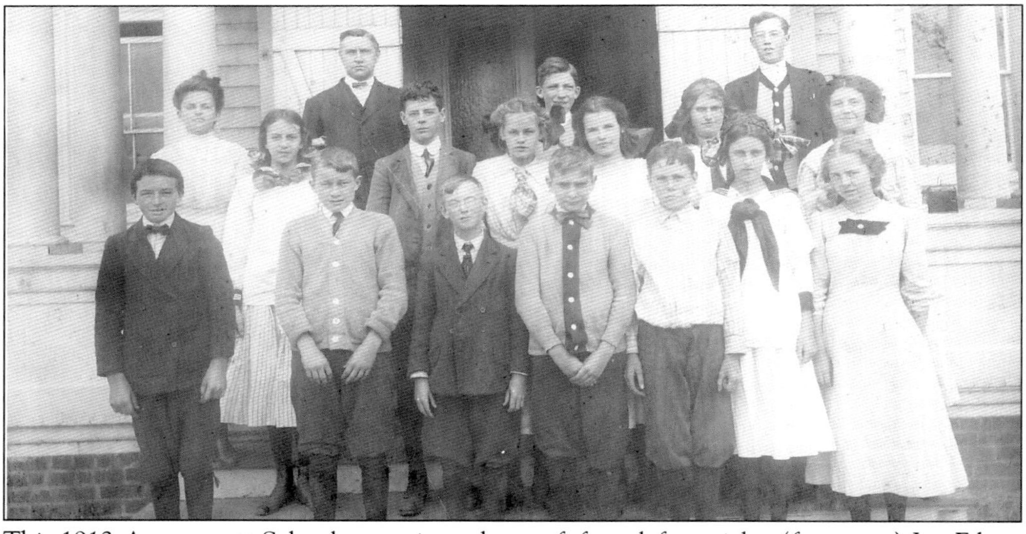

This 1912 Amagansett School group is made up of, from left to right: (front row) Joe Edgar, Vernon Kelsey, Nat Leek, Blanchard Barnes, Norton Griffing, Florence Terry, and Maude Bassett; (middle row) Mary Cozzens, Louise Mulford, Howard Eichorn, Alice Osborne, Marietta Murray, Ada Smith, and Angie Miller; (back row) Mr. Ellery Southard, Charlie Jackson, and Clyde Hand. Louise Mulford, whose mother Anastasie ("Tassie") was a great friend of "Miss Amelia" Schellinger's, was one of the first young women to leave Amagansett for college. After graduating from Mount Holyoke, she ran the Windmill Cottage summer inn with her mother, taught piano, and served as a beloved church organist for four decades. Her cousin, Catherine Mulford, worked as a librarian in Honolulu; her cousins John Wesley and Carrie, married Rosa Belle Edwards and her brother, "Dr. Dave," respectively.

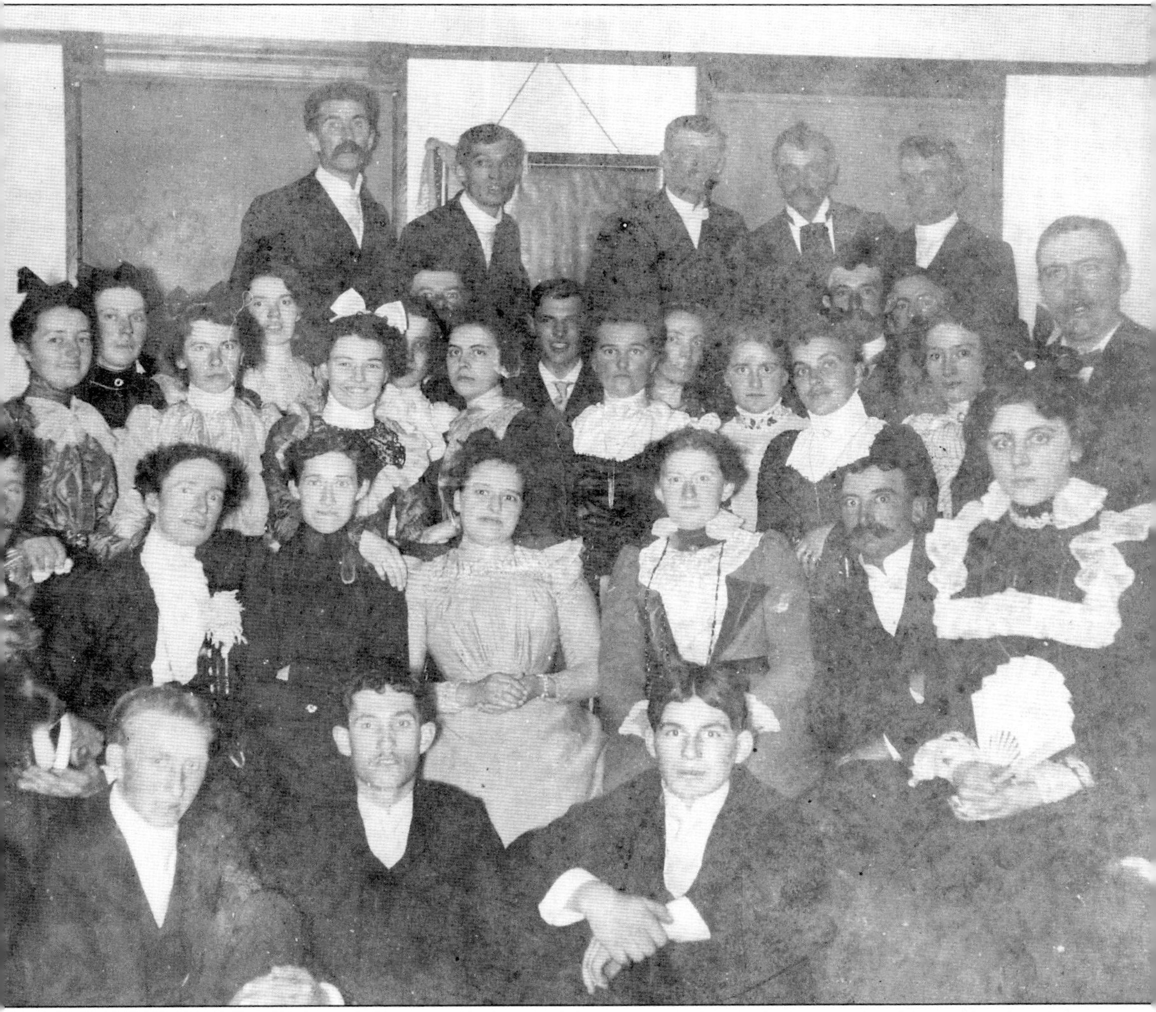

Schools were not the only centers of learning. The Chatauqua movement, begun at the turn of the century as a training camp for Sunday school teachers, developed into a nationwide system of adult education and entertainment . Miss Amelia Schellinger held a Chatauqua diploma, but we do not know whether it was earned at the Lake Erie camp, by correspondence, or extension course. East Hampton was a regular stop on the "circuit." Members of the unidentified Amagansett group shown here might have attended one of the many autumn offerings that Chatauqua brought to local halls, from concerts and plays to travelogues and "self-help" lectures ("How to Live 100 Years," for example). One lecture was advertised as being a "sure cure for the blues. It beats a vacation at the seashore for the fellow who thinks he doesn't like lectures. It exterminates pessimism. It brushes the cobwebs off the mental machinery and starts the wheels of thought revolving. It fires up and blows the whistle for spiritual factories that have been shut down. It prods communities into concerted action and sends individuals barking on the trail of opportunity. It skins sham, swats hypocrisy, and slams selfishness. It exalts virtue, glorifies labor, and shows inspiration. It is as invigorating as a mental bath." If nothing else, the lecture would have taught the audience everything it needed to know about mixing metaphors!

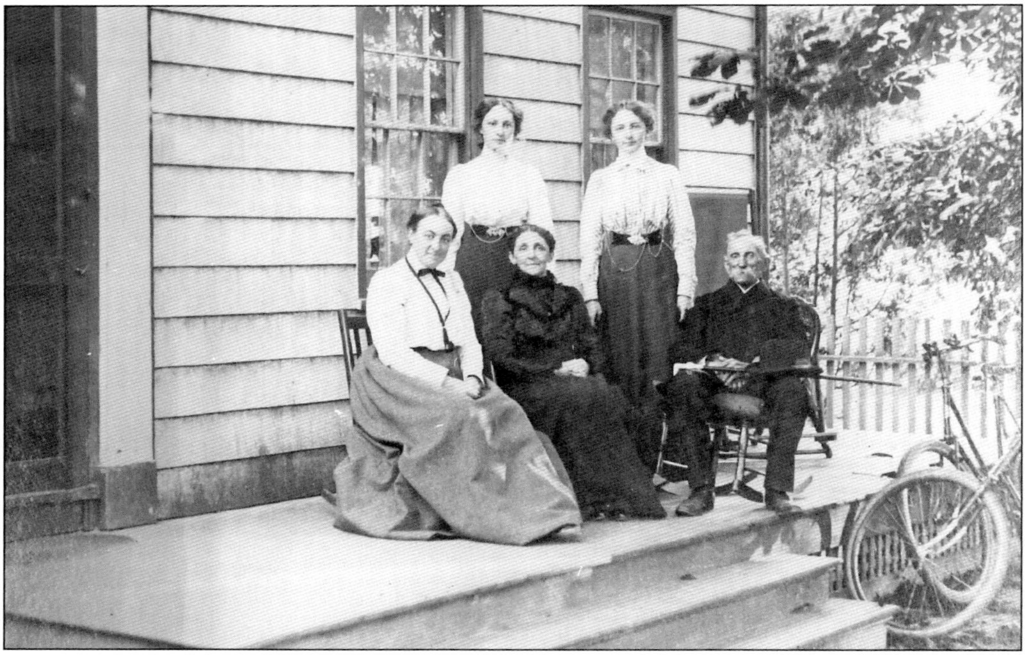

Reverend Dr. James B. Finch came to Amagansett in 1879 and served as its Presbyterian minister until 1903. He edited the *Caesar's Gallic War* volumes in the *Completely Parsed Classics* series which was published through the Cooper Institute in New York. His daughter Adelaide edited the long-popular 1897 *Finch Primer*; she was also principal of the Normal Training School in Lewiston, Maine. This photograph, taken at Reverend Finch's parsonage, shows Adelaide, her sister Bertha, Mrs. Finch, her daughter Maude, and Reverend James Finch.

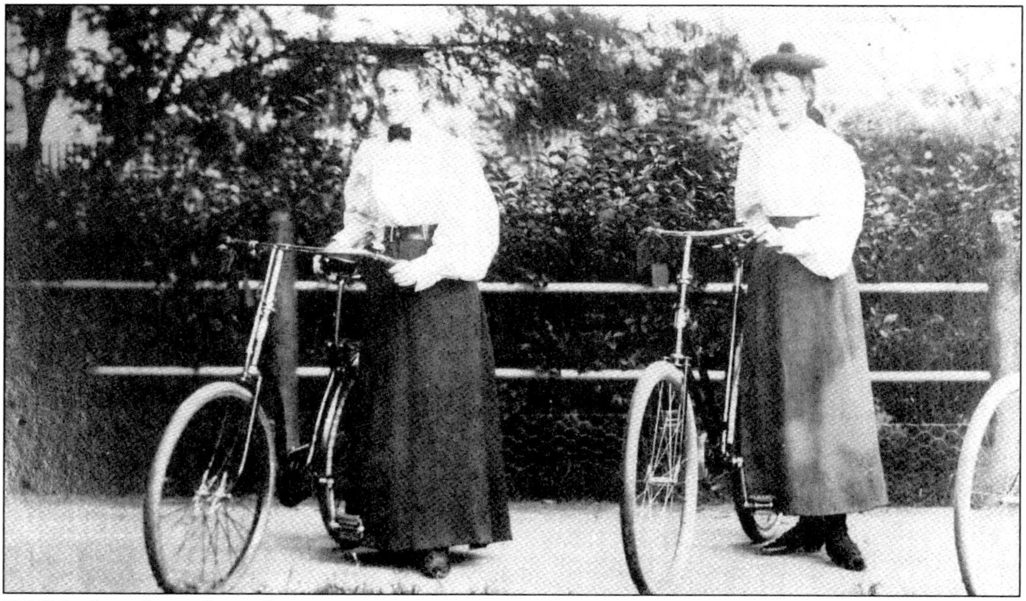

Well before the influx of city visitors, Amagansett had a tradition of responding to new trends. This 1896 Fred Parsons photograph shows Dr. Finch's daughters, Bertha and Maude, looking a very dignified part of the bicycle "craze."

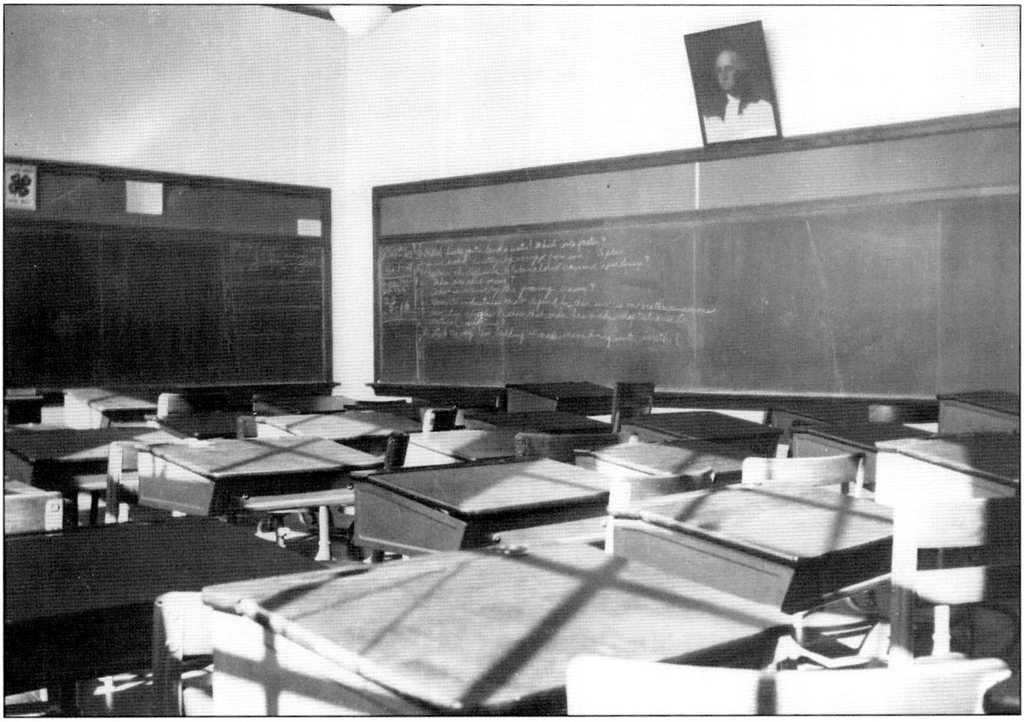

Carleton Kelsey's seventh-grade schoolroom is shown here in 1936, just after the move to the new school building. These geography questions are on the board: 'Which heats faster, land or water? Is air heated directly by energy from sun? Explain. Explain the difference between a land breeze and a sea breeze. When does each occur? What is meant by the growing season? Name (3) industries that depend for their success upon weather conditions. Give two examples to show that man has made adaptations to natural conditions. State one way that building is made easier during winter months."

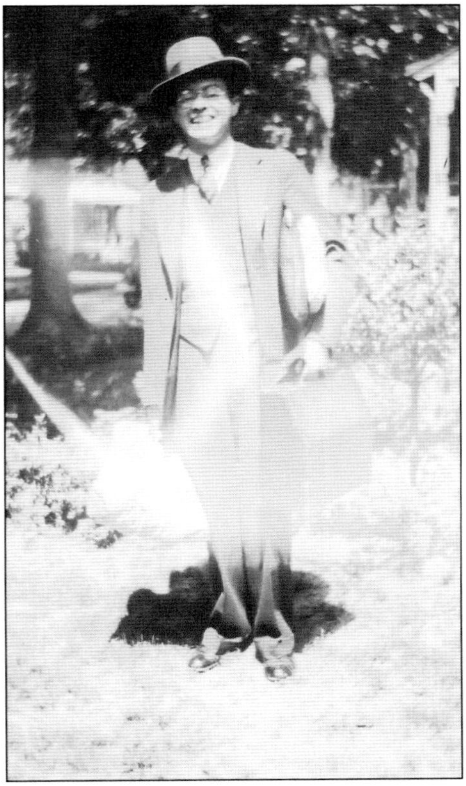

By the time Carleton Kelsey was celebrating his graduation from the Teachers College at Westchester, Pennsylvania, in 1935, many more Amagansett students were college bound. Carleton taught at the Amagansett and Southampton Schools, and at a private academy.

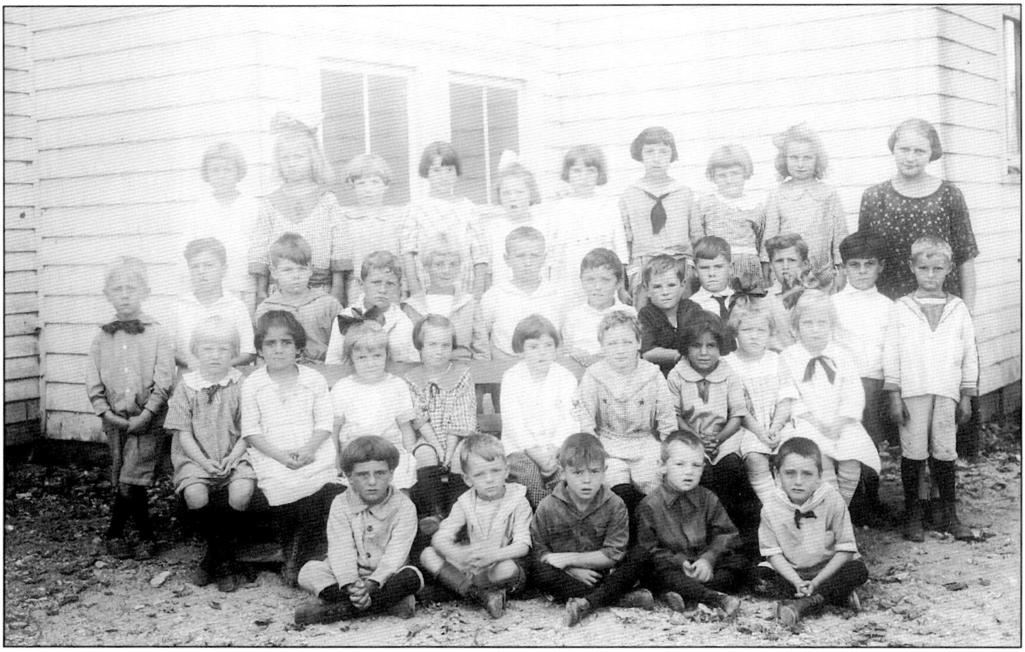

This 1923 photograph of Miss Dickson's grade school class, taken in a corner of the 1905 addition, includes Milton Miller (third row, fifth from right), whose recollections of the work and lives of Amagansett baymen are a vivid part of Peter Mathiesson's book, *Men's Lives*.

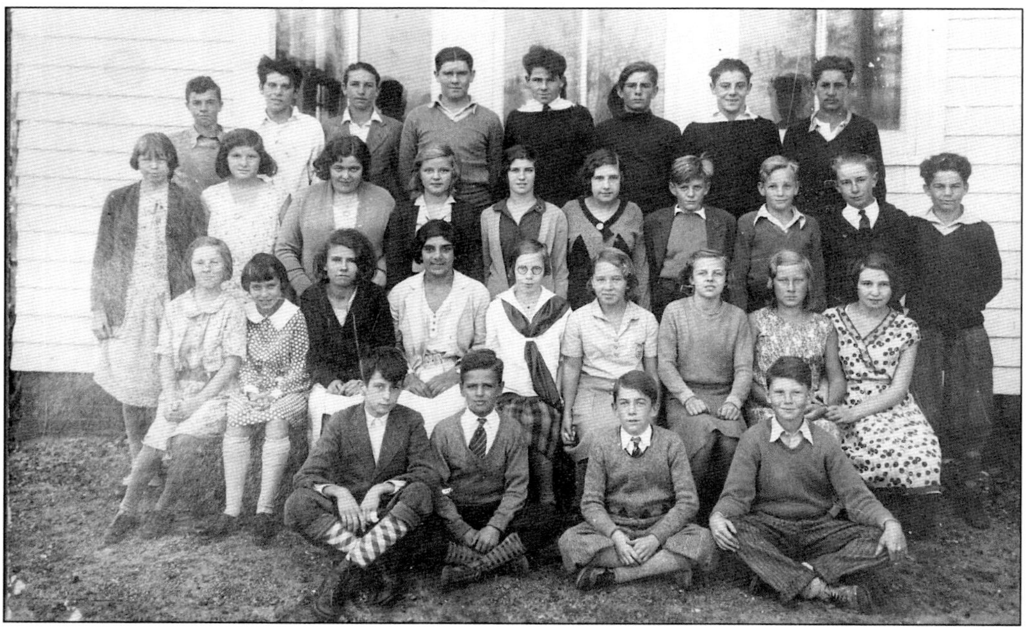

Milton Miller (fourth row, third from right) also appears in this eighth-grade school picture, taken in 1930, along with his wife-to-be, Etta Midgett (second row, third from left). Etta, born in Kitty Hawk, North Carolina, came to Amagansett at age ten when her father joined the Coast Guard and was stationed here. Several of her uncles followed, and worked as bunker fishermen for years.

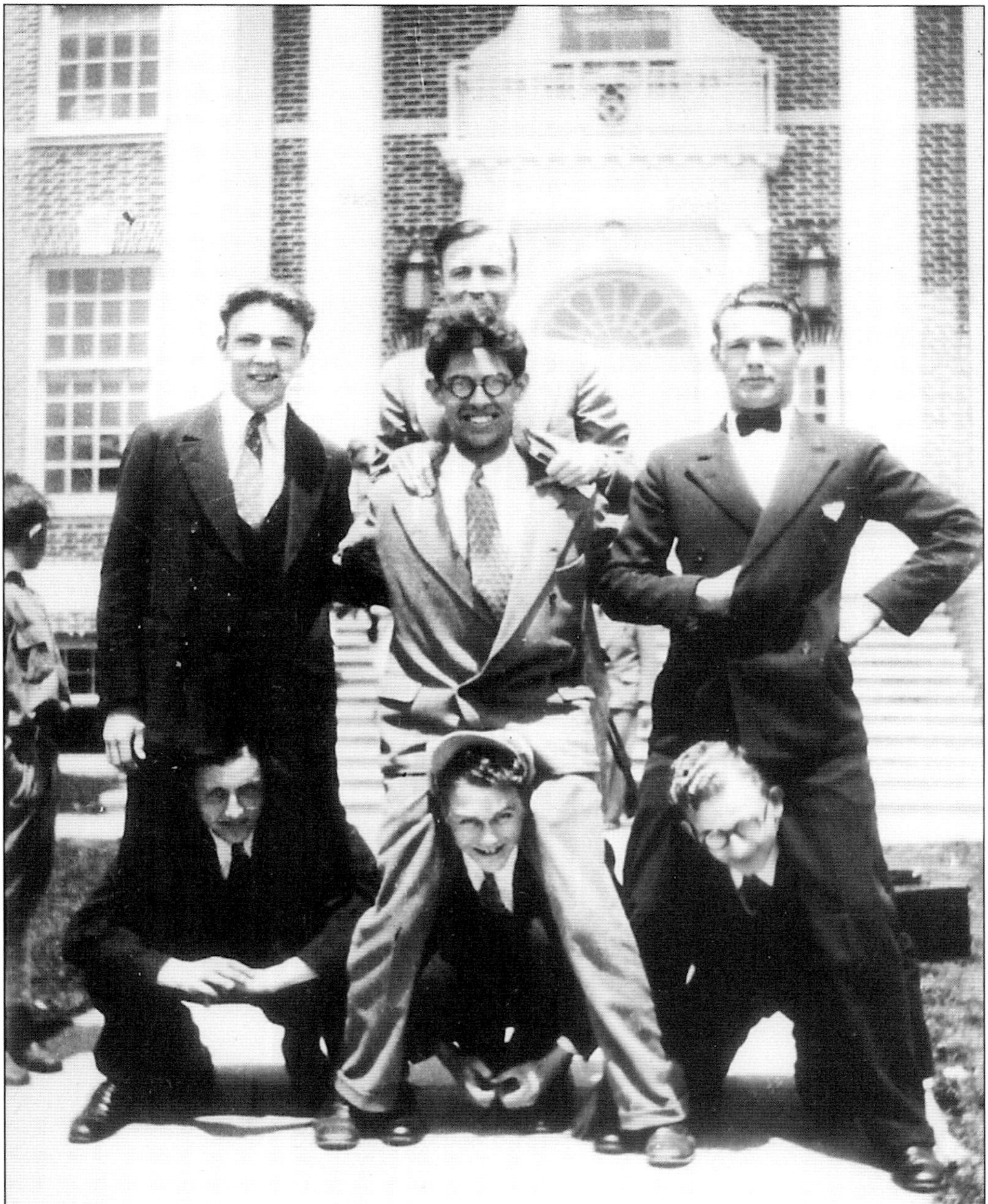

Amagansett students have always attended high school in East Hampton. The first high school, a wooden structure, was built in 1893, and a brick addition to that building—which still stands—was made in 1905. The present building, which appears in this photograph and owes its fine masonry to an Amagansett craftsman, was constructed in 1921. These 1928 graduates from Amagansett and East Hampton are, from left to right: (front row) Bill Granger, Gilbert Dayton, and Earl Gardell; (back row) Coolidge Hand, Charles Mansir, Byril King, and Dick Barnes (top).

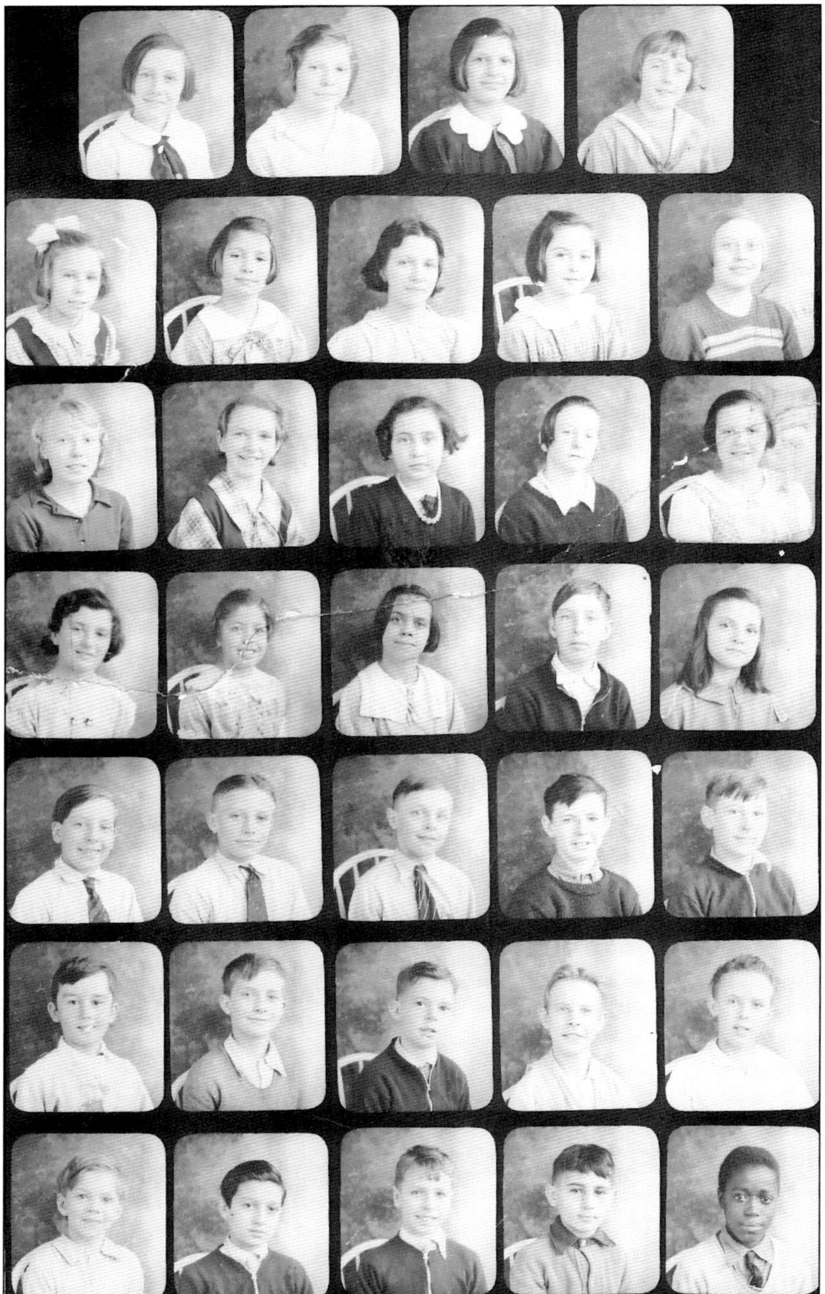

This 1938 Amagansett School group includes, from left to right starting at top row, Mary Natale, Agnes Napolillo, Mary Dellapolla, Ruth Griffing, Esther Midgett, Geraldine Miller, Marie Napolillo, Jeannette Loper, Janet Rogers, Edith James, Barbara DiSunno, Harriet Oxenham, Alice Morgan, Aileen Payne, Lucy Napolillo, Marian Scoville, Josephine Stella, Osmond Mannes, Irene Cote, Cornelius Mannes, Durwood Midgett, Gilbert McCalley, John Merrill, Arnold Eichhorn, William Walling, Sidney Payne, Edward Raynor, Hubert Topping, Leigh Finch, George Payne, Michael Riggio, Charlie Browne, Joseph DiSunno, and Lee Hayes.

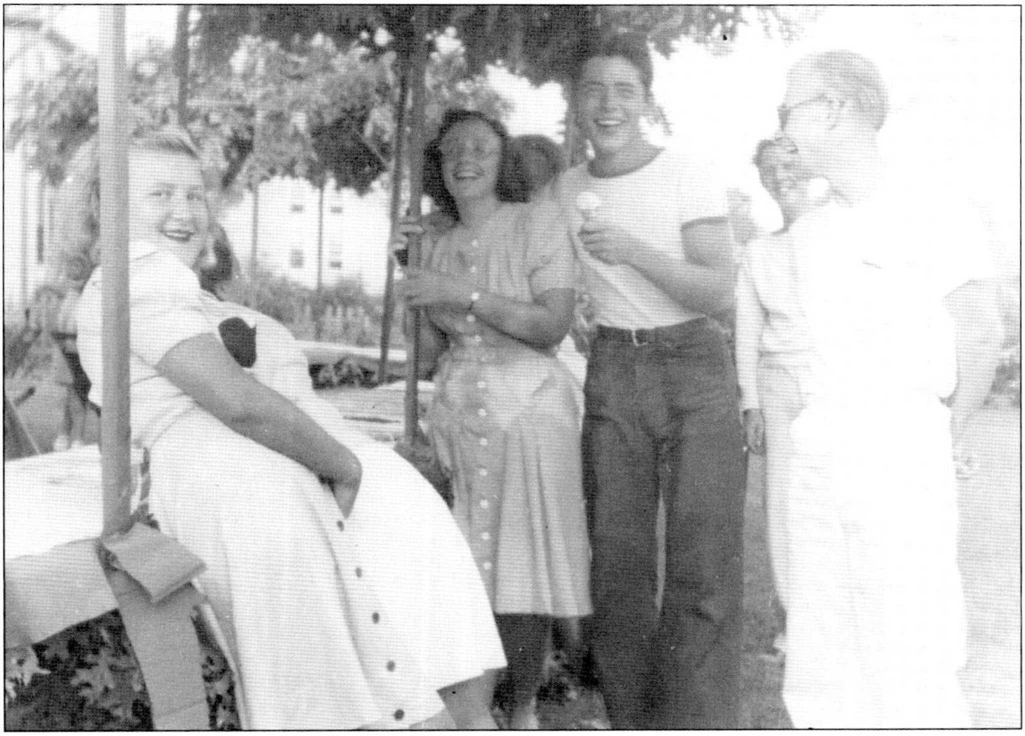

This is an "extracurricular" view of some of the same students who appear in the previous group. From left to right are Sarah King, "Babe" Bennett, "Ale" Edwards, Alfred Oxenham, Leigh Finch, and Durwood Midgett.

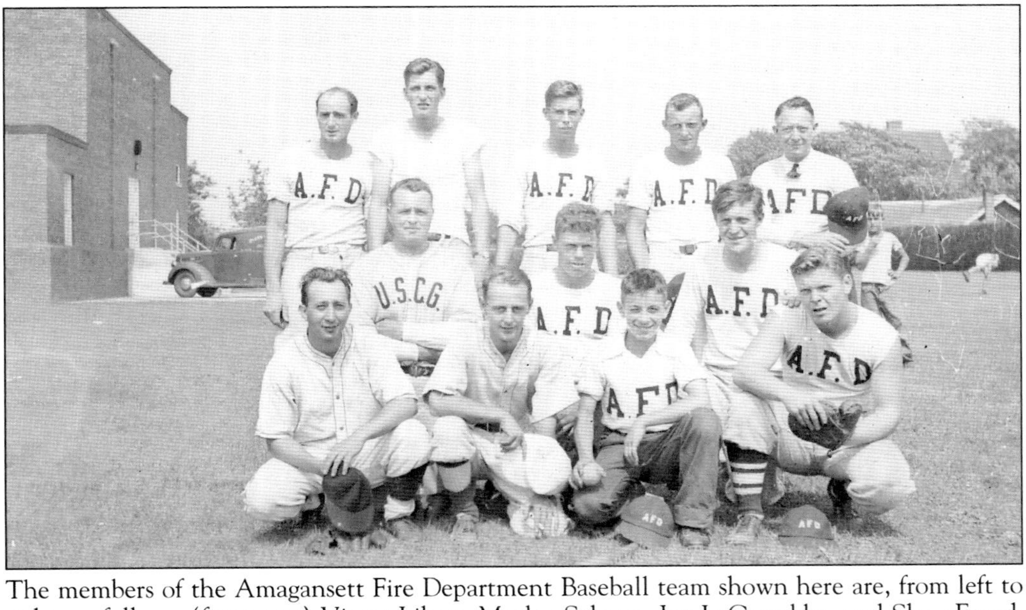

The members of the Amagansett Fire Department Baseball team shown here are, from left to right, as follows: (front row) Victor Libert, Morley Schapp, Joe LaCarrubba, and Shep Frood; (middle row) Amy Brooks, Bobby Burns, and Charles Ryan; (back row) Louis Ialacci, William Milligan, unknown, Harold King, and Mr. Arthur Ryan, the manager.

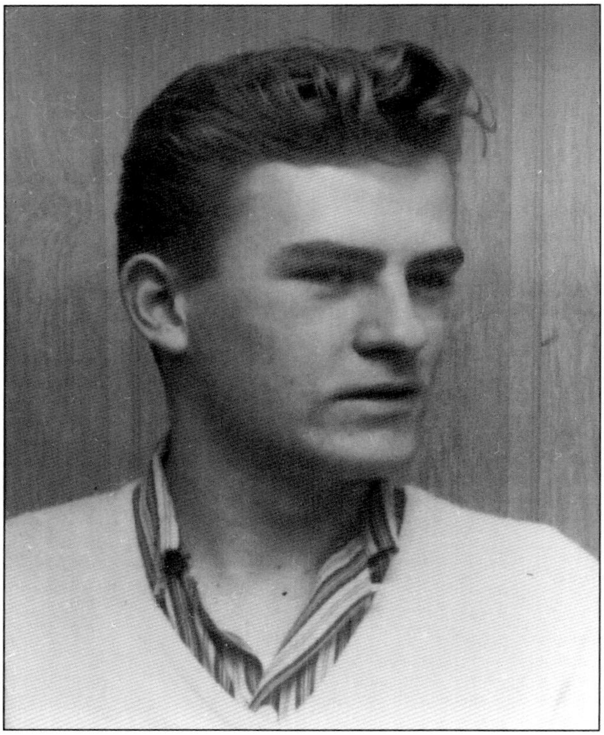

The distinct family resemblance between Milton Miller Jr. and his father (Milton Sr.—seen in several earlier school groups) helps to account for Librarian Carleton Kelsey's uncanny success rate—and the attendant surprise of several generations of children—at "guessing" at first sight from which Amagansett family a child descends.

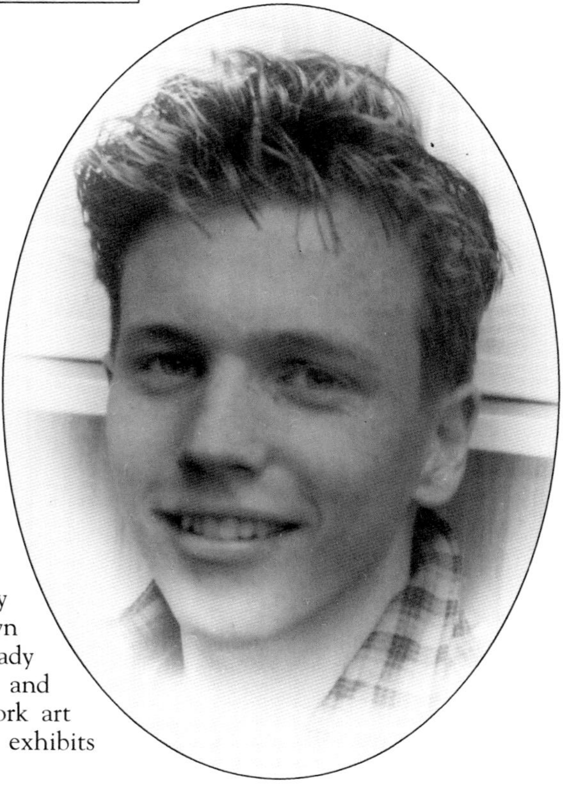

Tony Prohaska is the son of well-known illustrator and painter Ray Prohaska—who, with his wife Carolyn, was one of the first New York artists to make their year-round homes on the East End. Before the Prohaskas bought the Colonel Samuel King house on Main Street, it was rented one summer by Mrs. Guggenheim to a group of famous surrealist artists, including Max Ernst. Tony spent his early years around the horses and horse-drawn vehicles which were still a familiar, if already nostalgic, Amagansett sight in the 1950s and '60s. He and his sister Elena, a New York art consultant, have collaborated on several exhibits that revisit those times.

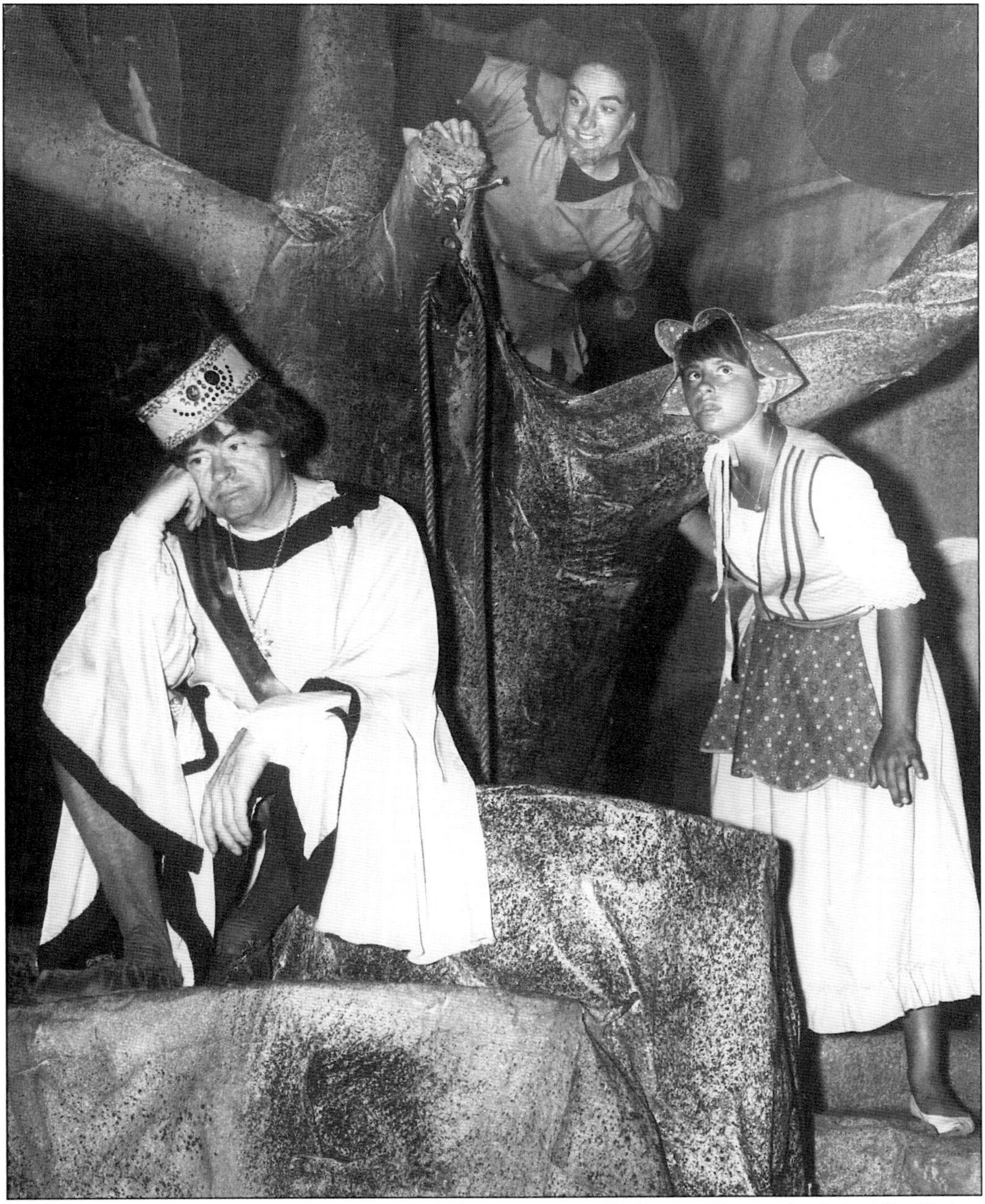

The Guild Hall Players produced *Rumpelstiltskin* in 1963, with Connie Bossey (right), Alba Farber (center), and Carleton Kelsey. The Players, founded in 1931 by the Barnes, Dayton, and Edwards families and lasting into the late 1970s, was the sturdiest of several local community theater groups which drew from Amagansett talent, and presented many memorable productions.

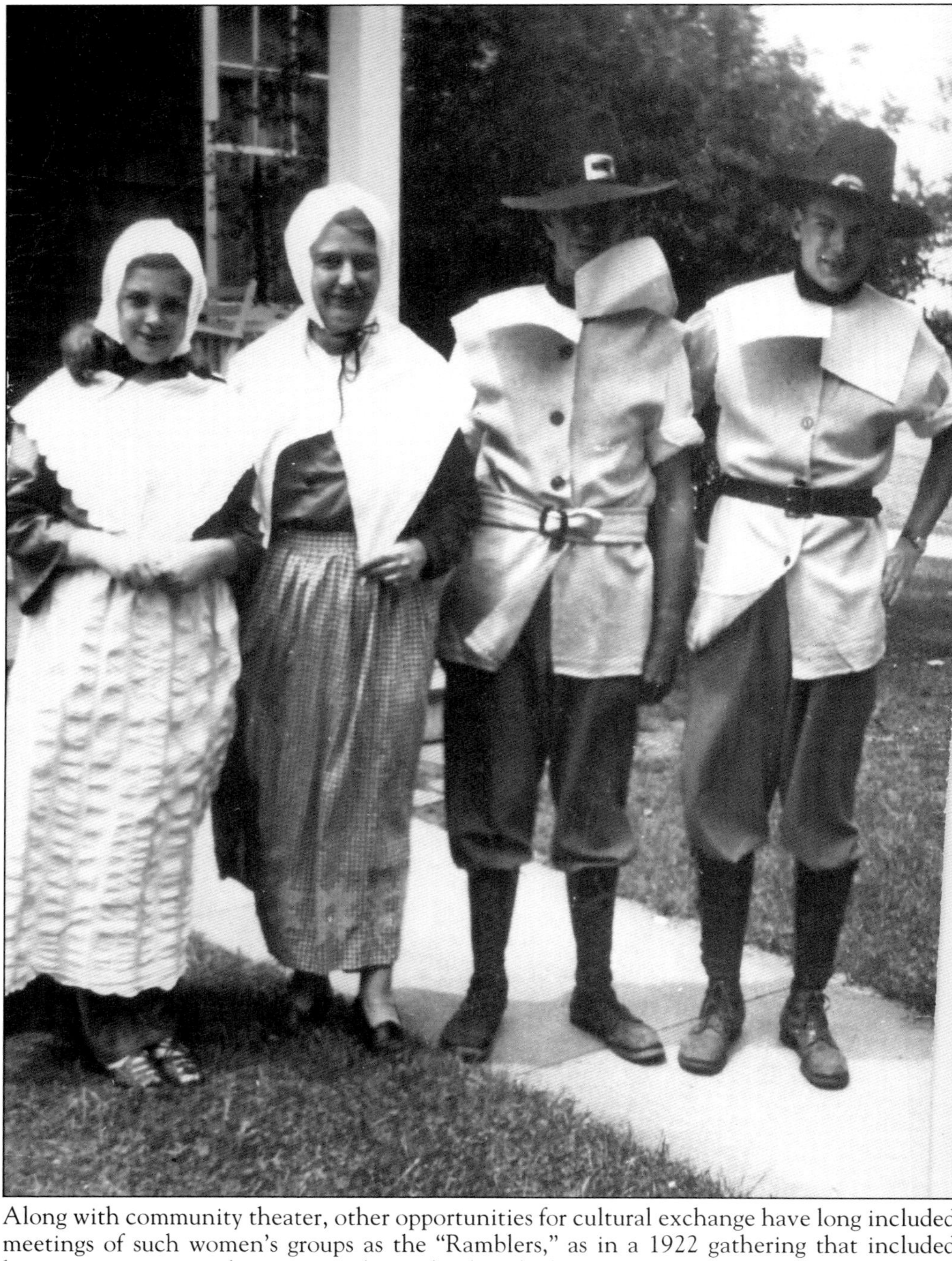

Along with community theater, other opportunities for cultural exchange have long included meetings of such women's groups as the "Ramblers," as in a 1922 gathering that included literary papers, victrola music, and "a ridiculous bedroom scene" from *The Pickwick Papers* presented by Mrs. Tiffany and Mrs. E.J. Edwards. Ambitious townwide "pageants" celebrated the community's heritage and were another chance to dress up. Beth (Barnes) Gray (now director of the East Hampton Free Library), Louise (Clark), and Otis and Thomas Barnes are shown here on their way to a "pilgrim" reenactment in 1948, part of the town of East Hampton's tercentenary celebrations.

Eight

Order and Chaos

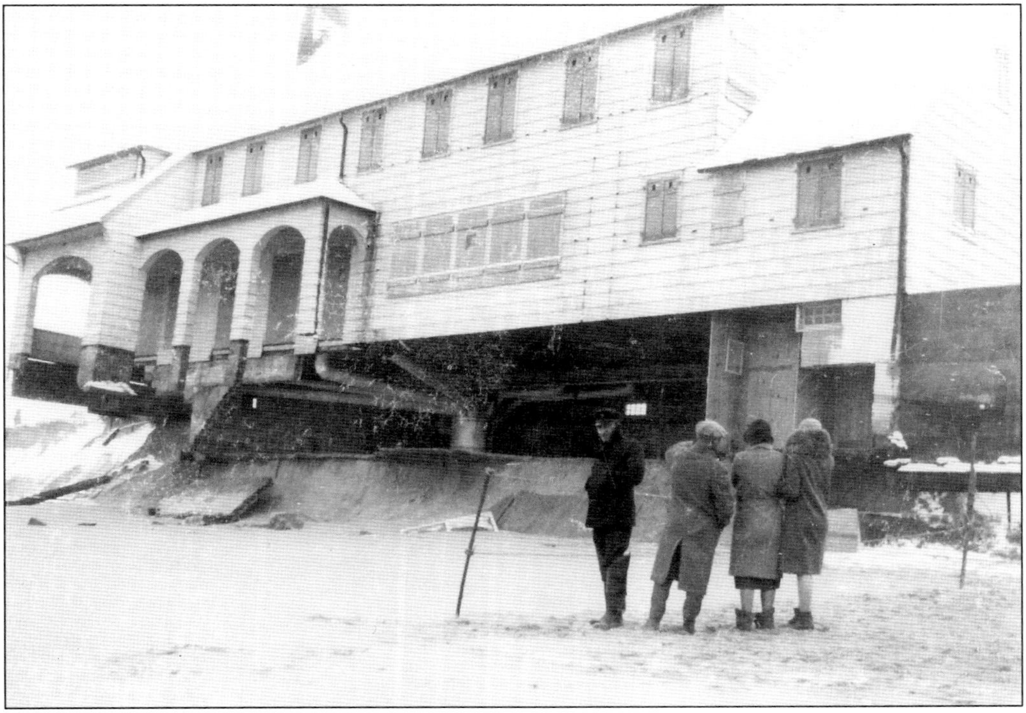

"Long Island's south shore is a long strip of soft, clean white sand; very different from the rocky New England coast to the northward, and from the hard sandy beach down in the Carolinas and Florida." In bad weather it receives the full force of the Atlantic; the summer homeowners who have built on the beach have inevitably discovered the power of a northeaster. This was the writer Ring Lardner's house, on the beach west of East Hampton.

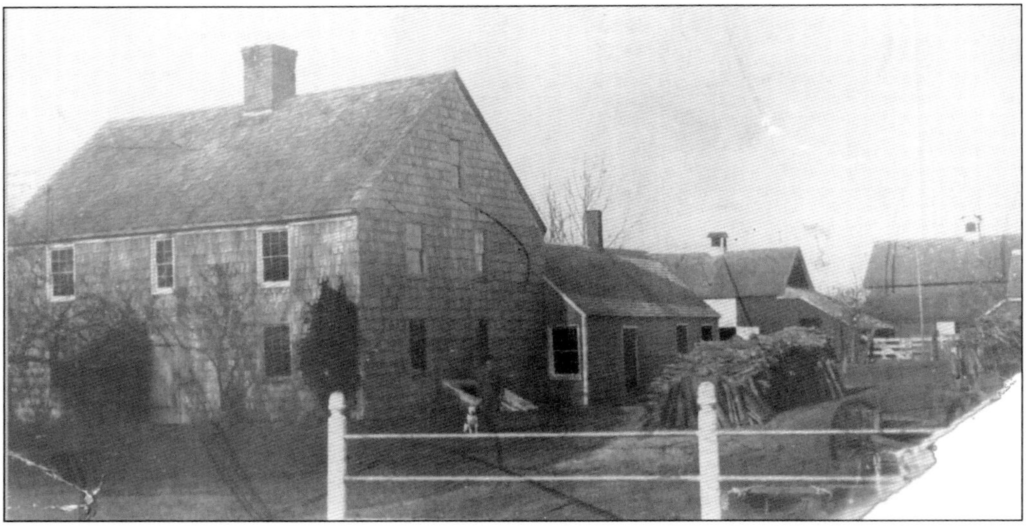

The Jeremiah Conklin house, built in 1690, is one of the local schoolchildren's favorites on walking tours, thanks to the legend that the two youngest children of the house were put into the large brick oven for safety, when "a party of roistering British soldiers" came to the house in 1779. Jeremiah, not a tall man, allegedly wielded his ox-goad in the face of British Major Cochrane during the occupation, and Cochrane later called him "the bravest little rebel on Long Island."

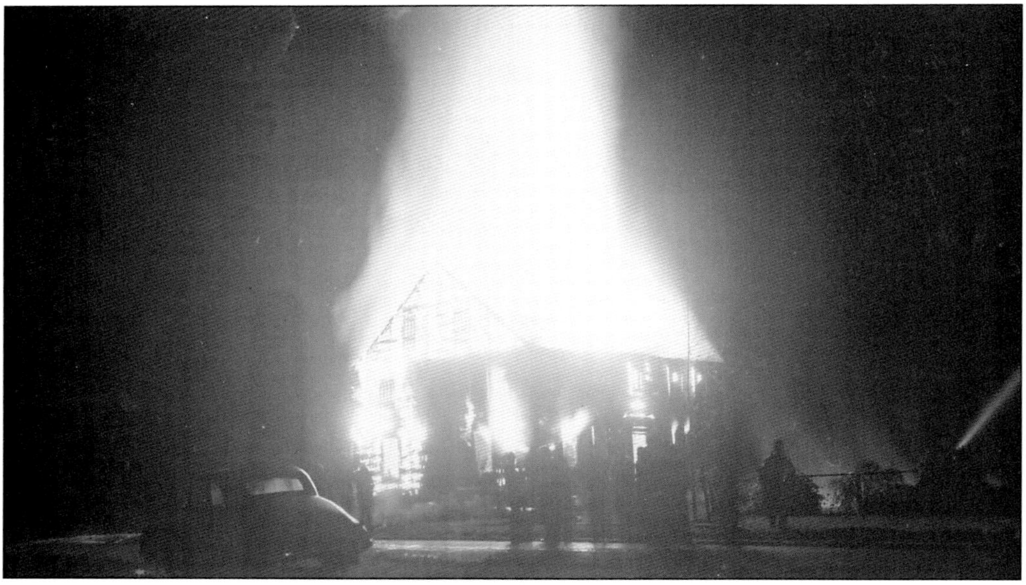

The Ananias Conklin house burned in 1940. Luckily, the historic building had been recorded in measured drawings under the "WPA." This was a planned demolition, part of the Amagansett Fire Department's exercises. Another Conklin house burned to the ground in 1821: its owner died from injuries sustained while attempting to save his household effects. His widow, with nine small children, was aided by neighbors, who went into the woods, cut timber from her land, and built her a new home. One of the nine Conklin children, Rebecca, married Erastus Barnes; another was the legendary David Van Renssalaer ("Uncle Rance"), who was ostensibly last seen going out to sea on a whale's back.

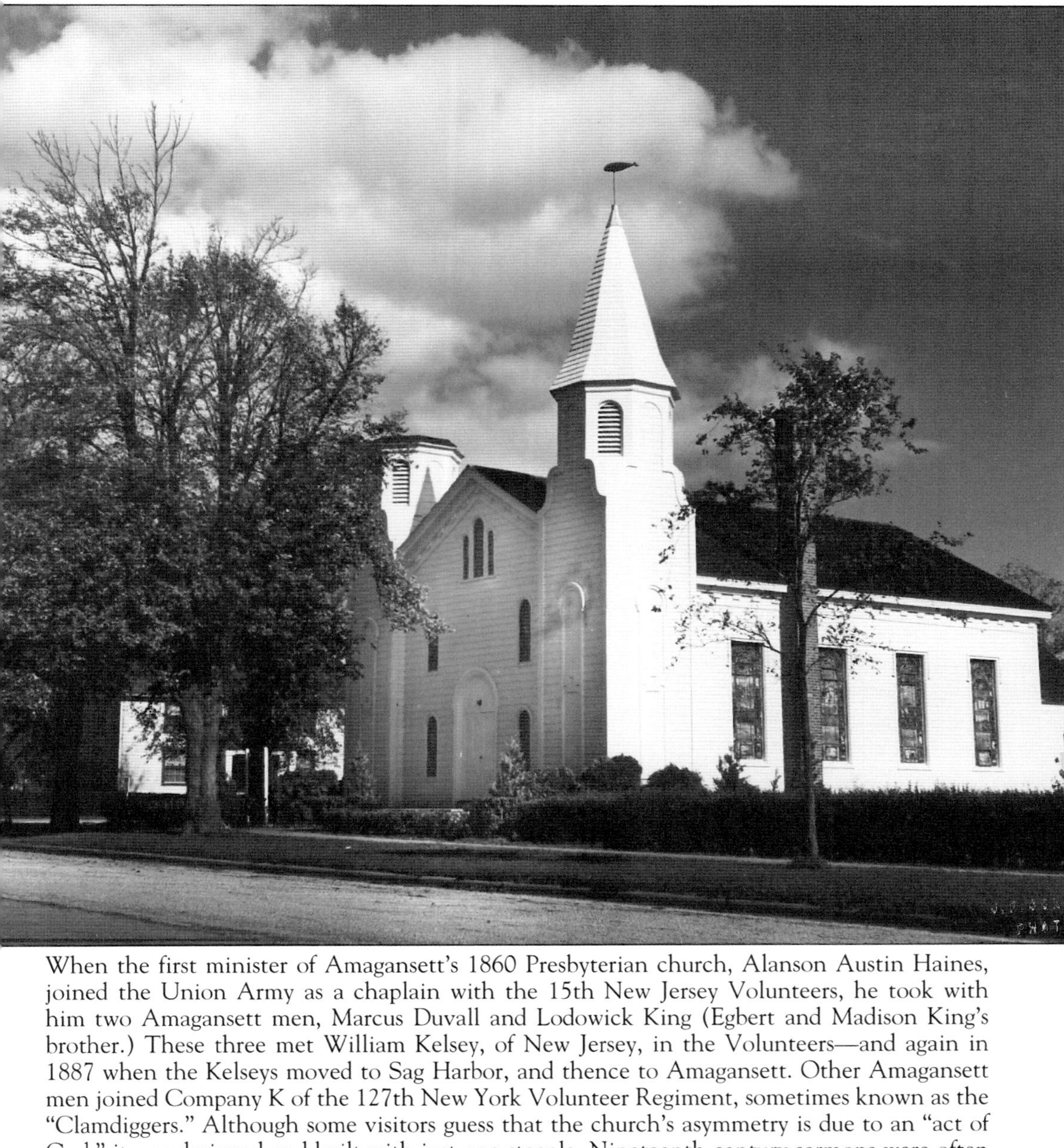

When the first minister of Amagansett's 1860 Presbyterian church, Alanson Austin Haines, joined the Union Army as a chaplain with the 15th New Jersey Volunteers, he took with him two Amagansett men, Marcus Duvall and Lodowick King (Egbert and Madison King's brother.) These three met William Kelsey, of New Jersey, in the Volunteers—and again in 1887 when the Kelseys moved to Sag Harbor, and thence to Amagansett. Other Amagansett men joined Company K of the 127th New York Volunteer Regiment, sometimes known as the "Clamdiggers." Although some visitors guess that the church's asymmetry is due to an "act of God," it was designed and built with just one steeple. Nineteenth century sermons were often hair-raising. As evangelical movements within Protestant churches spread, rhetoric such as that inscribed on an Amagansett bible box might make a "true believer" of anyone (the lines form an "endless knot," so that the reader may pick up the warning message at any line.) ". . . If thou a true believer be, The knot is broke and thou art free, . . . Oh man behold and thou shalt see, How many folds thy evils be, Thy flesh without thy heart within, Is wrapt about with woful sin, And sin has tied an endless knot, And death and hell which faileth not, And Justice ceaseth not to cry, That soul that sins that soul shall die."

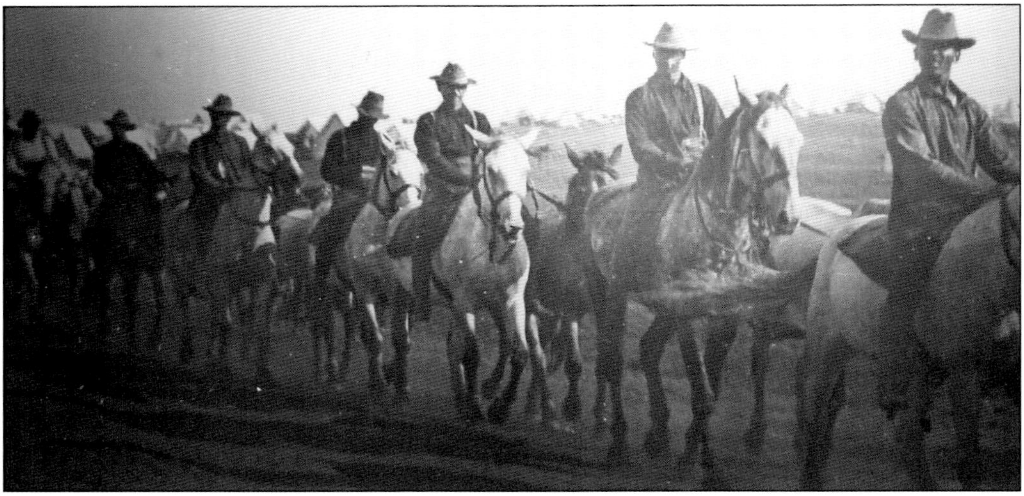

Amagansett turned out on August 14, 1898, when Lieutenant Colonel Theodore Roosevelt and the first of his 29,500 ailing "Rough Riders" arrived on the transport ship *Miami* at Montauk's Camp Wyckoff, to recover from malaria, typhoid, and yellow fever contracted in Cuba. Residents "petted and made much of the soldiers," and, one contemporary writer notes, even adopted the fashion of "ten-gallon" hats. Another account tells us that, at the camp's closing, many Amagansett homes benefited from materials and supplies left behind—including bedsheets. "It's a wonder the whole village didn't get yellow fever!"

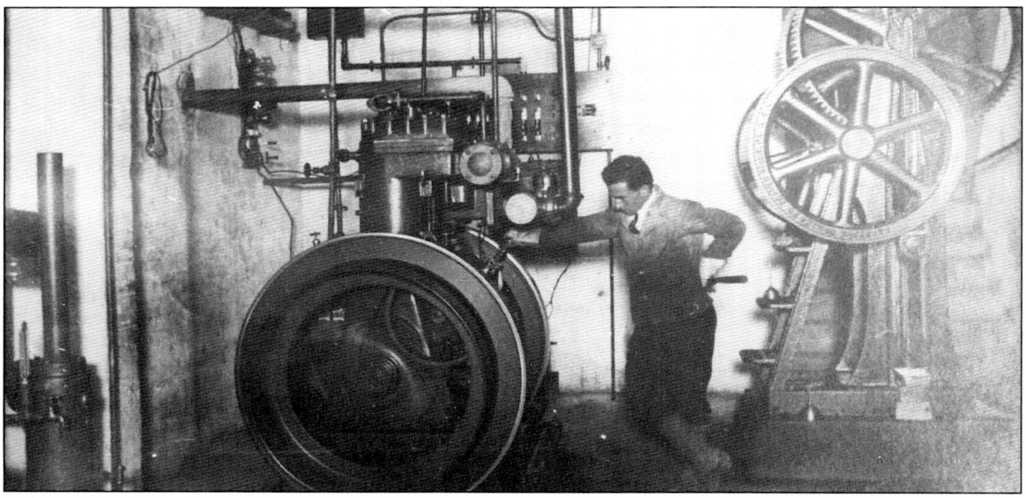

When the first captains of finance and industry built summer homes at "Devon," northeast of the village, their decision was more in a spirit of "rough rider"-dom than of Edwardian ease. Having traveled to the area, mostly from midwestern cities, for turn-of-the-century hunting trips, the Leverings, Proctors, Rawsons, and Rowes really did carve their "colony" from a wilderness. To make the transition from rugged camps to splendid family summers, they needed the best tradesmen, and the Devon homes (most still owned by the founding families) stand as historic reminders of the phenomenal labor and logistics which created them. To keep the "infrastructure" going, there was Jack Ciochetti, shown here in one of the homes' private power plants. During World War I, Jack served as head electrician on the German ocean liner *Deutschland*, which the U.S. had confiscated in New York harbor, renamed the *Leviathan*, and used as a troop ship.

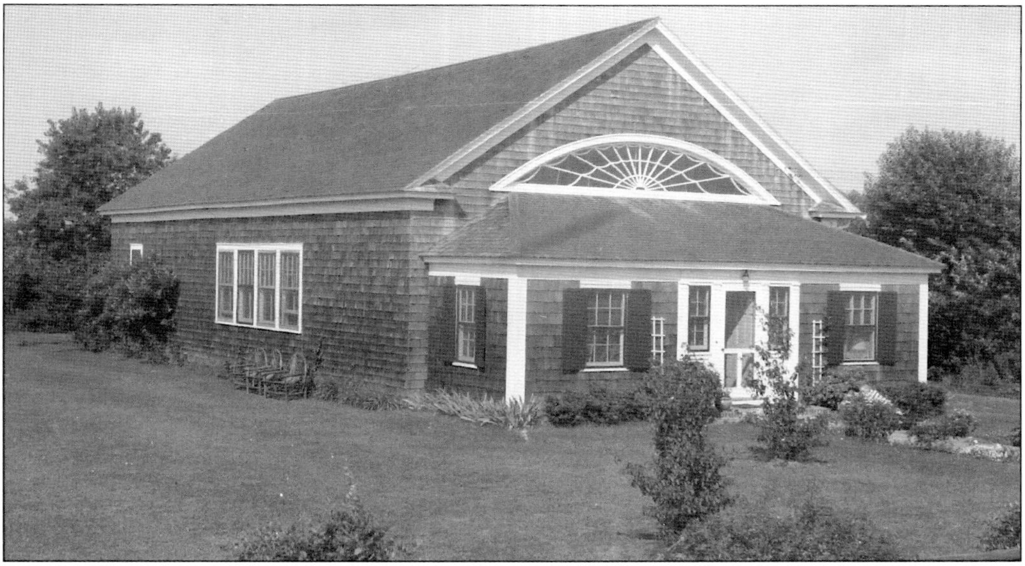

In 1903, as part of the national growth of women's groups for socializing and activism, "grassroots" civic improvements, and political crusades, the Ladies Society of Busy Workers was formed, with Mrs. Frank Tillinghast Sr. as its first president. And they *were* busy—by 1904, they were able to have Frank Griffing build Miankoma Hall, with funds raised by handiwork fairs and "socials." The society then rented the hall—for dances, card parties, and suppers. Miankoma Hall, like the Conklin & Co. store, was equipped to manufacture its own carbide gas for illumination.

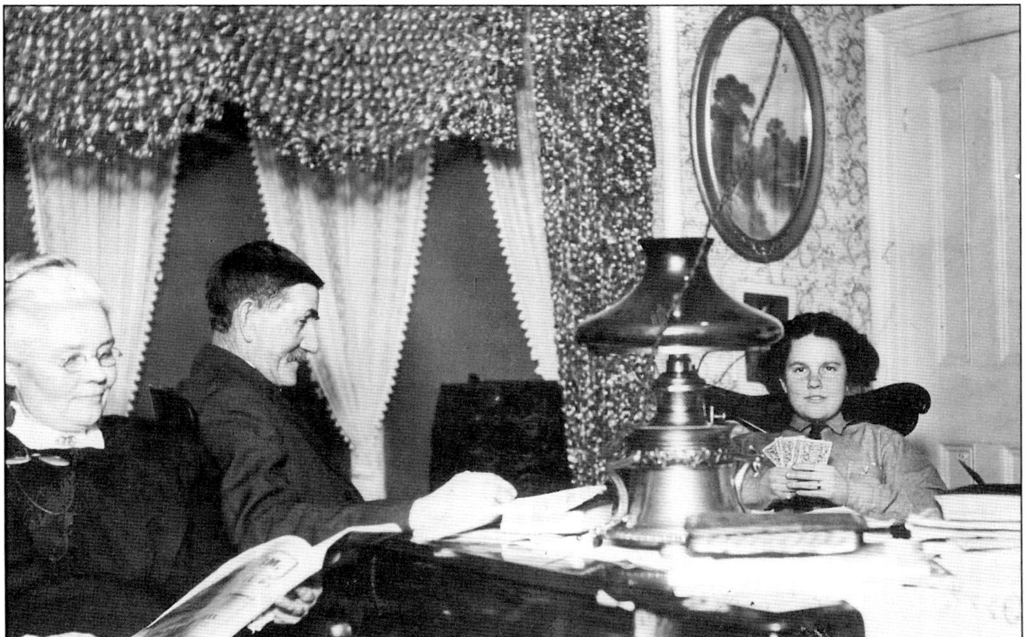

Phebe (Hedges) and Jeremiah Mulford are shown here with their daughter, Eleanor Rose. Jeremiah's sister wrote a memoir, *An East Hampton Childhood,* which includes such exciting stories as the shooting of their father, Captain Jeremiah, on the Sag Harbor Road.

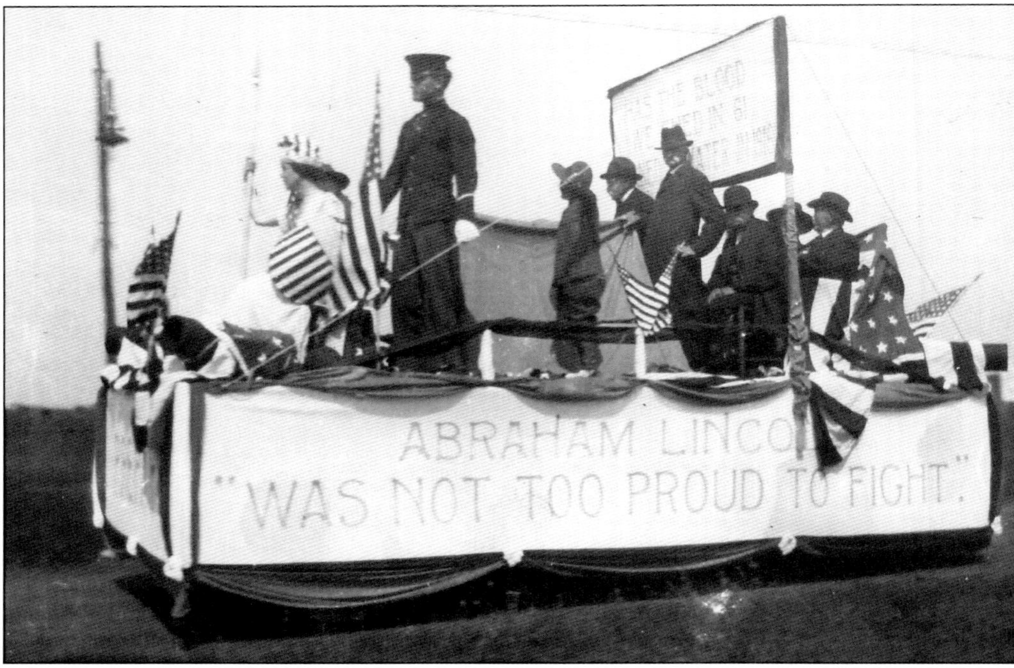

William Kelsey, Civil War Veteran, sits at the rear of this 1916 Memorial Day float which, along with advising preparedness, admonishes the citizenry with the question "HAS THE BLOOD WE SHED IN 61 TURNED TO WATER IN 1916?" Approximately twenty men from Amagansett fought in the War Between the States, and Charles G. Bennett, Myron T. Bennett, William J. Bennett, Claudius H. Hamilton, and William P. King gave their lives.

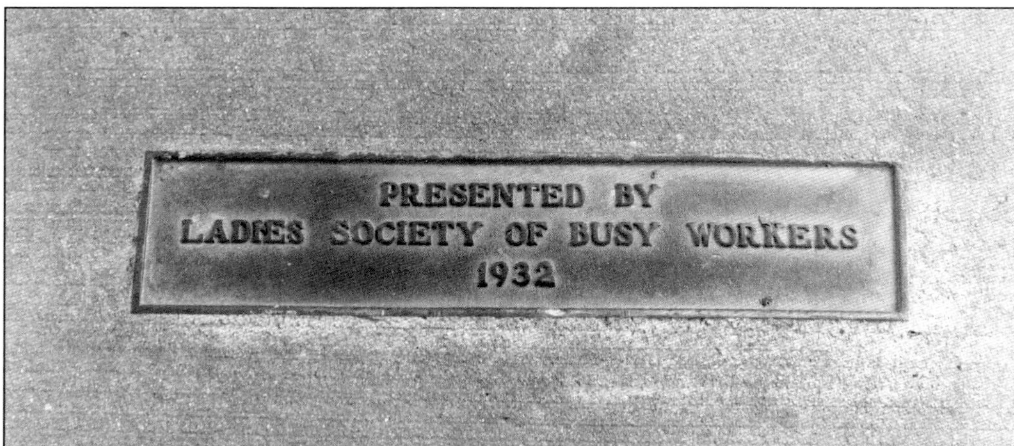

With Miankoma Hall thriving as a community center, the busy Ladies Society responded to a need—and a hidden agenda or two—on Main Street. In 1932, William Kelsey, husband of the secretary-treasurer, began work on the villages' sidewalks, pouring the initial concrete at the home of Mrs. Eva Edwards (the society president) on Montauk Road, and working east. The plaque which was inserted in those first nepotistic footpaths can still be seen in front of the Grade School; Amagansett strollers can find another in front of the Atlantic Avenue tennis courts.

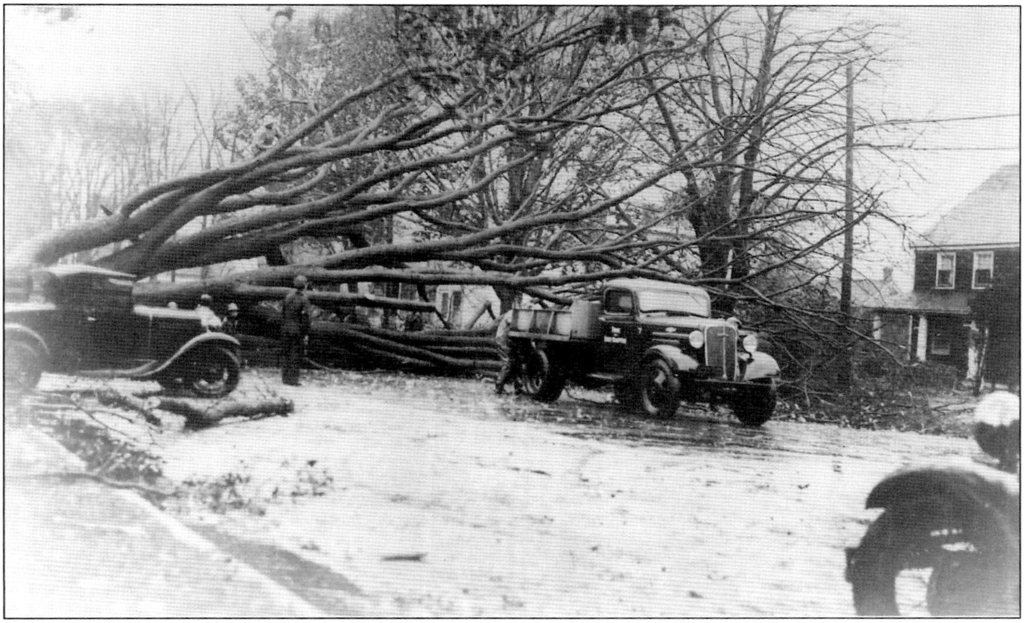

The 1938 hurricane wrought the most appalling havoc on the south shore—it came unannounced, and for three hours during the afternoon of September 21 devastated the 1880 elms, blew the roofs off several homes, and flattened small buildings. These photographs of the swift and concerted cleanup work celebrate the fortunate fact that no one in Amagansett was killed or injured, and that such early buildings as the library were barely harmed. Here, Harry Conklin stands by one of the many elms fallen across Main Street, on the day after the storm.

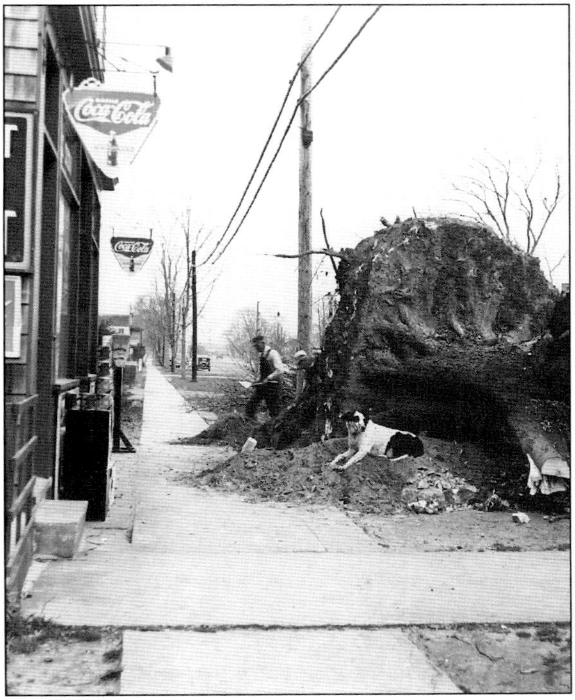

The landscape of Long Island was irreparably changed in one afternoon, and many communities were not nearly so lucky as Amagansett. The 1938 hurricane was one of the major catalysts for the sophisticated tracking systems now maintained by the national weather service. Locally, the hurricane's aftermath continues to promote gratitude for the environmental, as well as the civic, endeavors of the A.V.I.S.—the Amagansett Village Improvement Society, formed in 1921 and responsible for the refoliation of Main Street. This gives us a "dog's-eye view" of a once-towering elm.

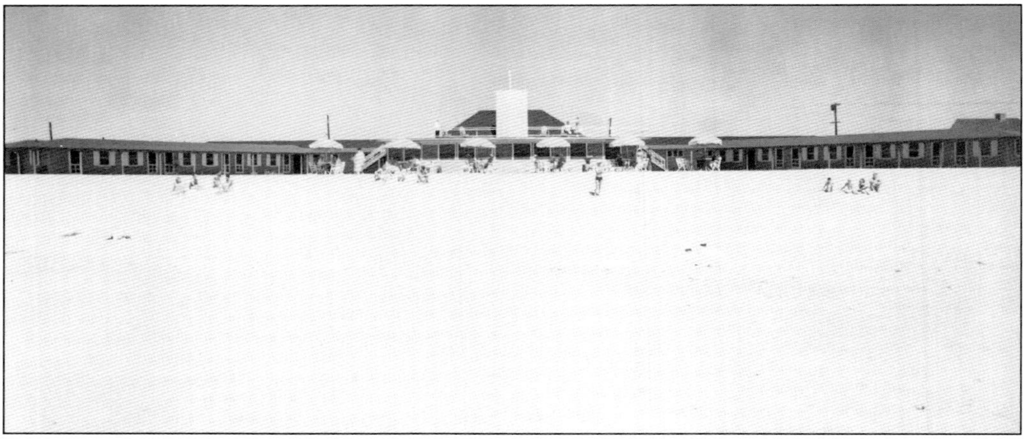

The entire Atlantic Beach Club in "Beachampton" disappeared in the 1938 hurricane. The club's "moderne" restaurant, run by Mrs. Barbour, had been a popular spot in the new residential area on the ocean shore.

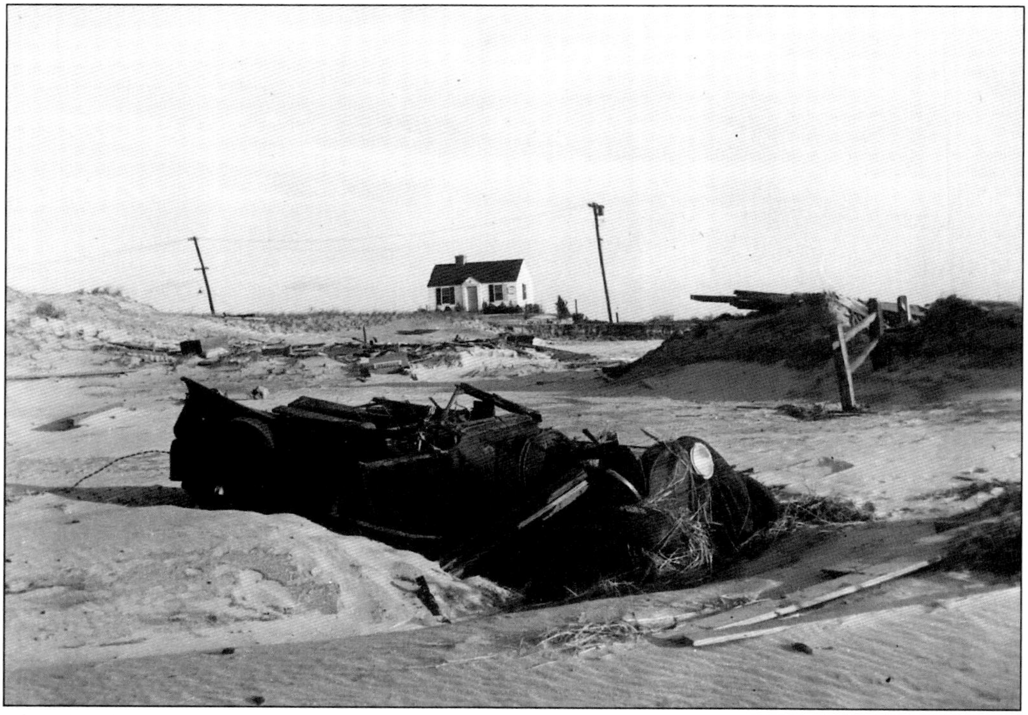

The Beachampton development office stands on the dunes, with a battered truck in the foreground, after the hurricane.

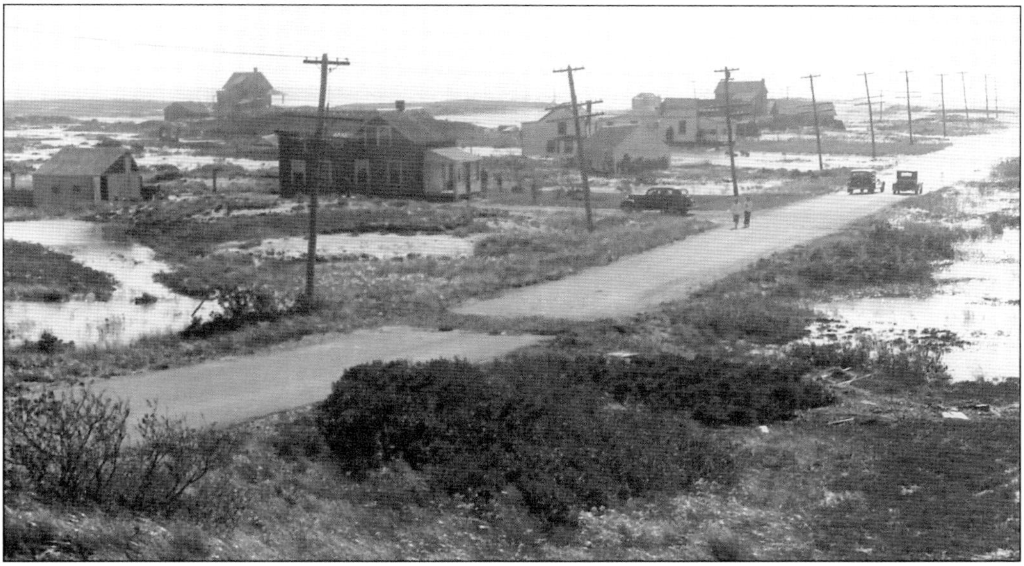

Early in the morning of June 13, 1942, eight saboteurs, whose soon-thwarted efforts were supposedly directed at crippling the metals plants in the Tennessee Valley, landed from a German submarine on the Amagansett beach—just west of where this photograph was taken. Note that in this photograph, taken after the 1938 hurricane, the road to the beach is marked with "scree" or debris left by the storm—to the left, you may also see the garage from the Coast Guard station, which was picked up, floated, and blown eastward approximately 300 yards.

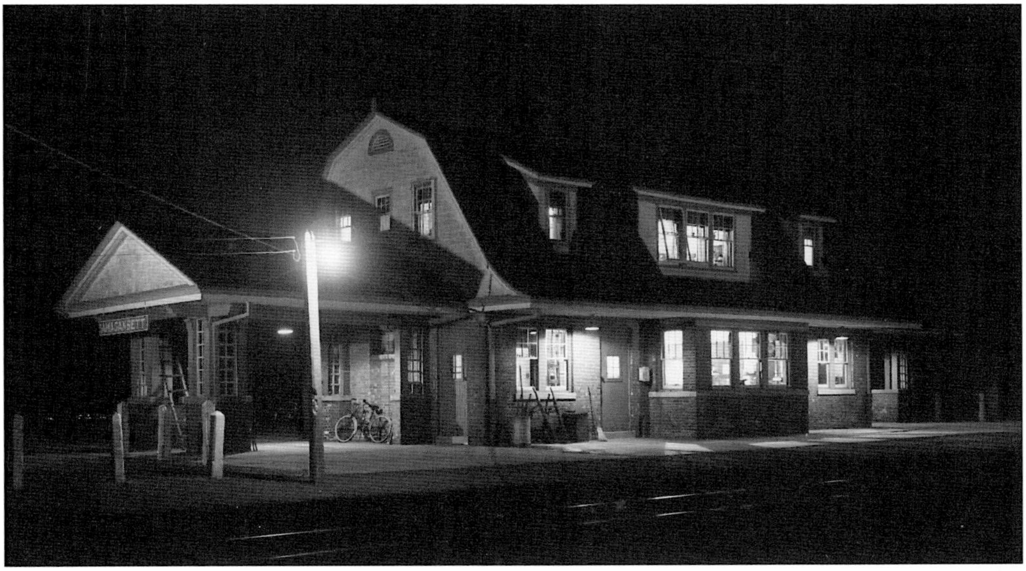

Although they "were under strict instructions to overpower" anyone they might meet on the beach, and take the "body or bodies" back to the boat, one saboteur, George Dasch, had a peaceful exchange with a coastguardsman on patrol before leading the others to the Amagansett train station and buying tickets for New York. For several days, they plotted strategy at such meetingplaces as Horn & Hardart's, Grant's Tomb, and Radio City. Dasch then traveled to Washington to be "shuttled from office to office" before turning himself and the others of the mission in to the FBI.

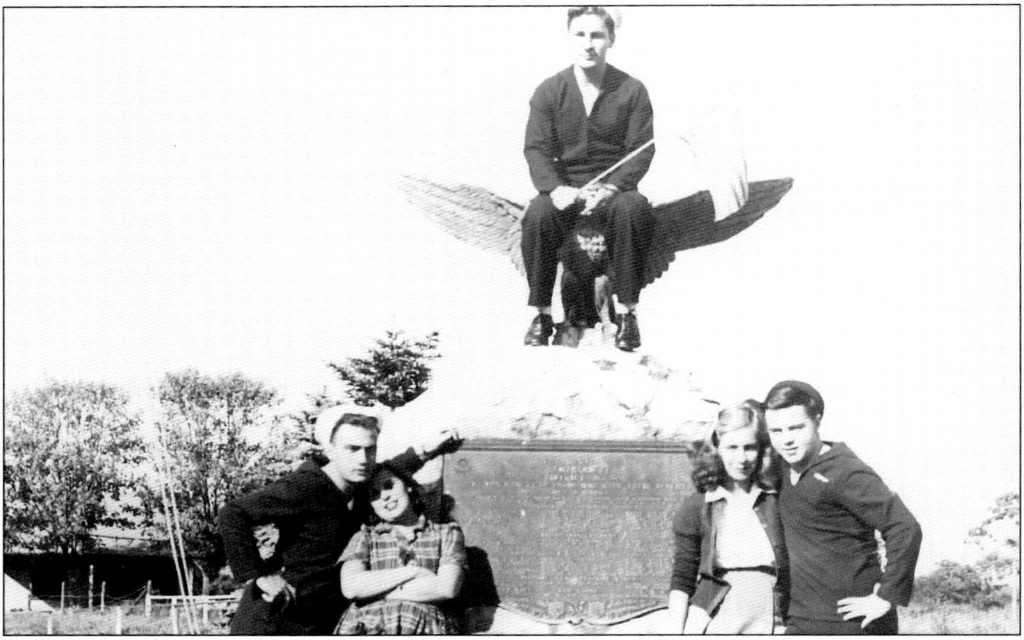

Pictured at the Village War Memorial Monument are Vito DeMai and Ernestine ("Babe") Bennett, Eleanor Scott and Harry Priest, and Don Ivins (at top), who married Eleanor Scott.

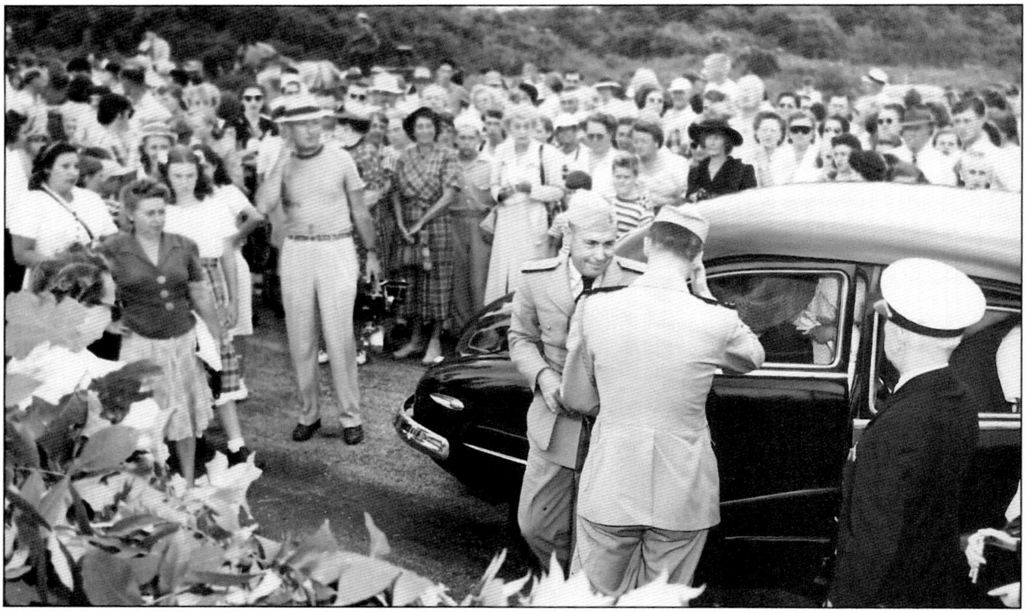

The tercentenary of the founding of the town of East Hampton precipitated an ambitious schedule of Amagansett events, including the dedication of the stone on Indian Wells Highway which celebrates "the place of good water." The *East Hampton Star* estimated that a crowd of between three and four thousand attended the "most spectacular" parade and dedication. Here, Rear Admiral Edward H. Smith, Commandant of the Third (now the First) Coast Guard District, arrives for the dedication, in August 1948. Also in attendance was Alex Haley (author of *Roots*), who served as public relations officer for the district.

James Griffiths helps Grace Finch with refreshments at the 1956 American Legion Convention.

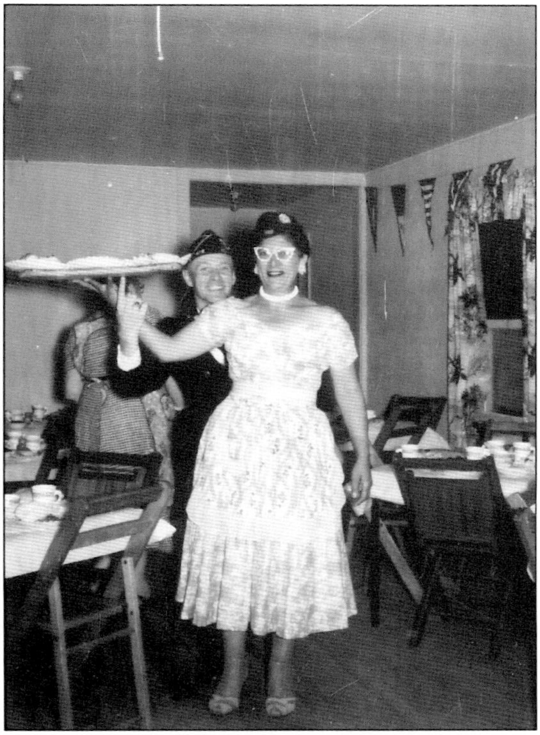

Steve Dellapolla supervised a community-built addition to the American Legion Hall on the corner of Abrahams Path (named for Abraham Schellinger) in 1962.

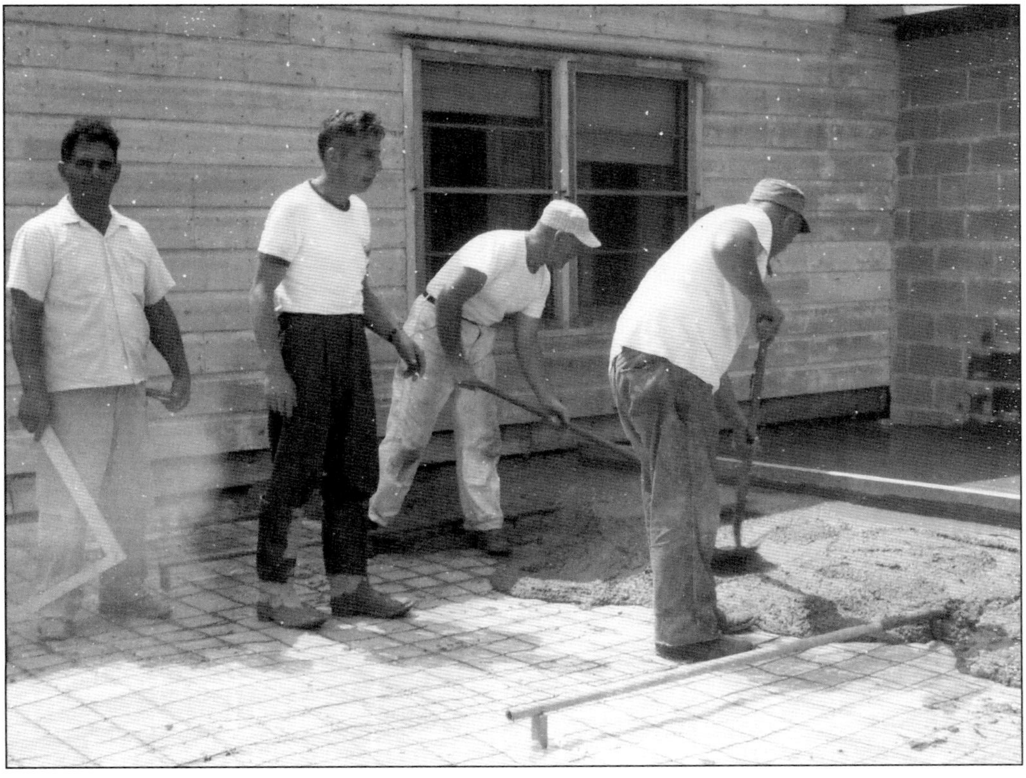

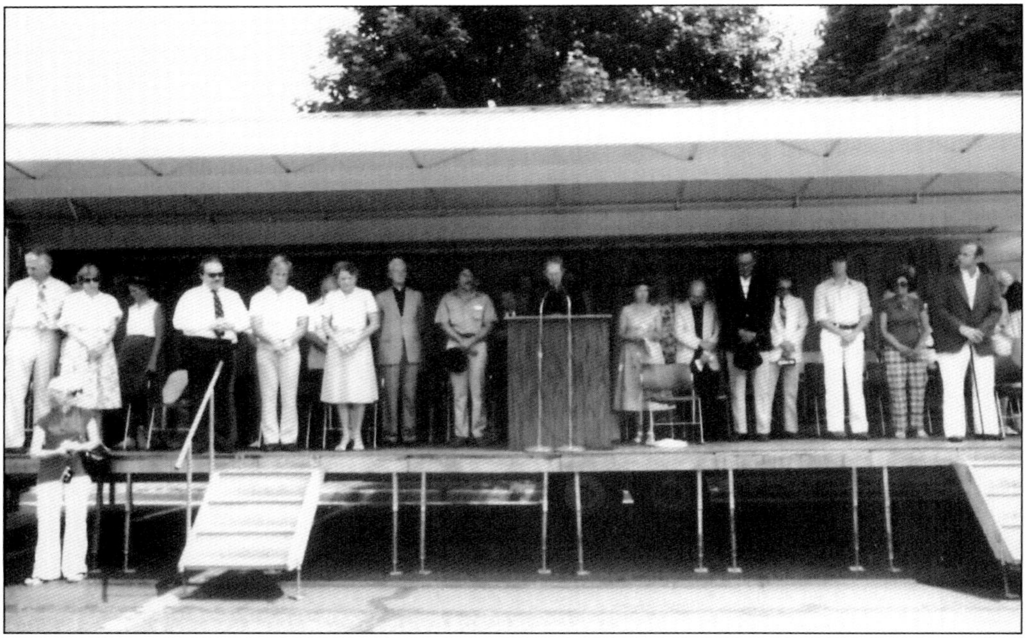

The viewing stand for the parade celebrating the1980 Amagansett Tercentennial, with Reverend Sam Davis at the podium, also shows such prominent state and local politicians as John Behan, Larry Cantwell, Mary Fallon, and Mary Ella Reutershan. Carleton Kelsey stands to the left of Reverend Davis, and John Rowe of the Devon Colony is third to the right from the podium.

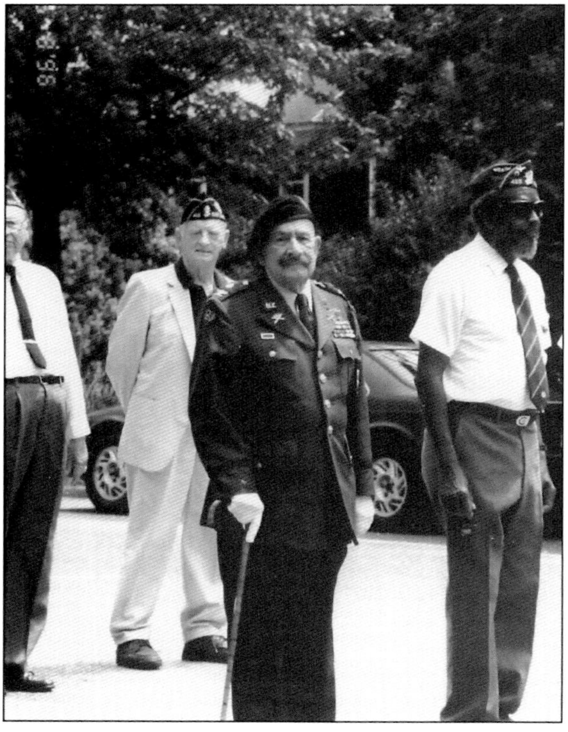

Colonel G. Harding Isaacson and Trevor Kelsall were among the marchers in the 1996 American Legion Convention parade.

Nine

Supply and Demand

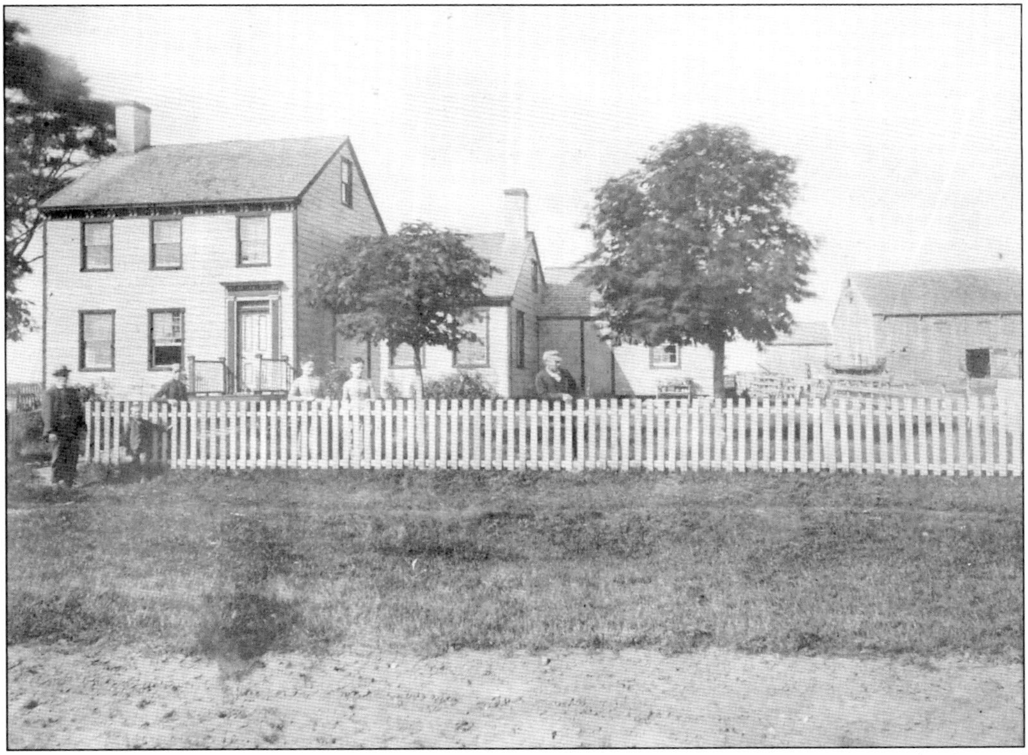

This house, located on Indian Wells Highway, belonged to Captain Lorenzo Leek. One of Captain Leek's recollections was that of an uncle who had deserted from a whaleship at Samoa, where he married and spent the rest of his life. A bit closer to home, his father, Erastus Leek, was second mate of the whaleship *Hamilton*, which sailed to the California gold fields. Abraham Leek was one of the crew, and Henry L. Van Scoy a passenger. Also aboard were Silas Sherman, George W. Schellinger, and William Strong (who married Margaret Baker and lived in the Baker house now at Stony Hill) of Amagansett, and John Miller of East Hampton. They sailed on October 5, 1849, from Sag Harbor, arriving in San Francisco March 14, 1850, around the Horn, never touching land except at Juan Fernandez (Robinson Crusoe's island). Erastus Leek died in California, soon after their arrival.

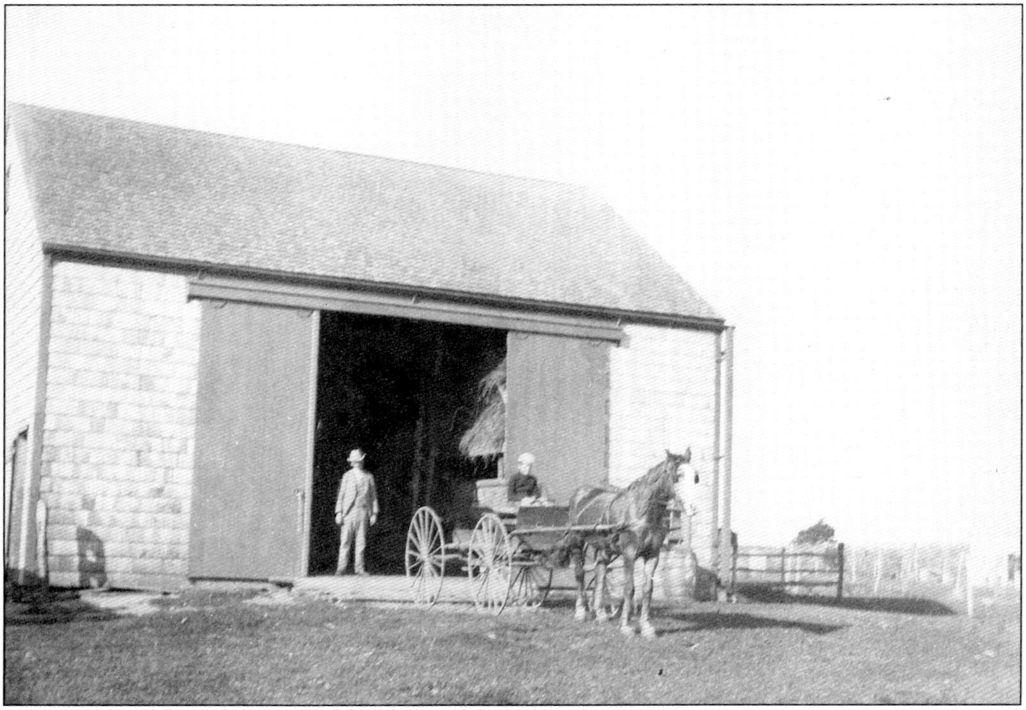

Erastus B. Leek, Lorenzo's son, was briefly a storekeeper on Main Street. He is standing in front of the Leek barn.

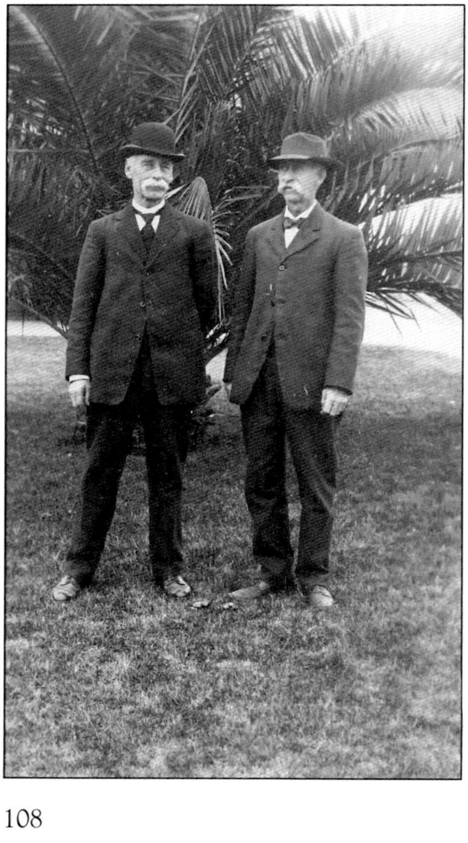

Erastus B. Leek is shown here while visiting John Baker Strong (William Strong's son), who had moved to California. Some time before this visit, the *Star* reported on the next generation: "Nathaniel Leek sent a wireless from Key West last week Thursday to his parents in this village. His in on his way home by boat from Mexico. The wireless was received at a station in New York and sent down from there by telegraph." Nathaniel Leek was a very successful patent lawyer. He eventually settled in Florida.

Joseph Knowles Smith kept a meticulous daybook of his carpentry work, and an equally conscientious record of his transactions at the "Fordham & Edwards" store. From the latter we learn that, in 1865, he purchased everything from bluing (10¢) to butter (2 and 2/16 pounds for 64¢), from paper and envelopes (12¢) to samp (also 12¢).

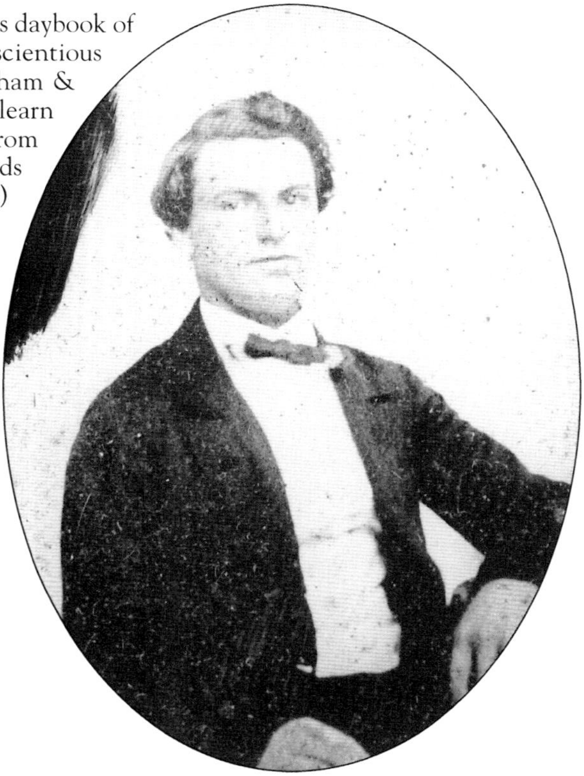

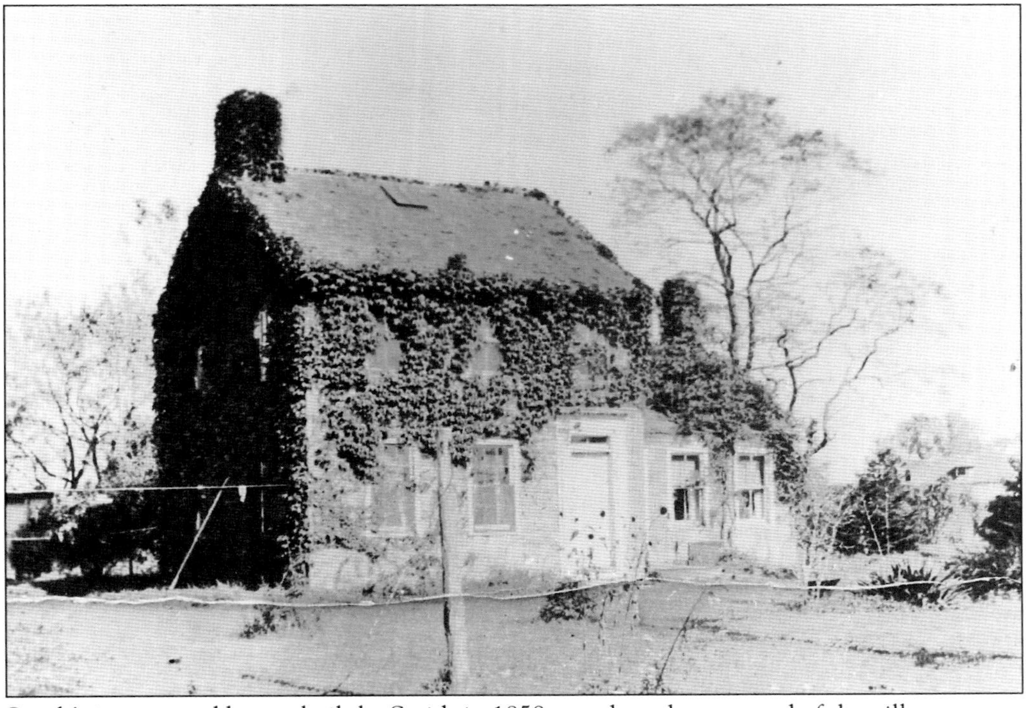

Smith's ivy-covered house, built by Smith in 1858, stands at the west end of the village.

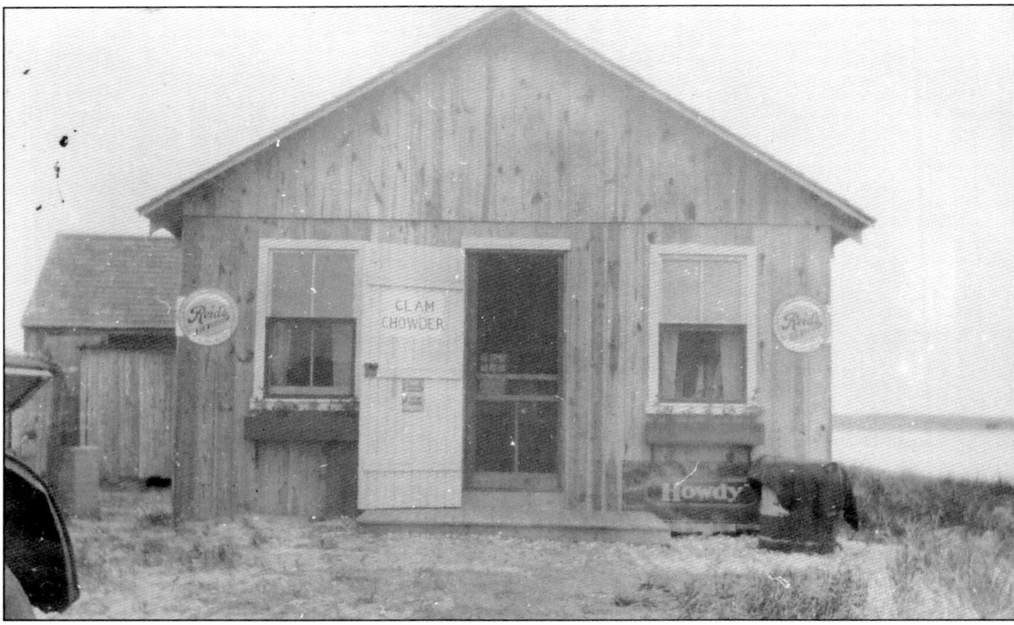

Before the days of shopping centers, businesses were spread throughout the area, and there are many stories of local shoppers who bypassed a closer store for a friendlier one. Well into this century, "East Side" was considered a part of Amagansett rather than Springs, and Fred Conklin's at Louse Point was one of the village's outlying stores.

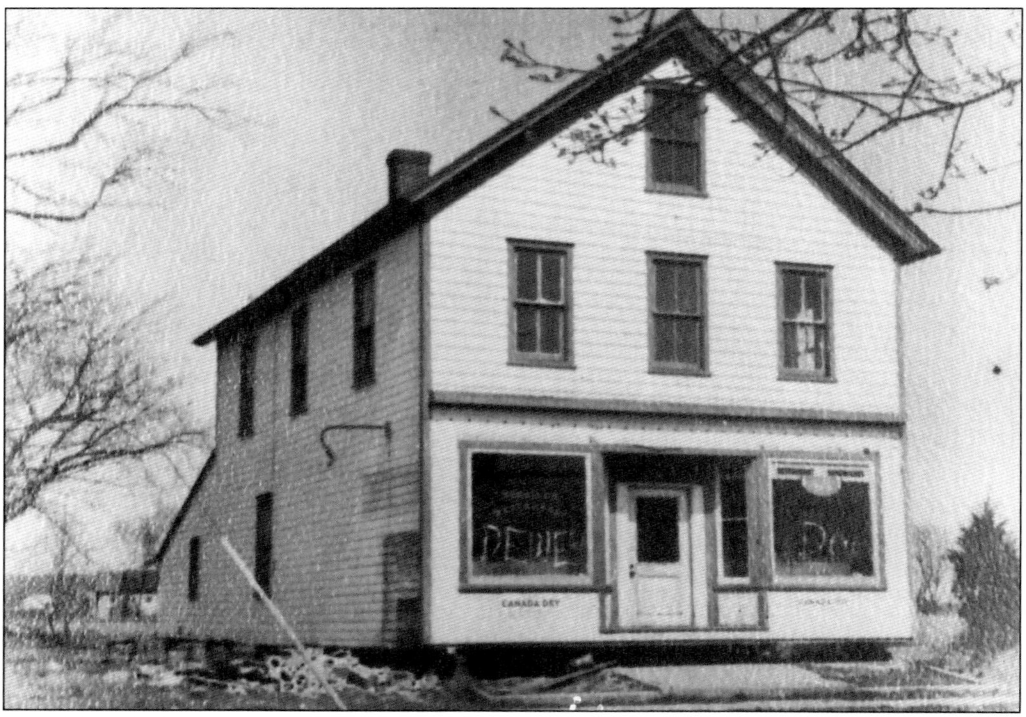

The Edwards Brothers store on Atlantic Avenue is shown here, ready to be moved to Old Montauk Highway. Notice the election graffiti.

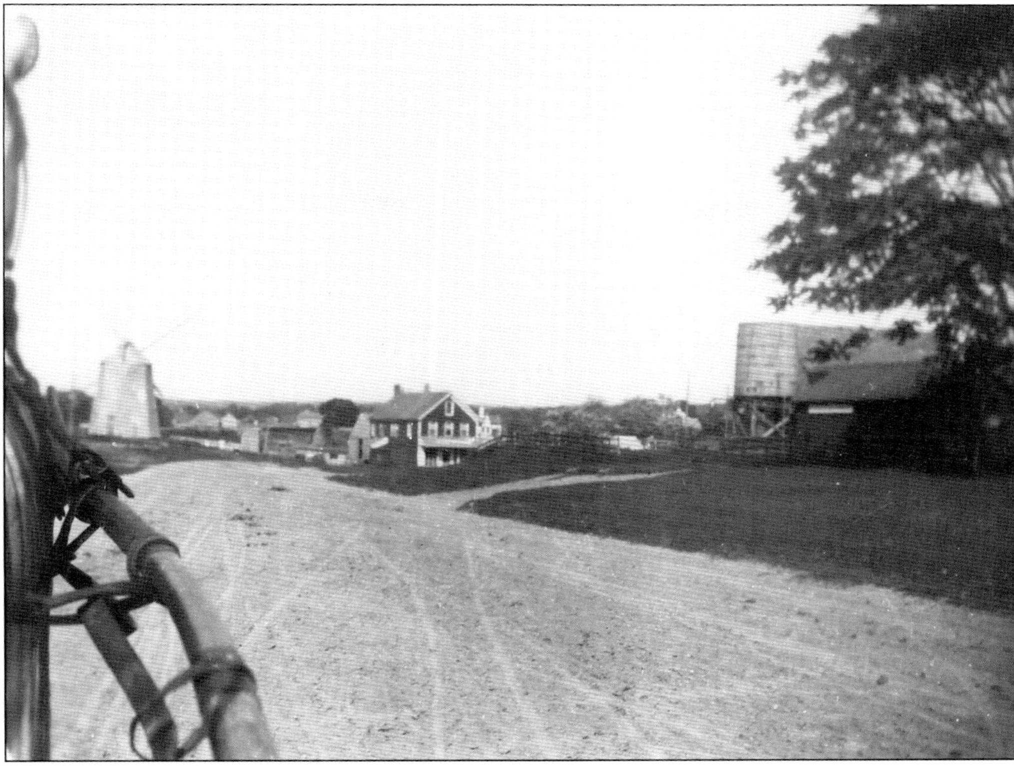

Trips to East Hampton were more likely to be family visits than shopping excursions. This photograph was taken on the drive back from East Hampton, in the area known as "the Hook."

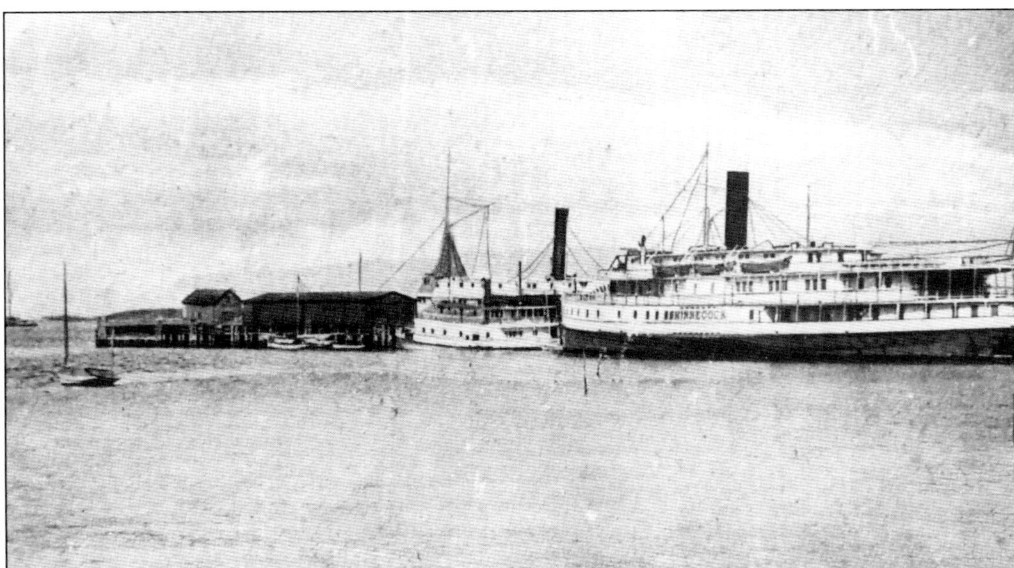

In the days of Jerry Baker's stage line, and before 1895, when the railroad came to Amagansett, a trip to New York would involve taking a steamer from Sag Harbor to Greenport, where the train would take travelers to Long Island City.

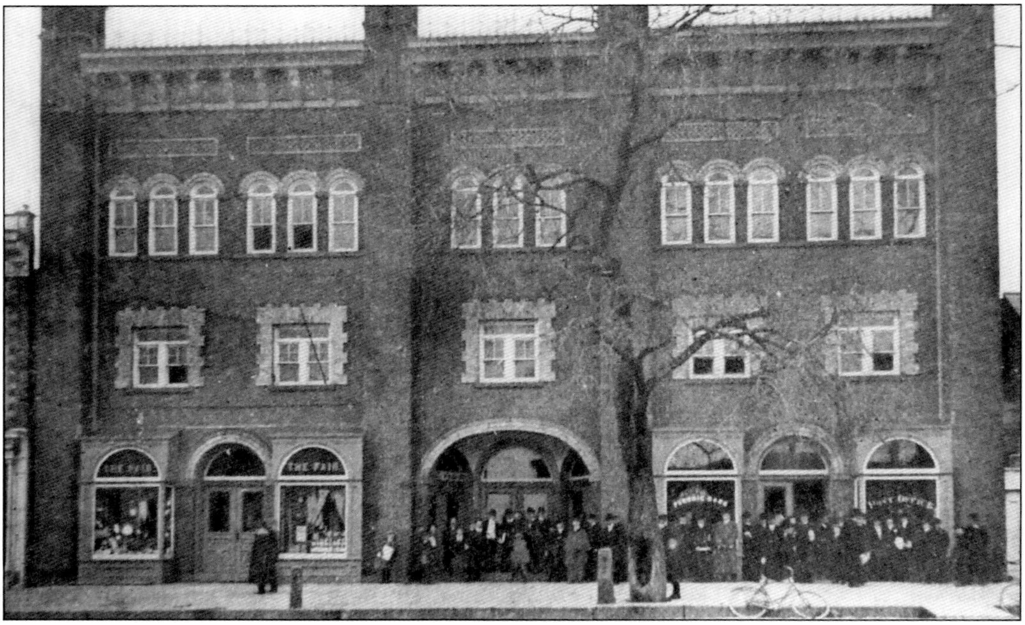

Compare the Amagansett post office (located at the Conklin & Co. General Store) with Sag Harbor's (above) during the same era. Although Conklin & Co. had a community hall and later a movie theater on its top floor, a *Star* item confirms our sense that it was more a "country" store:

"Any one who was up and around last Wednesday morning, just before 6 o'clock, might have seen two young maidens clad only in thier nightdresses slowly rambling along Amagansett Main street happily singing to themselves. After a jaunt of about a quarter of a mile they were stopped and questioned by Dimon Conklin, of the firm of Conklin & Company. Their answers were very non-committall, so Mr.Conklin enticed them . . . to the store, with pledges of candy, . . . then led them to their yard and told them to go back to bed! The young ladies in question were Miss Virginia Barnes, age three, and her little guest, Miss Gwen Vaughan. They had not been missed by their mothers, who were still sleeping soundly!"

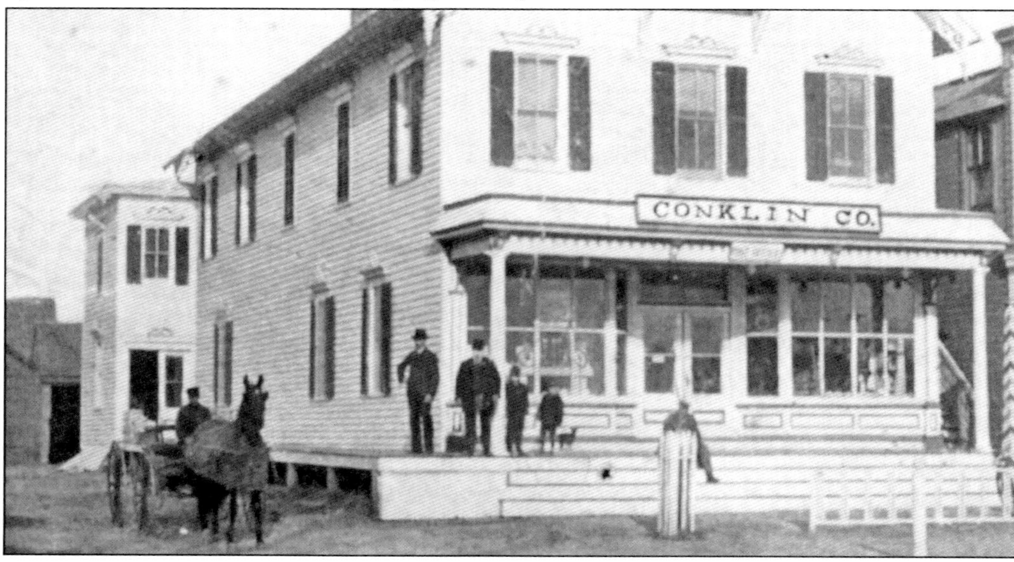

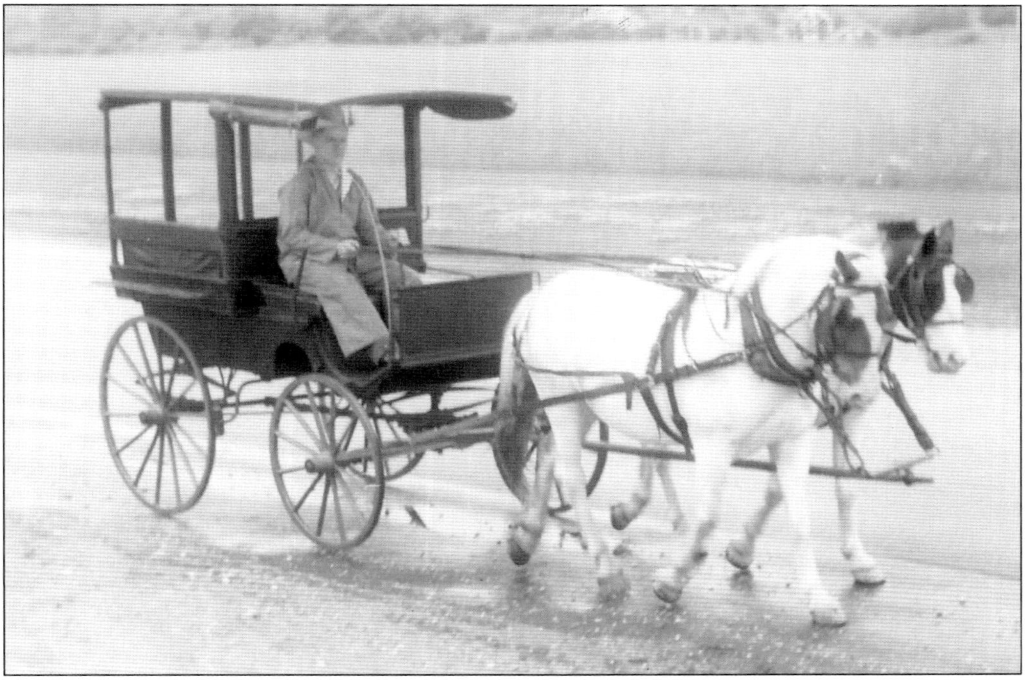

If something was needed from Sag Harbor, it was likely to be delivered by stage. Here, horses "Omaha" and "Pawnee" are drawing a "Rockaway," similar to Jerry Baker's stagecoach, with Frank Tillinghast driving.

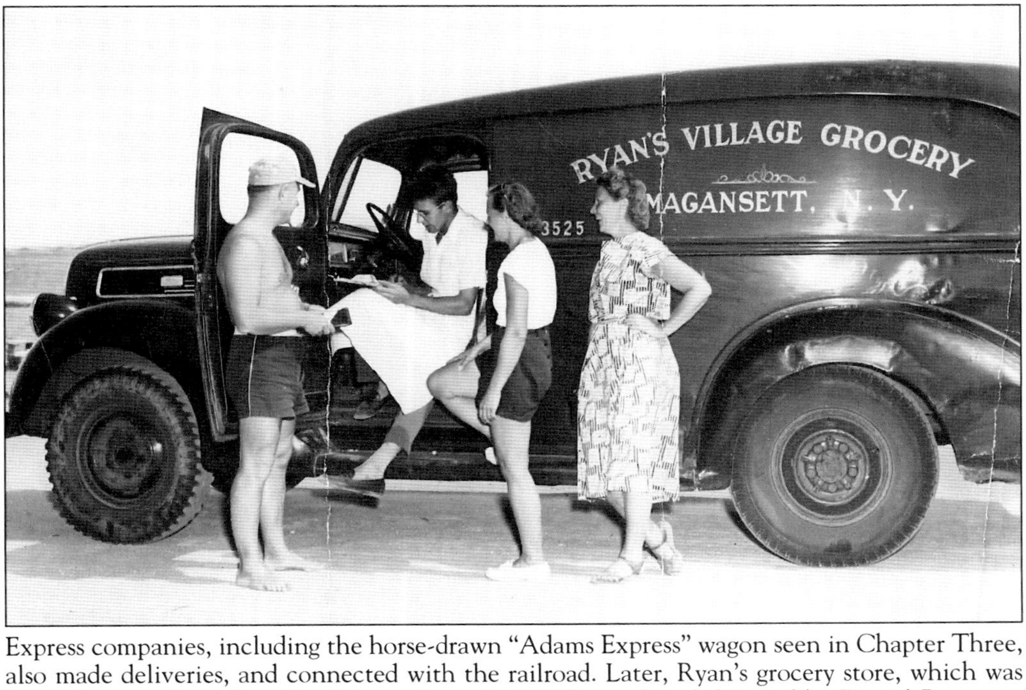

Express companies, including the horse-drawn "Adams Express" wagon seen in Chapter Three, also made deliveries, and connected with the railroad. Later, Ryan's grocery store, which was located across from the school (torn down in 1965), employed drivers like Daniel Bossey to make deliveries to the summer community.

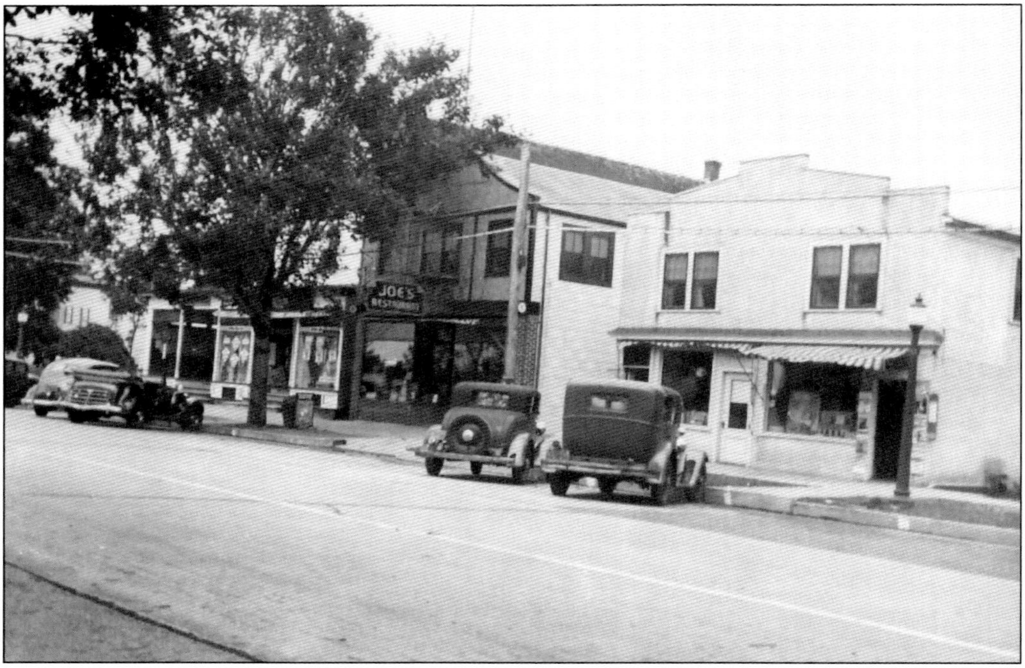

Most daily commerce was conducted on the Main Street of the village, and these two photographs, taken a decade apart, show the difference between the business districts of Amagansett (above) and Sag Harbor (below). Well into this century, Amagansett families were more likely to go to Sag Harbor, the nearest port, than to East Hampton for special purchases.

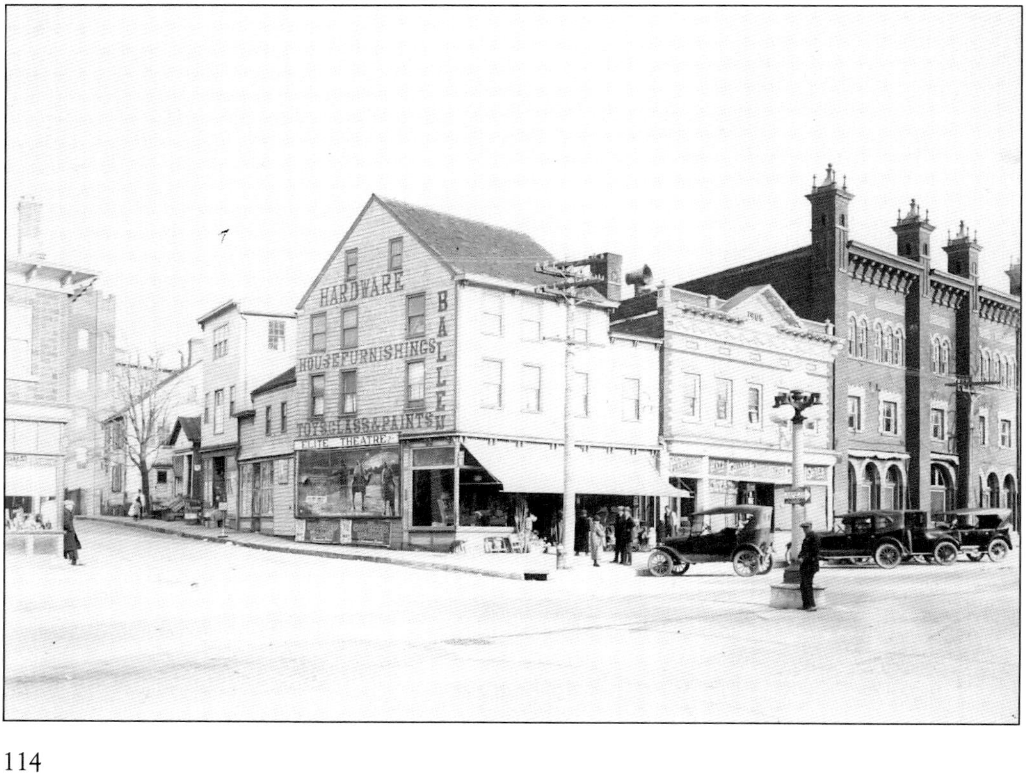

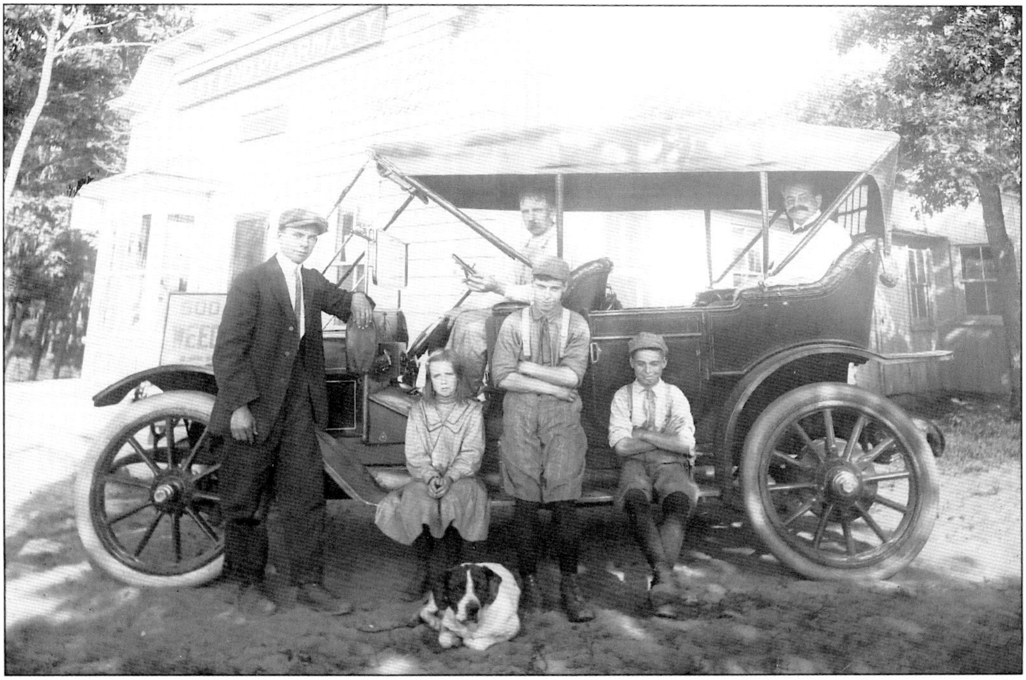

On the corner of Main Street and Cross Highway stood the West End Pharmacy. George, Edith, Floyd, and Edward Hamilton pose here, with David Hamilton at the wheel of the car, and Mr. Fisher, the pharmacist, in the back seat. The building later became a poolroom.

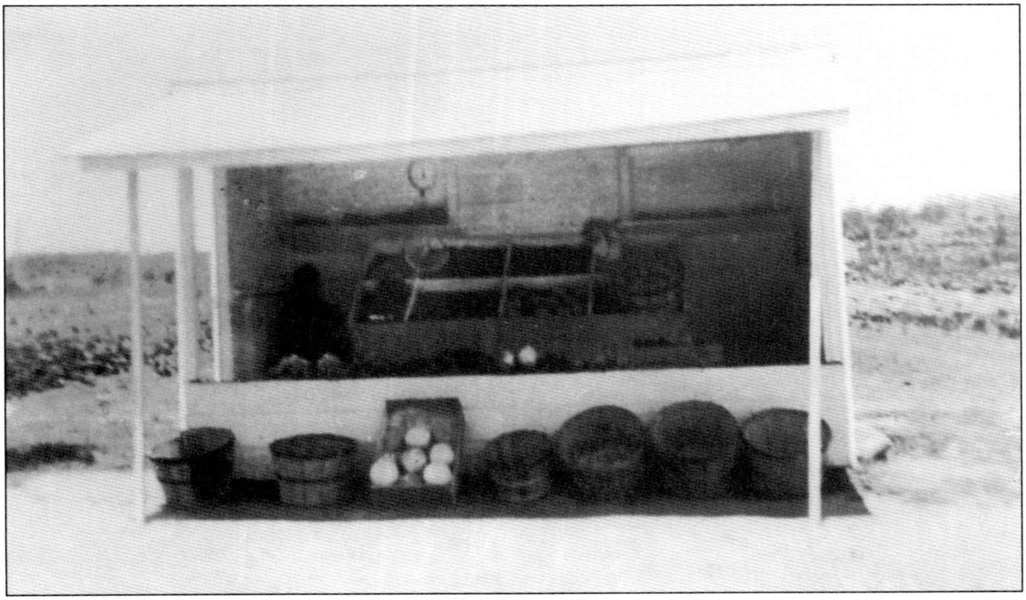

Store records beginning in 1811 are available, but fresh vegetables appear in none of them. Families either produced their own, traded for them, or purchased them from a neighbor. This first vegetable stand was opened in 1934 by Jack Stella. Stella joined the U.S. Army almost immediately after arriving here from Italy (and was one of the eighteen survivors of the Argonne's "Lost Batallion"). After working on the railroad, he farmed 80 acres in the village.

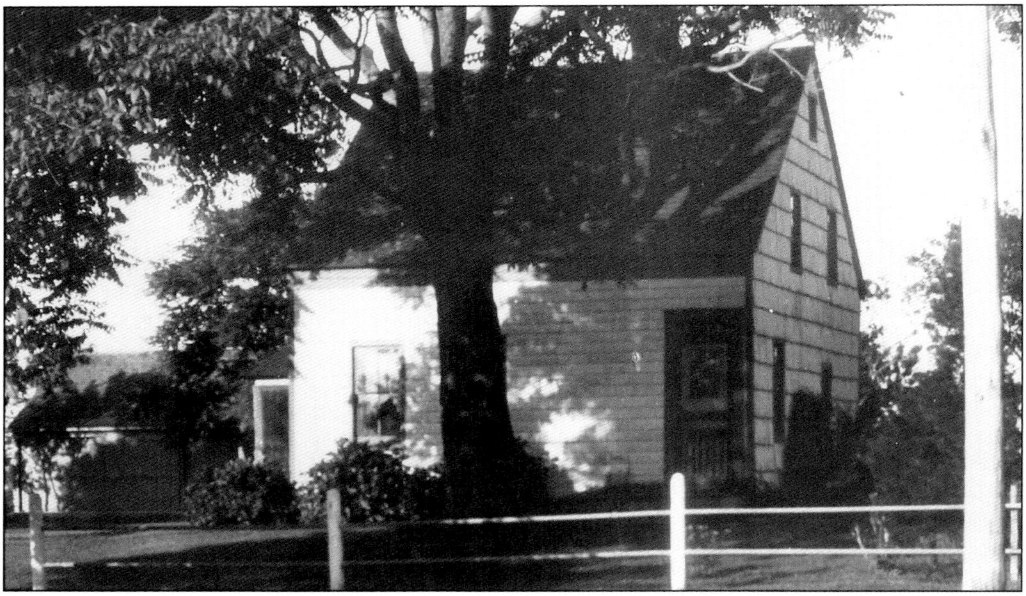

Nathan Hand, a Revolutionary soldier and sheep herder at Montauk, built this house on Atlantic Avenue. Then, his "narrow means" forced him to emigrate, in 1792, to the eastern shore of Lake Champlain, opposite Fort Ticonderoga. That new wheat-growing region had become known to Captain Barnes (his father-in-law) while he was serving in the French war. Hand bought a 200 acre farm there, but his family continued to spread out: his son Isaac and Issac's wife moved to Albany; his daughters married and moved to Brooklyn and Connecticut; his son Augustus stayed in Vermont, but *his* son became a physician in Illinois.

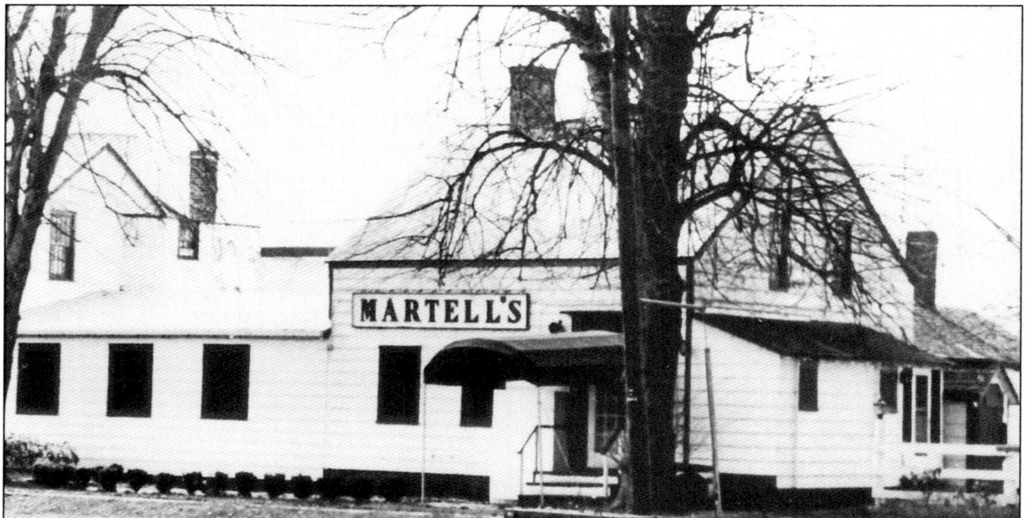

The 1825 Nathaniel Hand house, similar in design to Nathan's, has gone through a number of transformations unimaginable to its original inhabitants. It was built on by Frank Eck and became the popular nightspot, the "Elm Tree Inn" (when, before the great hurricane, there were still elm trees). Later, through the 1970s, it was a legendary "singles" gathering place, Martell's. It has been further enlarged, into a restaurant building just east of the Amagansett Farmers Market.

Ten

New and Old

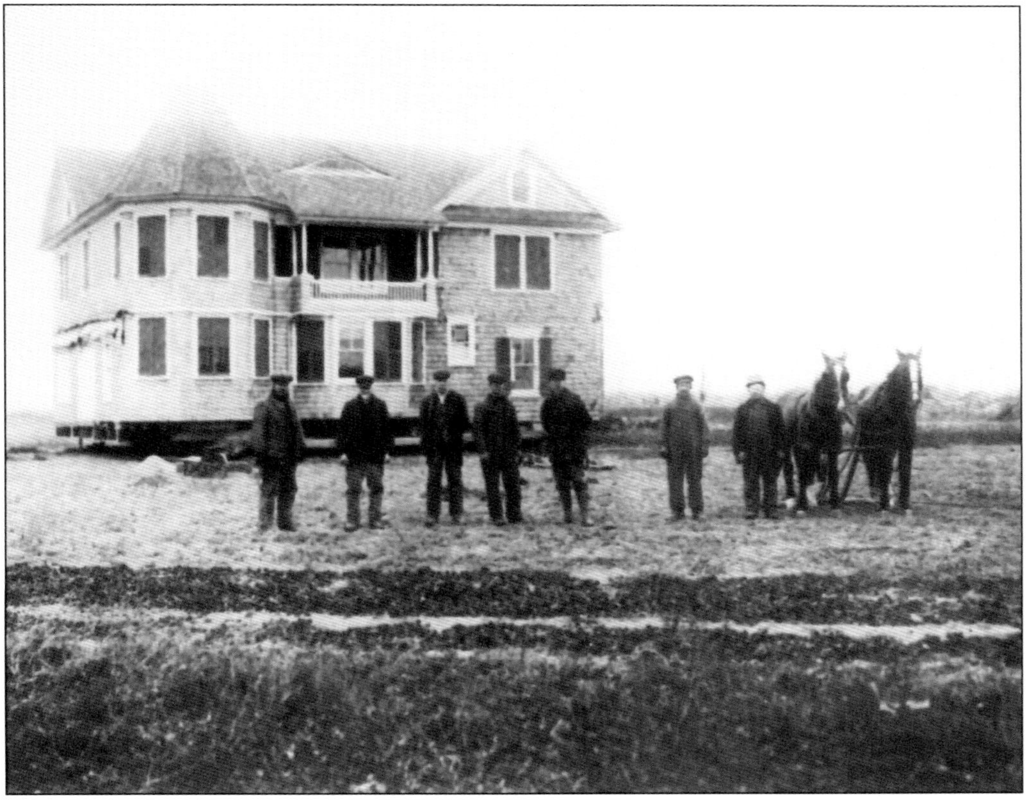

While Amagansett families were generally prosperous, they built according to their household needs—there was no impulse toward ostentatiousness; sturdy comfort was valued. Amagansett residents also moved buildings to meet immediate needs: one was relocated five times. This crew, moving a summer house with horses, carries on the tradition.

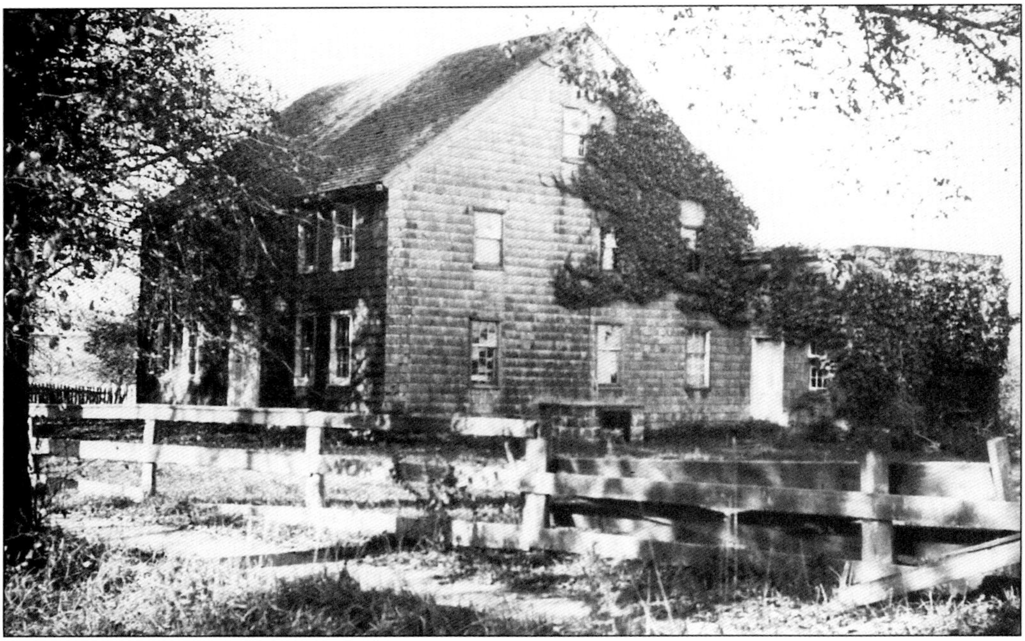

The Edwards-Hand House is shown first *in situ* on Main Street, then after its move by Robert Kennelly to Adelaide deMenil's property. A group of actors rented the house one summer, and a whimsical local led them to believe that a Hand family fortune (some say the amount was $40,000) was hidden somewhere in the house. The thespians literally tore the place apart—even the chimney was pulled down—so the house's restoration was particularly ambitious.

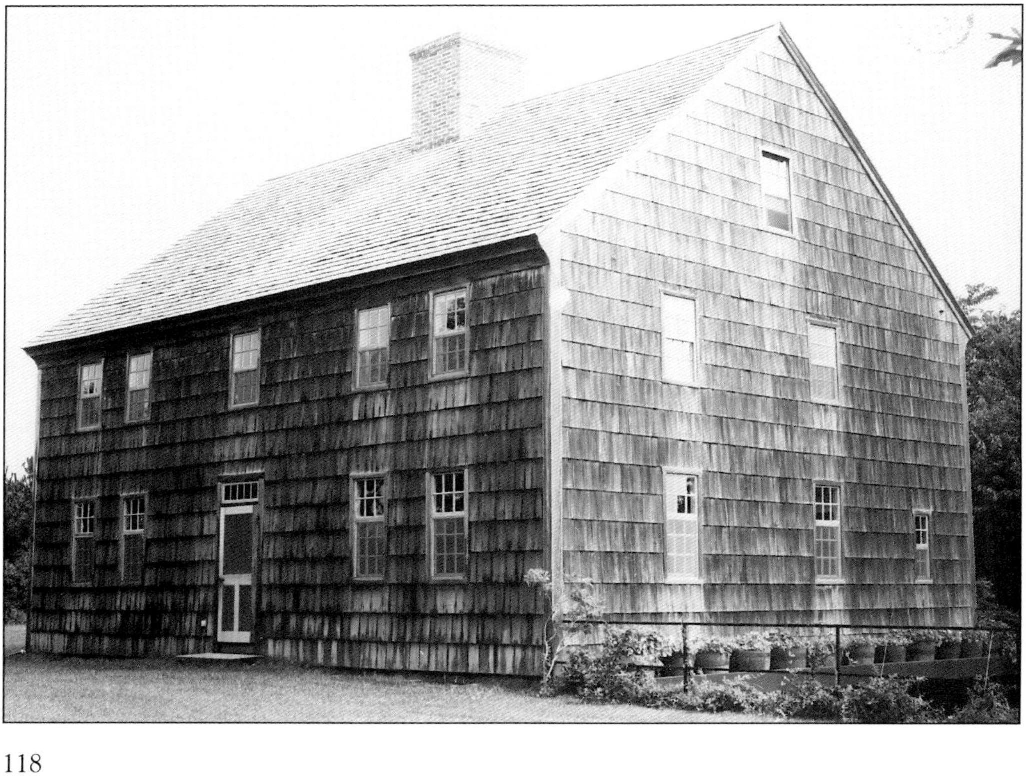

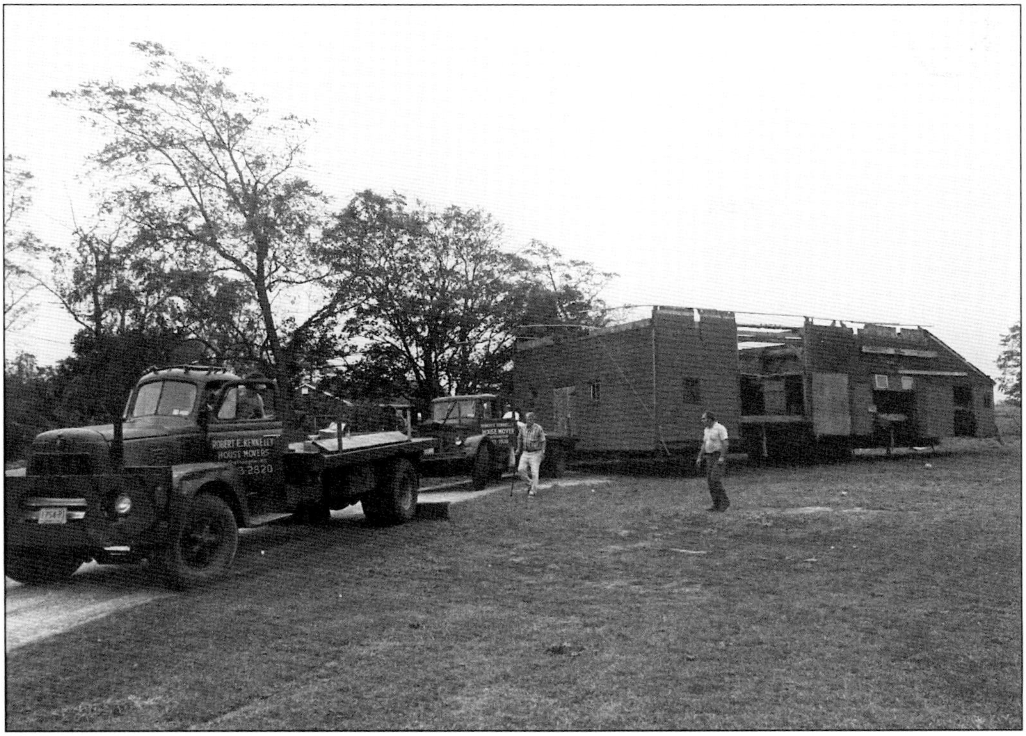

Robert Kennelly moved the Roy Lester Barn from Pantigo to the Miss Amelia Cottage grounds in 1979.

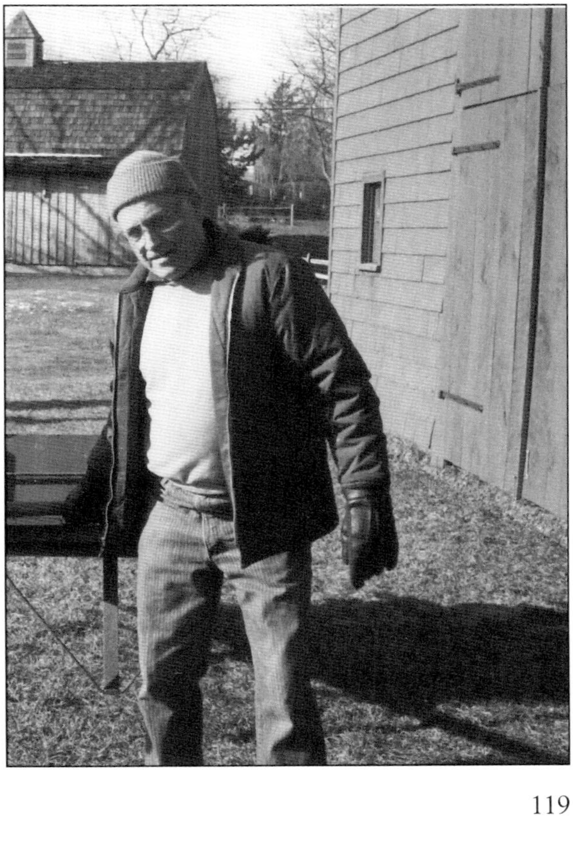

William Compton is shown here on the Miss Amelia Cottage grounds, with the newly built Jackson Carriage House in the background. Among the horse-drawn carriages in the museum's collection is David Edwards' "doctor's buggy", which he used to make his rounds.

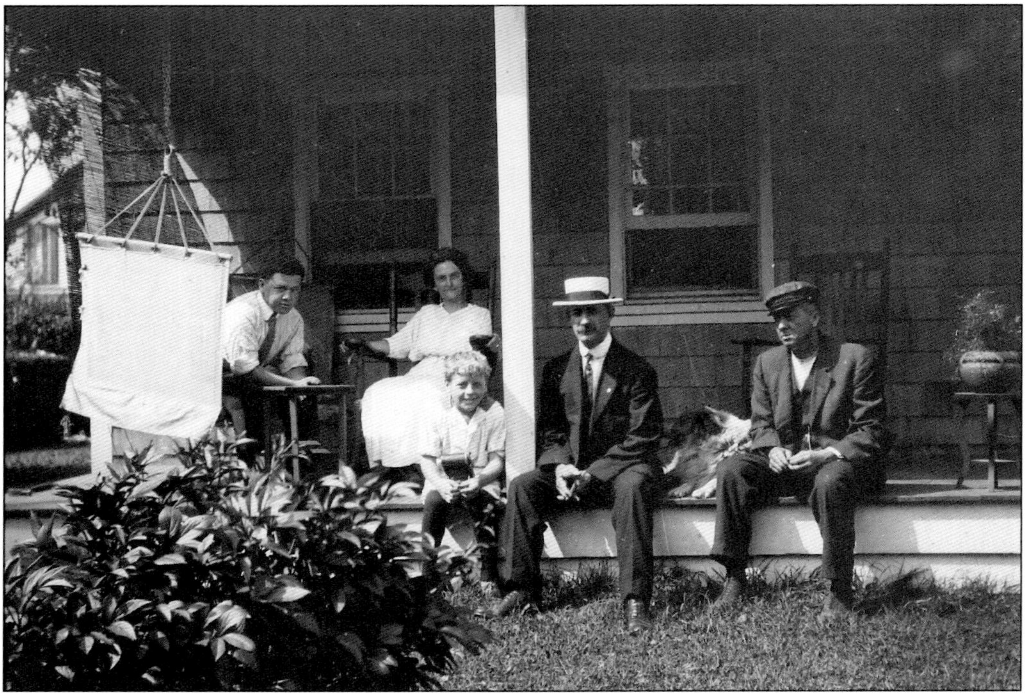

When Florence Eichhorn became the village librarian, she worked in the Samuel Schellinger building, where she and her family had lived. Here on the porch are George Eichhorn (far right) and "Paddy" Murray (in the boater hat). George, his father James, and Patrick Murray all had long careers as Long Island Railroad engineers.

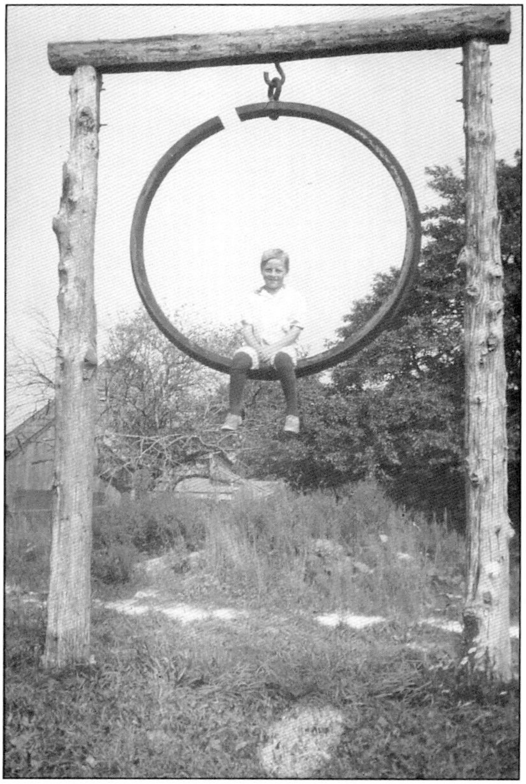

This 1914 photograph shows nine-year-old Clement Eichhorn sitting on a locomotive tire, given to his father by the Long Island Railroad. The metal tire was cut to make it "clang" more vehemently, and it served as the village fire alarm. It stood next to the library building.

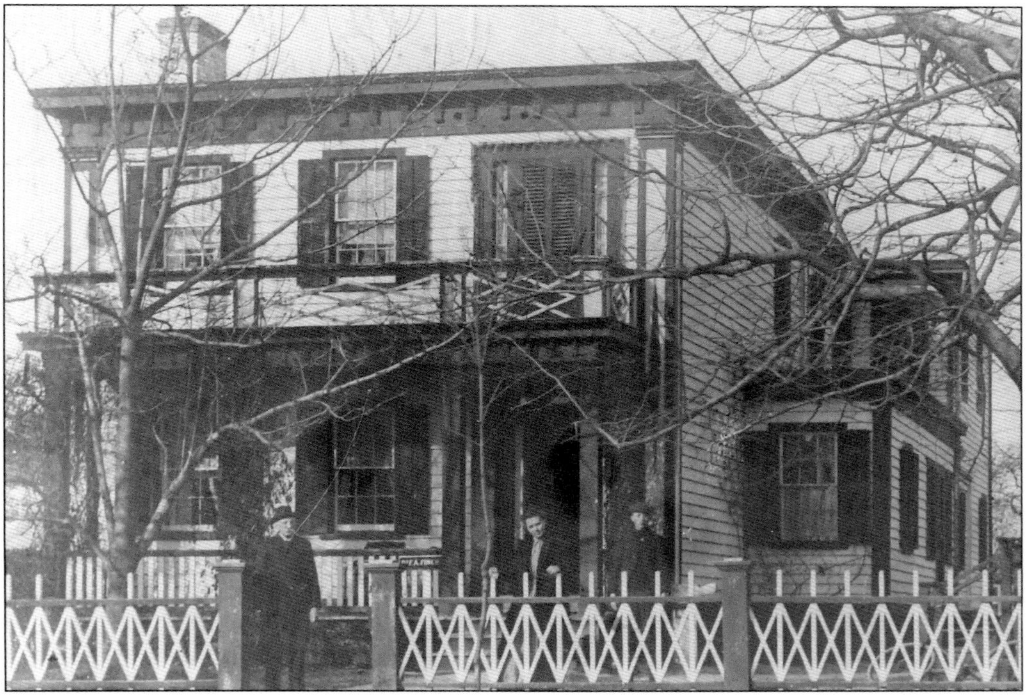

The Captain George Brown house, built in 1850 and destroyed by fire in 1910, stood on what is now the entrance to the parking lot next to the library. A whaler out of Sag Harbor, Captain Brown was supervising the cutting of whale "blanket pieces" one day when a huge mass of whalemeat fell, and he was crushed to death.

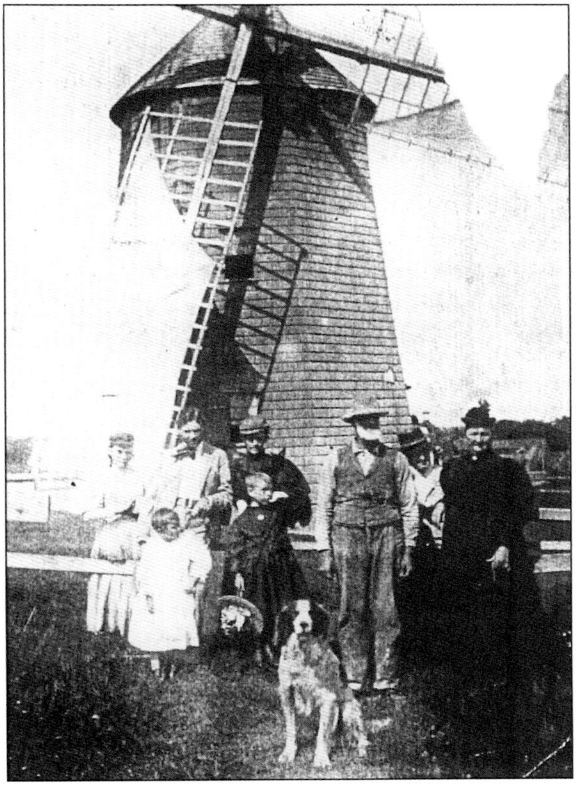

A structure that moved from one end of the village to the other was the Amagansett Windmill, built by Samuel Schellinger at Miller Place in 1814. In 1829, the Amagansett Mill Company moved it by water to the landing at Gardiner's Bay, and from there to a site near where the flagpole now stands. (Atlantic Avenue was simply called "the road from the mill to the ocean.") An English speculator, R.W. Ashby, bought it in 1871 and moved it "out of the village" to what is now Windmill Lane. He sold it to Abraham Stratton Parsons, who appears here with his family, in 1878. The mill burned down in 1924.

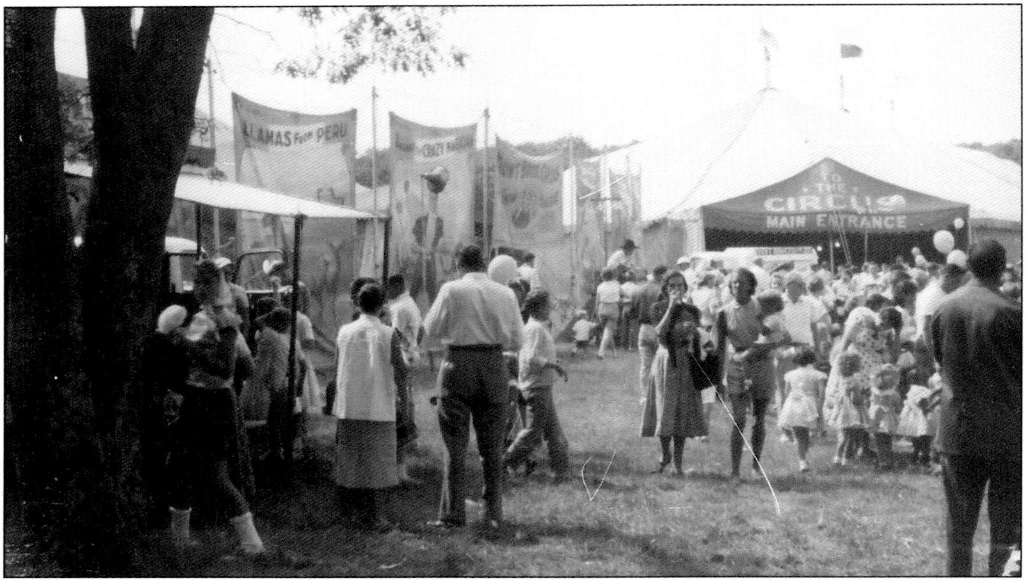

Entertainments of every variety were perhaps more accessible to residents a century ago than they are today. People could read thrilling accounts in the *Star* of "Barnum's Museum and Menagerie," but the arrival of the Hunt Brothers' and other traveling circuses to the American Legion property created a special stir in the village well into the 1950s.

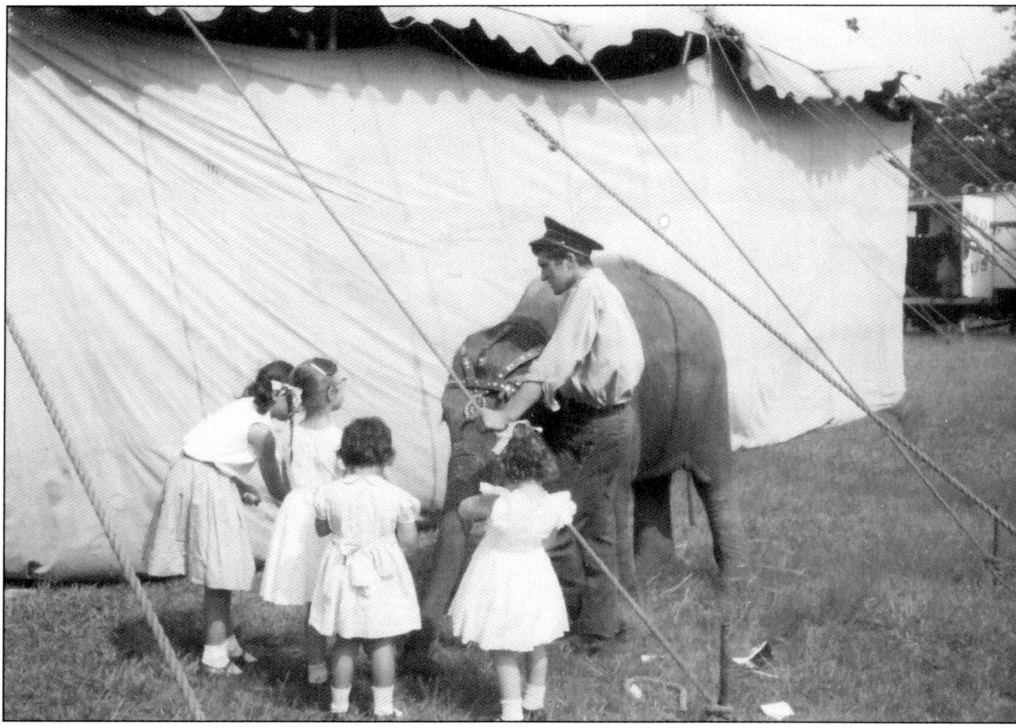

When it was no longer a stop for the circus, the corner was the site of hugely attended carnivals through the 1970s, but it has been a while since anyone could "go out and see the elephant" in Amagansett.

Fanny (Miller) Payne's daughter Mary Ann married Jonathan Schellinger (making Fanny Miss Amelia's grandmother), and her daughter Eliza married Jonathan's brother, Alben Derby Schellinger. Such neatly extended families were not uncommon: one local source noted that five Osborn sisters married five Hedges brothers. On the back of Fanny's portrait a descendant wrote, "died April 22d 1882 aged ninety-five years fifteen days."

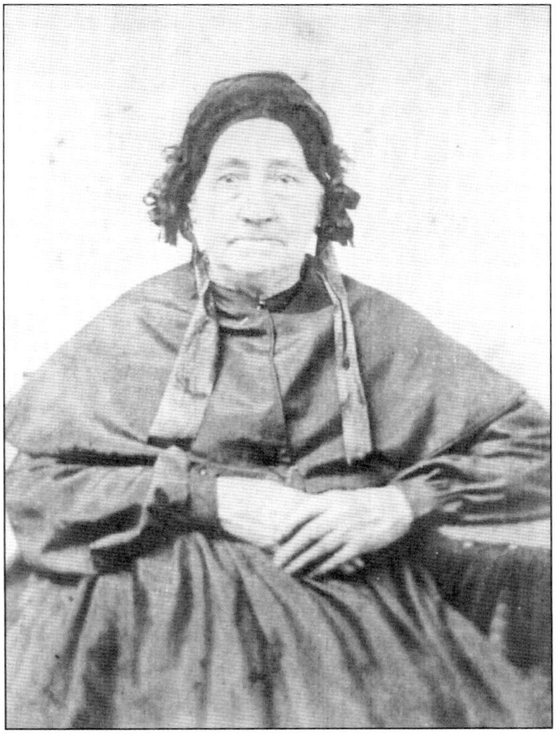

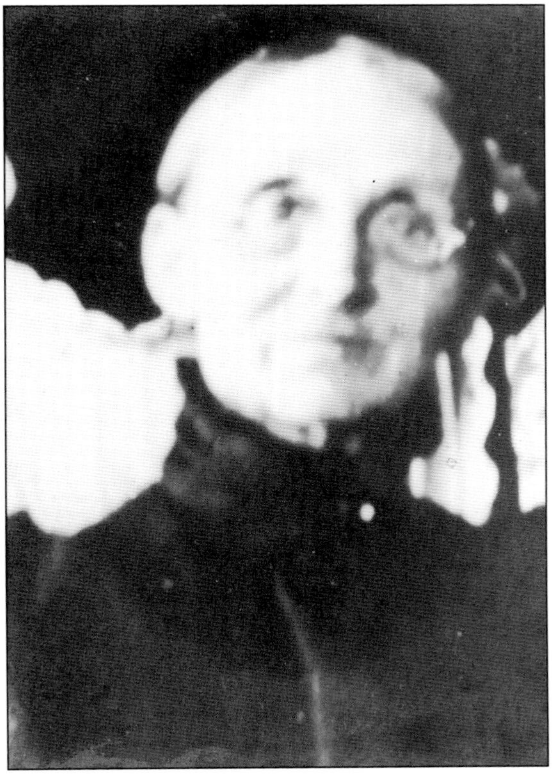

Ellen (Schellinger) Parsons was the daughter of Alben and Eliza (Payne) Schellinger.

Julia, the daughter of Alben and Eliza Payne Schellinger, was Theodore H. Hand's first wife. After her death, he married Carrie Edwards, who appears in the 1902 photograph of the Nathaniel Hand house.

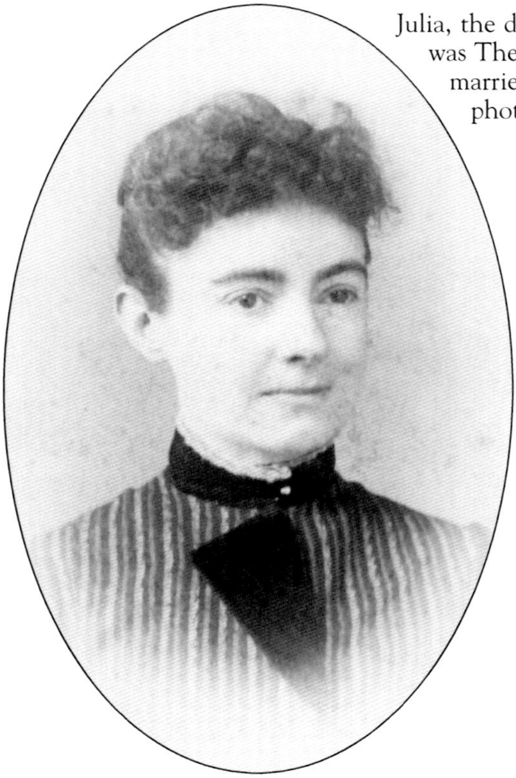

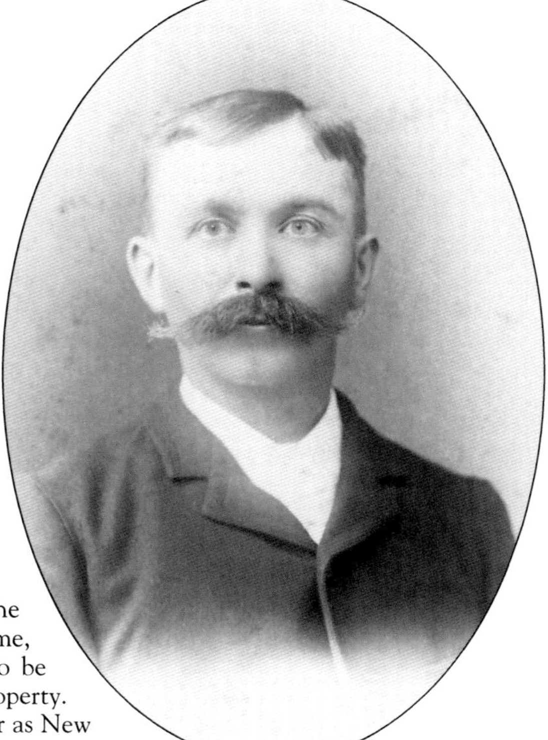

The Hands were famous as tanners from the earliest days. During Theodore Hand's lifetime, a barn, where bark had been ground up to be used in tanning leather, still stood on the property. Shoes from the East End were shipped as far as New Bedford and Newport.

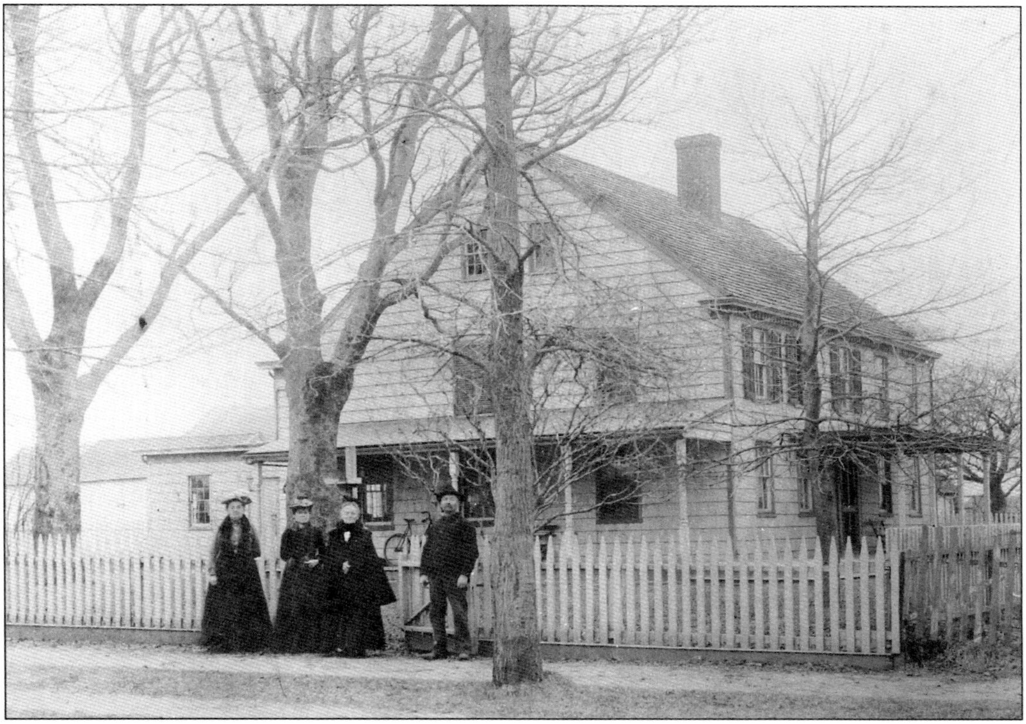

This house was an inn from Revolutionary times. His Majesty's Commissioner for Indian Affairs, Sir William Johnson, stayed here in 1772 when he was advised to take healthful "sea baths." In this 1902 photograph the village dressmaker must have been calling when the photographer arrived, and she is included in the group. From left to right are Carrie (Edwards) Hand, Emma Bridgens (dressmaker), Phebe (Conklin) Hand, and Theodore Hand.

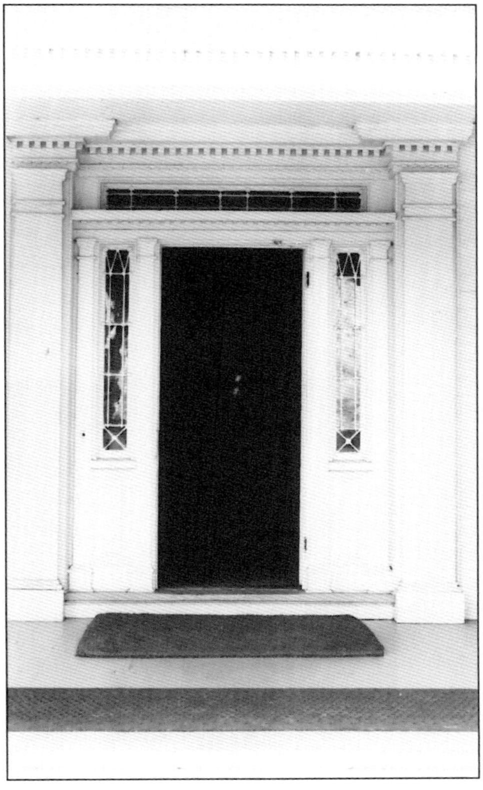

The William Hand house has the only Greek Revival doorway in the village.

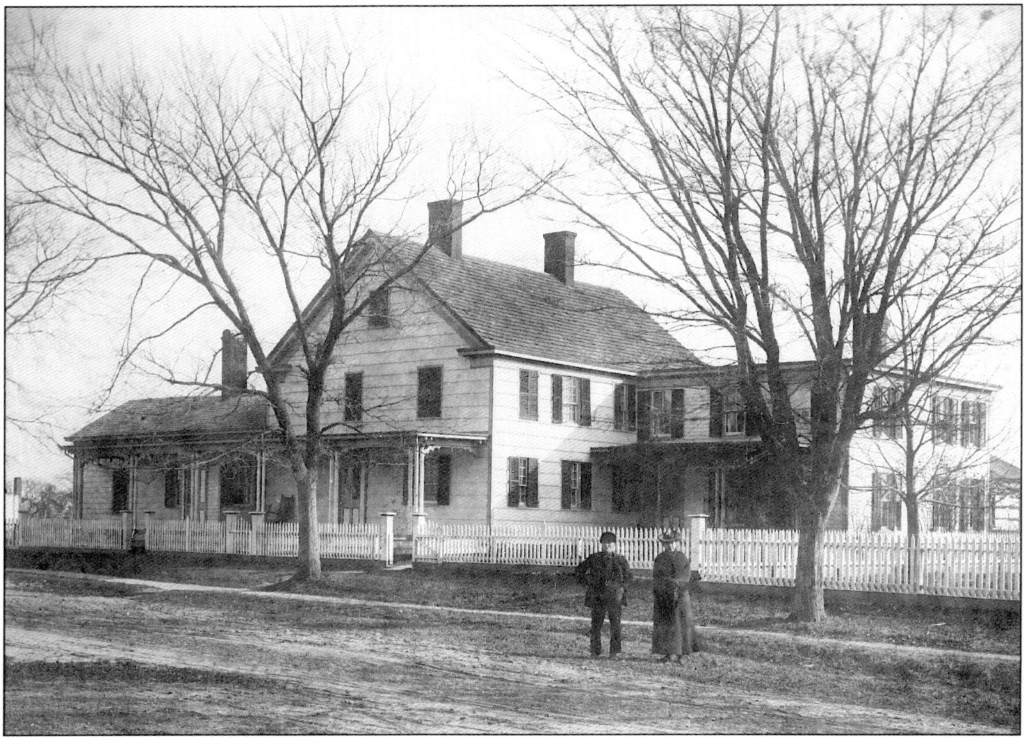

Hester Schellinger married Thomas Osborn in 1720 and moved into this house. It remained in the Osborn family until its 1832 purchase by Benjamin Hedges, after he stopped herding in Montauk. In 1840, both of Hedges' children died of "fish fever," probably a measles-like disease. The house is now part of the Amagansett Square shops.

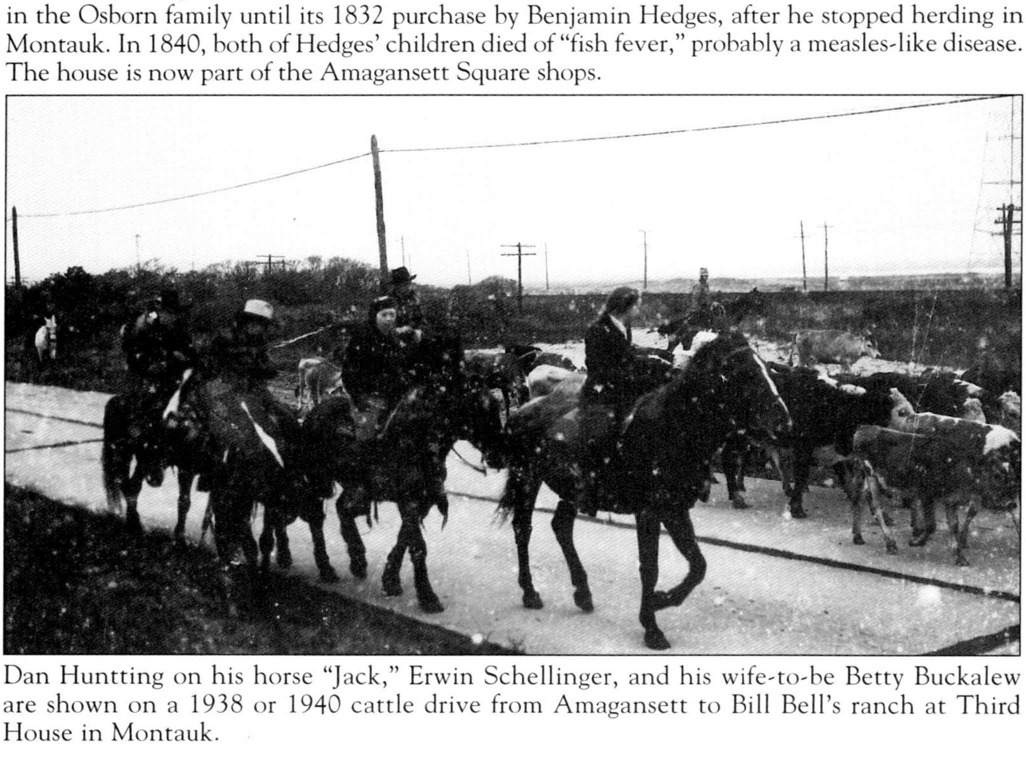

Dan Huntting on his horse "Jack," Erwin Schellinger, and his wife-to-be Betty Buckalew are shown on a 1938 or 1940 cattle drive from Amagansett to Bill Bell's ranch at Third House in Montauk.

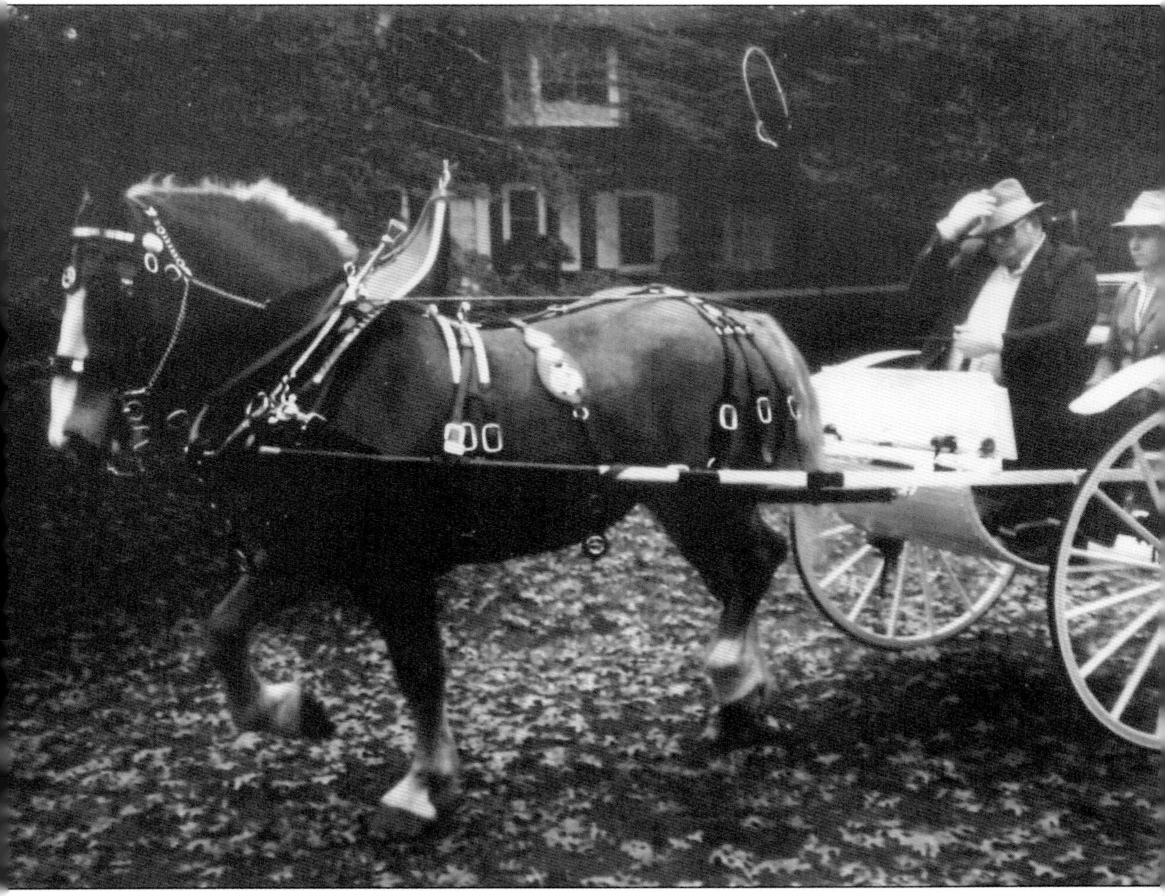

Bob and Doris Willumson were photographed in a cart drawn by one of their Scorpion Farms' horses. Participants in many carriage events, the Willumsons have also provided Sunday pony rides to Amagansett children, on the grounds of the Miss Amelia Cottage and Roy K. Lester Carriage Museums.

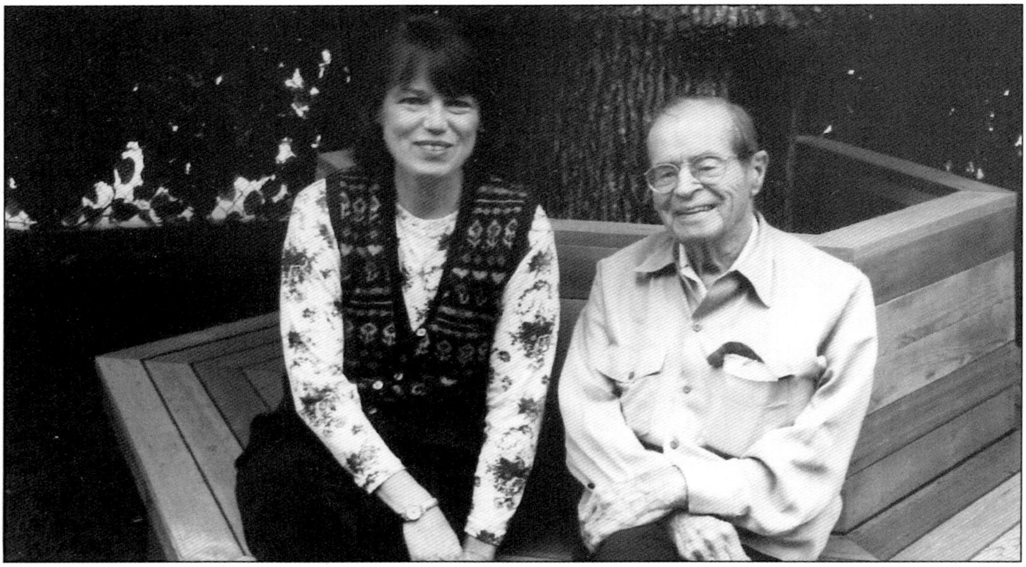

Carleton Kelsey, whose lifelong research and collection of photographs is the reason for and heart of this book, is a founding trustee and officer of the Amagansett Historical Association. He has been the Director of the Amagansett Free Library since 1964, and is the author of *Amagansett: A Pictorial History* (1986). He is currently at work on an encyclopedia of East Hampton town government, and, with Lucinda Mayo, on a monograph detailing the history of Amagansett's Edwards family.

Lucinda Mayo, who researched, selected photographs, and wrote the text for this book after long consultation with Mr. Kelsey, is a 12th generation descendant of the Barnes family, which helped to found Amagansett. She has lived on the East End for fifteen years, twice serving as Director of the Amagansett Historical Association, and has worked as a museum professional and arts administrator in Australia, California, and Connecticut, and as a teacher in Mexico and New York. The recipient of two New York Council for the Humanities fellowships, she is continuing explorations, with Carleton Kelsey, into Amagansett's family histories, and into East End connections with her childhood hometown of Wethersfield, Connecticut.

Photo Credits

All photographs by, or from the collection of, Carleton Kelsey, with the exception of those graciously given or loaned by these individuals and collections: the estate of R.B. Allen, p. 102; the Barnes Family Collection, courtesy of Beth Barnes Gray pp. 17 and 48; the Barnes Family Collection, courtesy of Mary Louise Barnes Mayo, p. 94; Josephine Stella Crasky, p. 115; C. Frank Dayton, p. 98; the *East Hampton Star*, p. 45; the Edwards Family Collection, courtesy of Mrs. Anne Roberts, pp. 69–70, and 99; Lucinda Mayo/Amagansett Historical Association, pp. 15 and 119; Lucinda Mayo/Richard Wands, pp. 10 and 60 ; Cal Norris/Amagansett Historical Association, pp. 119 and 127; Tony Prohaska, p. 4; John Reed, p. 93; Mr. and Mrs. David Schellinger/Amagansett Historical Association, p. 22; E. Shank/Amagansett Historical Association, p. 11.